Timothy Shay Arthur

Three years in a man-trap

Timothy Shay Arthur
Three years in a man-trap
ISBN/EAN: 9783743335295
Manufactured in Europe, USA, Canada, Australia, Japa
Cover: Foto ©ninafisch / pixelio.de

Manufactured and distributed by brebook publishing software (www.brebook.com)

Timothy Shay Arthur

Three years in a man-trap

PUBLISHERS' PREFACE.

It is nearly twenty years since the author of this volume gave to the public "Ten Nights in a Bar-room"—a revelation of the evils of liquor-selling so true to nature, so vivid in pictorial effect and so strong in its delineation of character and incident, that it took the people by surprise, and it has ever since held its own among the most popular books of the day, the demand for it being still unabated.

In "Three Years in a Man-Trap" he grapples again with the monster Intemperance, but in a new field, and with enemies more thoroughly disciplined and organized. From a quiet country village with its "Sickle and Sheaf" he turns to a great city with its six or seven thousand saloons and dram-shops, and uncovers the deadly ulcer that is eating steadily down toward the vitals of the people.

From the first page to the last of this new book the reader will find himself drawn on and on by a series of rapidly-recurring pictures, some of them so intense and vivid, yet so true to real life, that he will almost hold his breath while he follows the author from canvas to canvas through the whole.

It cannot fail, the publishers believe, to make a profound impression. Its scenes, its facts, and, above all, its deep pervading earnestness, will powerfully impress every one, and awaken the people to a new sense of their duty and their danger.

THREE YEARS IN A MAN-TRAP.

CHAPTER I.

A SHARP retort was forming on Lloyd's tongue, when I noticed a look of blank surprise, almost terror, break suddenly into his face. His eyes were on the door. I turned, and saw that it was pushed open just a little by a woman's small white hand. Through the opening I could see, indistinctly, a woman's face, pale and wild-looking, but was not able to make out with certainty the features. Almost in the instant I saw it, the door was shut again and the face hidden. When I turned to Lloyd, his countenance was blanched.

"Who was it, Tom?" I asked.

He did not stir nor speak for several moments.

"Who was it? Do you know?" I repeated my question.

He shook his head.

"I think I do," I said.

"Who?" He spoke eagerly, leaning toward me like one in great suspense.

"If I'm not mistaken, it was the wife of Ellis Granger," I returned. "He's been going to the dogs for a year, as we know, and about as fast as the devil wants him. I heard some young fellows talking about him at the theatre the other night, and they said his wife was almost distressed to death about him, and that her friends were afraid she'd lose her mind. They've only been married a couple of years."

"And you think it was her?" Lloyd queried, the look of suspense and fear beginning to pass from his face.

"I'm almost sure of it," I replied.

"Where have you seen her?"

"At the theatre with her husband. She's one of the handsomest women I ever saw, or was some time ago, but has changed so much of late that you'd hardly know her as the same person. Granger is breaking her heart, so they say."

"But I can't understand what should bring her down here at this hour and on such a night," said Lloyd.

"Nor I, except on the theory that she is out of her head," I replied.

"I don't like the look of it."

The fear and anxiety came back into Lloyd's face. Then, after seeming to debate with himself for a while, he stooped and took from a closet under the counter his overcoat, and as he drew it on said,

"I must see who it is. She might perish in the cold and snow."

He went out hastily, much to my surprise, for Tom Lloyd was not given to caring for other people. If the woman, whoever she was, had come in and said or done anything he didn't care to have said or done, he would have turned her out into the wild storm, unless hindered from doing so, with as little feeling as if she were a brute, so hardened had he become in the few years we had kept this tavern together.

He came back in about ten minutes, stamping the snow from his boots and shaking it from his clothes. The sober look was still on his face.

"Did you find her?" I asked.

He shook his head, and then, in a half-dogged sort of way, went slowly back to his place behind the bar.

"Who do you think it was, Tom?" I asked.

I saw the muscles of his face quiver a little.

"No idea in the world," he answered, with the tone of one who would be glad to push the whole thing out of his mind.

The day had been unusually cold and boisterous. Toward evening it moderated a little, and the snow began to fall—not in large soft flakes, but in fine grains almost as hard as hail. The wind kept high, and blew the snow about in blinding gusts.

The streets were almost deserted until a little after nightfall, when men of business, workmen, clerks, factory and store hands began hurrying homeward, some packing themselves into the overcrowded cars, and others bending to the storm, that almost took the breath away in its wilder eddies.

And now business, which had been dull for some hours, grew brisk again. As the men poured forth at six o'clock from the bindery and printing-office, a larger number than usual came in for something warm to fortify themselves against the bitter cold they were to encounter on their way homeward. Most of them took spirits instead of beer. For nearly half an hour Lloyd, myself and our bartender were kept as busy as bees.

Then came a lull, and our rooms were nearly empty of guests.

"We shall have a poor evening, I'm afraid," said Lloyd.

"Yes," I replied; "a man's home must be dreary enough if he doesn't prefer staying there to going out to-night. We shall miss the faces of some of our friends."

"Some, I'm thinking, that we'd like to miss altogether," said Lloyd. "There's old Jacobs, the pressman. I dread to see his face. He's sure to get up a row with some body. A glass or two makes him as snappish as a cur."

"I'd rather see him a dozen times over than Ashley's son," I replied. "That boy's going to ruin as fast as the devil can carry him."

"I wouldn't, then," was returned. "John's a

good-natured, quiet fellow, and never gets into trouble with any one. He is a little wild and fast, it is true, but he'll grow out of that."

"I wish I could be sure of it; but when a young man under twenty gets switched off the track, ten to one against his ever getting on again. That's my observation."

"It isn't mine, then," said Lloyd. "I can point you to a dozen steady family-men who were once among the wildest young fellows I ever saw."

"A great deal depends on character and temperament," was my reply. "In the case of John Ashley, a weak, good-natured, social boy—we can hardly call him a man—the chances are all against him."

"I shouldn't wonder if they were," returned Lloyd, in a tone of indifference. "But that's none of our business."

"I'm afraid we shall have trouble with his father yet," I remarked.

"His father go to ——!" said Lloyd, angrily. "What can he do? Let him keep his son at home."

"That is more easily said than done, I imagine. You can't keep a fellow at his age in leading-strings. But he is a minor."

"Well, what of that?"

"The law against selling liquor to minors is an ugly one. I don't like it."

"Law!" A derisive laugh rang through the bar-room. "I'm not afraid of liquor laws. They've all got a loophole. Our friends in the Legislature know how to manage that business."

"But if one should happen to get tripped, it wouldn't be so pleasant to be fined and jugged. There's a good deal of stir among these confounded temperance men just now," I replied.

"Oh, well, they'll only kick up a little dust. It won't amount to anything."

"Maybe not; still, I don't altogether like the look of things. Did you see the judge's charge to the grand jury yesterday?"

"No."

"It is nearly all about us liquor-sellers."

"Indeed?"

"Just so. Here it is;" and I took an afternoon paper and read:

"Gentlemen of the grand jury: There are two matters to which I wish particularly to call your attention at this time, viz.: *First.* To the flagrant violations of the law respecting the sale of intoxicating liquors."

"That doesn't mean us," said Lloyd; "we pay our license—we are law-abiding."

"We shall see;" and I read on:

"The grand jury for the December session, in their presentment of Saturday last, have uttered the following emphatic language:

"'The jury would state that seven-eighths of all the cases of assault and battery brought before us can be traced to the too free use of intoxicating liquors, and would most earnestly recommend a more stringent enforcement of the license laws.

"'Besides the mischiefs which inevitably flow from the licensed sale of liquors, the evils which follow the unlawful traffic in liquors are of great magnitude, and require the stern application of law to them to suppress them. That you may be informed what is prohibited by law respecting the sale of liquors, I propose to give you a summary of the law on that subject.'"

"That'll do; you needn't read any more of his stuff. We pay our license;" and Lloyd waved his hand impatiently.

"There's something here about minors and drunkards—an extract from the law the judge speaks of. I guess you'd better hear it."

Lloyd bent his head to listen, and I went on:

"Willfully furnishing intoxicating drinks, by sale, gift or otherwise, to any person of known intemperate habits, to a minor or to an insane person, for use as a beverage, shall be held and deemed a misdemeanor, and, upon conviction thereof, the offender shall be fined not less than ten nor more than fifty dollars, and undergo an imprisonment of not less than ten nor more than sixty days; and the willful furnishing of intoxicating drinks as a beverage to any person when drunk or intoxicated shall be deemed a misdemeanor, punishable as aforesaid."

"It doesn't amount to anything," was Lloyd's reply. "The judge only spread himself a little to gain popularity with the temperance men. As to grand-jury presentments, they never come to anything."

"I guess the judge was about of your opinion," said I, "for toward the end of his charge he lets the cat out of the bag. Hear what he says;" and I read:

"'Unfortunately, we are too much accustomed to consider that laws will execute themselves, or that the officers of the law should become public prosecutors, and too little attention is given by our citizens generally to the enforcement of the laws and the punishment of wrong-doers. In a republican government every citizen has a direct interest in the enforcement of the laws, and if a greater interest were manifest in their enforcement, our republican institutions would not be so often brought into question.'"

"Just so: what's everybody's business is nobody's business," replied Lloyd.

A fiercer blast than usual sent the fine, sand-like snow in a pelting gust against the window. In the pause that followed I heard a child's voice outside. Then the door was pushed slowly open and two little figures glided in, white with snow—a bright-eyed Italian boy not over ten years of age, and his sister, who was still younger. The boy had a violin and the girl a tambourine. They were shivering with cold.

"Off with you! Off with you!" cried Lloyd, advancing toward the children and waving his hand toward the door.

The girl looked frightened, but the boy stood his ground.

"I wouldn't turn a dog out on a night like this," spoke up a man who had come in a short time before, and was now sitting at a table reading and enjoying his glass of hot whisky punch.

Lloyd felt the rebuke, and returned to the bar. The children came forward, and, after shaking the snow from their poor garments, began warming their half-frozen hands at the stove. There was a pinched, hungry look in the girl's face, and something so wistful in her large, black, Italian eyes that I was moved to pity.

So I came round from the bar and said a kind word. It was as if a sunbeam had fallen on the child's face, it brightened so suddenly.

"Hungry?" I asked.

She nodded her head in reply, looking pleased but eager.

I took the two children into a back room, and gave them each some bread and cheese and a small glass of beer.

"You're a great fool," growled Lloyd. "We'll have a hundred of these vagabonds upon us before the week's out."

"We can deal with them as they come along," I replied, with some asperity of tone, for I was provoked at his utter want of feeling.

His eyes flashed. He was getting more and more irritable every day, and I found it sometimes as much as I could do to keep from an open quarrel. He drank more of late than usual. For the first year or so after we opened the house he indulged sparingly, but in the last few months his appetite for liquor had grown on him so fast that I began to feel concerned—the more so, as he was one of the men into whom the devil seems to go by the way of drink.

An hour later and customers began to drop in, but not as freely as on clear nights. Men with comfortable homes, and not too much given to drink, preferred keeping indoors to going out on such a wild and stormy evening. So, as a rule, we had only the hard cases that night—customers who must have their liquor if they had to go through fire and water to get it.

Old Jacobs the pressman was among the earliest of these. Not long after him came John Ashley, the foreman's son, and soon after, Joe Wilson, a young man who worked in the bindery, and who, though not yet of age, was fast going to ruin.

By nine o'clock we had in about a dozen men and lads, half of whom were up stairs in private rooms, playing cards, singing songs or in other ways amusing themselves, and every now and then ordering up liquor.

They were a thirsty set, and made frequent demands on the bar. The tongue of old Jacobs was getting oiled by this time, and he was in the midst of an argument with another man, and rather an ill-looking person, who was a stranger. Now, Jacobs, toper as he was, and always as full of beer as a keg, had a queer fancy for talking on the side of temperance, and the tipsier he got, the longer and stronger he talked, not unfrequently in pressing his case offering himself as an example and witness of the evil of liquor-selling and liquor-drinking. He was, strange to say, a real or pretended advocate of prohibition, and had a way of putting his argument that bothered a good many, silenced some and brought a few over to his side. I was always annoyed when he got going on this key, for he said a great many hard things and a great many true ones. As for Lloyd, it was generally as much as I could do to keep him quiet. He would have pitched him into the street long ago if he had not taken counsel of prudence and repressed his quick anger. Jacobs was generally liked among the men in the printing-office, and an indignity to him would have been resented to our loss in the loss of custom. So we had to bear with him, and our forbearance made him grow reckless of speech when the humor was on him.

"There's no good in it, sir, no good," I heard him say sharply to the stranger in a rising voice. "And if I had my way, there wouldn't be a rum-mill in the State."

"It's well for some people that you haven't your way," said the other, with just a shade of annoyance in his tone—"for our friends over there, for instance;" and he waved his hand toward Lloyd and myself.

"It would be better for some that I could tell of, and, if all the truth were known, better for 'our friends over there,' if they had never seen a beer-barrel or toddy-stick. I know. They've got a pile, I've heard; and I guess it's true. Many littles make a mickle, as the Scotch say. But there are two sides—"

The old pressman stopped in the middle of his sentence. A man wrapped in a heavy cloak, white with snow, had pushed open the door, and was standing just inside. The collar of his cloak covered his face to his eyes. I thought I knew him, but could not clearly make out who he was. He stood like a statue for several moments, looking keenly through the room, and then, without speaking, went out.

"Who was that?" asked one and another.

"Some poor father seeking in sorrow for a prodigal son," said Jacobs. "I've done it myself. Poor boy! But he's dead now;" and a sob and a quiver came into the old man's voice, half drunk as he was.

"I know," said one who worked in the bindery: "it was Ashley. He's after John."

"By George! that's so!" exclaimed Jacobs. "I thought I knew him. Hark!"

And down from one of the rooms above came a voice singing,

"Champagne Charley is my name."

"That's his young hopeful," said Jacobs, with a half chuckle. "I guess he won't find him. But it's hard;" and his tone changed. "I know. I've been there. I've traveled that road, and know all about it. 'Tisn't agreeable, no how you can make it. If I was Tom Lloyd and Hiram Jones, I wouldn't let the boy come here. He's a minor, and it's risky business, you see. The judge put that very thing to the grand jury yesterday strong, and I guess that's what's set Mr. Ashley going. If he'd pounced down on John to-night, there'd have been some court business, maybe, and maybe—*something else.*"

He drew down his mouth in a comical way. A laugh went round the room, but neither I nor Lloyd enjoyed it very much.

"As I was saying," resumed old Jacobs, turning to the stranger with whom he had been talking, "there's no good in it, and the whole thing ought to be stopped."

"How will you stop it?" asked the other.

"By law, sir—by law! It's the only way," returned the old man, slapping his hand upon the table at which he was sitting.

"Then you'll never see it stopped," was answered. "The people of this country are not going to pass laws that interfere with a man's right to eat and drink what he pleases."

"Of course not," said Jacobs.

"Then what are you talking about?" asked the stranger, with ill-concealed contempt of manner.

"About laws to stop whisky-mills," answered Jacobs, sharply. "The law doesn't say anything about my eating bad meat, but it says you sha'n't sell it. Why? Because bad meat makes people sick. So does arsenic, and so does whisky. If the law is right in one case, why not in the other? Can you tell me, my fine fellow?"

And the excited old man leaned across the table and glared at his opponent in a way that must have been felt very offensive, for I saw the stranger's hand move nervously, as if he were going to slap him in the face.

"Come, come, Jacobs," said I, in a coaxing voice, as I came round to where he was sitting, and laid my hand on his shoulder. "Let's have good-fellowship here to-night, and not wrangling."

"Who's wrangling, Hiram Jones?—who's wrangling, I'd like to know?" The old man pitched his voice to a higher key, and shook off my hand impatiently.

"You're not, of course," I returned, in as pleasant a way as I could speak.

"Who is, then?" sharply asked the stranger. I looked at him, and saw a devil in his eye—a devil that I did not care to provoke. Before I could reply, Jacobs turned to him and said,

"Ha! my fine fellow. Answer me that! You talk of law! I've got more sense in my toe nail than you've got in all your ugly head!"

I saw the blow coming, but was not quick enough

to catch or turn it away. In a moment after, old Jacobs fell with a heavy jar on the floor, and in the next instant his assailant was dropped at his side. I thought the men in the bar-room, all of whom knew and liked Jacobs, would have killed the man who struck him, so furious was their assault upon him. While he was struggling with them and showing the strength of a giant, but getting dreadfully punished by kicks and blows on head, face and body, I saw him draw a pistol from his pocket and try to cock it. Then a sharp crack rang through the room, followed by two more in quick succession.

The stillness of death followed, broken almost instantly by a savage oath from a fellow-workman of Jacobs, who kicked the stranger in his side with almost the force of a horse's hoof. I heard the ribs crack. The pistol fell from his hand, and he sank back with a groan. There was an ashen pallor on his face.

"Is any one hurt?" ran now from lip to lip. Happily, the bullets had done no harm. Our next concern was for the man who lay unconscious upon the floor with his ribs broken in.

Work like this is always bad work for saloon and tavern-keepers. It brings them into public notice in a way they desire to avoid. In most cases of drunken rows and violence, the uproar draws in a crowd, accompanied by police officers. Arrests are apt to be made, and indictments and appearances in court often follow.

On this evening the storm without kept the street clear, and no one heard the pistol shot or loud confusion of voices, so we had time to cover up our trouble and keep it out of the papers. The man, still insensible, was carried up stairs and laid on a bed in one of the rooms. After a little while he came to, and we learned from him his name and residence. He proved to be a man in the wholesale liquor trade. His name was Spencer. After consultation it was decided to have him taken to his boarding-place that night, which was done, the men who had beaten him in anger carrying him through the storm in pity.

As for old Jacobs, he was not seriously hurt, but a good deal scared. After taking another glass of ale he went home, and at a much earlier hour than usual.

CHAPTER II.

THE evening had worn on until it was nearly ten o'clock, the heavy storm continuing. The snow, which had fallen to the depth of several inches, driven by eddying winds, was piled up in some places several feet high. Only a few of the men who took Spencer home returned that night, and by ten we were nearly deserted.

Among those who still remained was John Ashley, the foreman's son, and he had drunk so much that he was unable to walk steadily. I was trying to persuade him to go home with a journeyman who worked under his father in the bindery, and who went past his house, when I heard an exclamation from Lloyd. It was full of pain and surprise.

The street door was again pushed ajar by a woman's small white hand. Through the partial opening I could see a woman's face and form, and beyond her, made visible by a street lamp, the fast-falling snow and its ghostly shroud upon everything.

Suddenly the door was thrown back, and the slender form of a girl, pale as death, stepped a few paces inside. Her light, abundant hair had fallen over her neck and shoulders, and lay about them in wet and tangled masses.

"Father! father! oh, father! don't do it, father!" she cried out in a piteous kind of wail, like one in cruel suffering.

By this time Lloyd had come from behind the bar, and was only a few steps from the girl, when, looking at him for a moment, she uttered a piercing cry, and turning, fled through the door with the fleetness of a deer.

"Stop her!" he cried wildly, "stop her!" I ran out, Lloyd following quickly. Just as I reached the pavement I saw the flutter of a garment at the corner of Harvey street, round which it disappeared. I sprang forward, but when I reached the corner no living form was visible. I ran to the next corner, but saw no one. As I turned from the baffled pursuit, Lloyd came up, bareheaded, as I was, and said huskily,

"My God! it's Maggy! What does it mean?" The name of God was often on his lips, but never with the solemnity, anguish and sense of helplessness with which it was then uttered. "Has she gone mad? Oh, Hiram! and out in such a night! Did you see which way she went?"

"I saw her go like a flash round into Harvey street," I replied, "but when I got to the corner she was not in sight."

We ran this way and that for a while, fruitlessly, and then returned for our hats and overcoats. Leaving the saloon in charge of our bar-tender, we started out again, taking different ways—Lloyd, that in the direction of his home. I asked all the policemen I met—not many were out that night—if they had seen anything of a young girl in a waterproof, and with only a handkerchief over her head, but could gain no intelligence of her. After searching about for half an hour, and until I was almost stiff with cold, I went back to the saloon, or "The Retreat," as it was called. As I turned into Harvey street I saw, just a little in advance, some one trying, with difficulty, to make head against the storm that beat in his face. He staggered from side to side, now coming up against the house, and now swaying to the curbstone. Just as I reached him his foot tripped against something, and he pitched headforemost into a bank of snow. I waited for a few moments to see if he could recover himself. But after a few feeble efforts to rise he lay still with his face downward.

I stooped, and taking his arm, tried to help him up, but he lay like a log.

"Come, come, sit up! You'll freeze to death!" I said, in a loud, commanding voice, jerking his arm at the same time.

"Oh, it's you, Hiram! Well, you needn't pull a fellow's arm off," growled the prostrate man, in a thick, drunken voice.

It was John Ashley. The poor, weak, good-natured fellow had taken a glass too much, and then started for home, against his will, as I afterward learned. But our bar-keeper, who had a grudge against him, put him out of the saloon after we left, and would not let him come back. So he started for home in the blinding storm, and unless I had come upon him as I did, he would never, I fear, have reached his father's house.

Nothing was left for me to do but get him home—a distance of many blocks—as best I could. So I raised him by main strength to his feet, and after steadying him, said,

"Come."

"Come where?" he asked, not moving a step.

"Home. I'm going to take you home," I said.

"I'll bet you a drink on that!" he mumbled thickly, and then broke out in an attempt to sing "We won't go home till morning."

I was in no mood for exercising patience, so I put forth my strength and drew him along. After his feet got in motion he kept on unresistingly. At the next street I hoped to get a car that would take us near his residence, but the snow had blocked the track, and no car was in sight. I waited for a while, when a policeman came up.

"Are the cars running?" I asked.

"No; they stopped an hour since," he replied, then, as he recognized me, added with a laugh,

"Taking home some of your work, I see."

"I wish he'd stay at home," I answered, impatiently. "Guess I'll have to turn him over to you, and let him have a night in the station-house."

"Who is he?" asked the policeman.

"Oh, it's Ashley's son," I replied.

"Not Ashley at the bindery?"

"Yes; and I wish he'd keep his boy at home."

"No, sir; it can't be done!" said the policeman, speaking strongly. "John's got to be taken home. I'll not put that disgrace on his father. You've made him drunk, and now you must take care of him. Don't let him get into a station-house to-night. If you do, there'll be trouble. He's a minor, understand."

I did understand, for the judge's charge to the grand jury was still fresh in my memory.

"You'll have to give me a lift," said I.

"There's no 'have to' about it," he answered. "I'm on my beat, and can't go off of it, if I cared to."

So I had nothing to do but to get the drunken boy home as best I could. It took me nearly an hour. Two or three times he fell down, when it was as much as I could do to lift him up. I was completely exhausted and out of temper when we reached his father's house. It was then after eleven o'clock. A light burned in one of the chambers and in the hall.

He was so stupefied with liquor and cold that he could not stand alone, and it was with difficulty I got him up the steps. Then I squared him round and leaned him with his back against the door, saying, in a low voice,

"Steady, now, John! Steady!"

As soon as I had him set firmly, I gave the bell a

violent jerk and ran down the steps, waiting a little way off to see that he was taken in. In a few moments the door was opened, and he fell heavily into the vestibule. A mother's cry of pain and terror rang out upon the air. Yes, it was a mother's cry; my heart told me that.

I hurried away, the cry ringing in my ears so distinctly that it seemed to be coming after me, and as I went I swore that John Ashley should never enter "The Retreat" again.

And he never did. But I am ahead in my story, and must go back a little in order that the reader may not only know how I came into this wretched business, but something of the characters I have brought before him.

CHAPTER III.

I WAS earning fifteen dollars a week at my trade—might have earned twenty if I had worked steadily, but would have been no better off, for my pockets had holes in them that let everything run out. I was not careful of my money, but spent it freely, and for the most part foolishly. I was fond of company, and that into which I drifted was not always the best for a young man. Too often the evenings found me in a drinking-saloon—not that I cared much for liquor, but I met good fellows there, and passed the time agreeably.

There worked beside me in the bindery—my trade was that of a bookbinder—a man named Tom Lloyd. He was ten or twelve years older than I, and had a wife and four children. I was single. Taking one week with another, Lloyd's wages did not reach an average of over sixteen dollars, though he could easily have earned from eighteen to twenty. Scarcely a week passed that he did not lose a day or an afternoon. He was always complaining about hard work and poor pay, and never received his wages on Saturday night without grumbling because the amount was so small. He was not what was called a drinking man, though he took his glass of beer two or three times a day.

As his pockets were generally empty by Monday or Tuesday, he often borrowed of me small sums, to be returned on Saturday night. At first these were promptly repaid, but after a while only a part was made up, and a promise given to square all by the next pay-day. He rarely kept his word.

"Never mind," I usually replied to his half-shame-faced apologies; "let it go over another week."

"I'm so dreadfully poor," he used to say sometimes. "How we are all to keep soul and body together is more than I can tell. Six mouths to feed! Just think of that!"

I pitied and forgave him all he owed me whenever he talked after this fashion. Six mouths to feed, and I had only one, yet Saturday usually found my pockets as empty as Tom Lloyd's.

Mrs. Lloyd was a clever sort of woman, and managed to do a great deal of hard work at home, and yet keep herself and house looking tidy. She had been very well educated in one of the public schools, and was rather intelligent. I liked both herself and husband so well that I often called in on Sunday afternoon and took tea with them.

If Lloyd had worked as faithfully and economized as carefully as his wife, their income would have been larger, and they would not have heard the wolf growling as often as they did. As it was, the signs of poverty were beginning to show themselves at home in many ways. The furniture and carpets were growing old and dingy, and could not be replaced, clothing was poor and scant, and everything was getting a sort of pinched look. Mrs. Lloyd's face often wore a dreary, anxious expression.

And yet Tom Lloyd would drop out a day for fishing, gunning or some other recreation almost every week. This recreation always acted in the wrong direction, as the day that followed found him so disinclined for work, either bodily or mentally, that ten hours rarely counted in his favor on the wages book for more than five.

So it went on until little debts here and there began to grow troublesome. Duns waited for him to come home at meal-times, or haunted him at the bindery. He put them off, and promised without hope of being true to his word. Strangely enough, all this failed to keep him more diligently at his post. The fact was, he had an idle vein in his make-up. He did not like work.

"I was born to be a gentleman," he would sometimes say, meaning by a gentleman one who had nothing to do.

One Sunday afternoon we were taking a walk together. It was warm, and we were thirsty.

"Come, let's have a drink," said I as we came in sight of a showy-looking saloon with LAGER BEER in large gilt letters above the door and on the window.

"I'm agreeable," was the ready answer. So we went in and drank each a mug of beer.

"Do you know that chap?" asked Lloyd as we passed out of the saloon.

"No," I replied, turning, as I spoke, to read the name on the window. It was "JOHN GLUM."

"Well, I do, then. I didn't know till now what had become of him. He's got a tip-top place here, and no mistake."

"Who is he?" I inquired.

"He was, when I knew him, one of the poor tools in Johnson's bindery. He never earned over seven or eight dollars a week."

"He makes more than that a day, judging from what we saw just now," I replied.

Lloyd made no answer, but walked along for some distance silent and with his eyes upon the ground.

"By George, Hiram!" he exclaimed, at last, lifting his eyes and looking at me with a new and excited expression on his face; "that fellow has put a new idea into my head. He isn't the poor tool we all thought him."

"A penny for your thoughts," said I, laughing.

"A gold eagle wouldn't buy them, if that were to lose them," he answered, with a strange earnestness of manner that surprised me. Then the new idea dawned upon my own mind. I understood what he meant.

"It's a blamed sight easier than work, Hiram."

"Drawing beer and mixing punches and cocktails?" I queried.

"Yes, and pays better," he said, with emphasis. I could feel in his voice the thrill of an unusual excitement. The blood was warming up his cold face. Light glittered in his eyes.

"Not a very reputable sort of business," I rejoined.

"Reputable! Faugh! It pays, and if you have money, you're reputable enough. A fig for all that!" and he snapped his fingers sharply. "Who cares for me now? Is Tom Lloyd anybody? Nothing but a poor miserable hack trying to keep soul and body together. If I were to fall sick to-morrow, who would look after me and the children? Nobody! We'd be packed off to the almshouse. Reputable!"

As he said this a handsome phaeton with two fine horses went dashing by.

"Do you know that party?" he asked, flinging out his arm in an elated manner.

"No," I replied.

"Billy Logan and his two daughters. Billy keeps the 'Logan House' in Briar street. Six years ago he peddled stationery, but that sort of thing was too slow for him, so he set up a bar in a small way. I don't believe he had ten dollars' worth of liquor in his shop when he opened. You see what he is now."

I was beginning to feel interested. A poor peddler transformed in six years to a gentleman sitting in his elegant phaeton behind a span of spanking black horses!

There was no such luck for a poor journeyman bookbinder. A feeling of envy and dissatisfaction crept into my soul.

"That's respectability, you see," Lloyd went on. "Money's the go; people don't ask how you make it. All right if you have it, and the more you get to spend and splurge on, the more respectable you are. It's the way of things in this world. Do you see that elegant house over yonder? Splendid enough for a prince."

"Yes."

"Well, do you know who lives there? I can tell you: that house belongs to Hart Hartley, Esq. He made all his money by liquor—not by selling it glass by glass over a counter to Tom, Dick and Harry. He isn't one of your John Glums and Billy Logans, but a manufacturer and wholesale dealer. Why, it is said that he furnishes liquor to half the saloons in our city, and piles up his hundred thousand dollars every year. Now, figure me out this, Hiram Jones: what makes Hart Hartley's business more respectable than John Glum's? If there is anything disreputable in selling a glass of beer or whisky for one man to drink, is it any the less disreputable to sell a keg or barrel for a hundred or a thousand men to drink? Maybe you can see the difference, but my head isn't clear enough."

I was a great deal more interested in what Lloyd was saying than I affected to be. A new line of thought had been opened, and my mind was busy looking over the ground it presented. I was not a bit fonder of work than Lloyd. Ease and self-indulgence came very natural to me, and work was accepted only as a necessity. I had cast about a great many times to see if I could not get into something better—that is, something that required less work and paid more—than bookbinding. But my education had been defective; I had no knowledge of accounts, and was a poor penman. Shut away from general business for years in a bindery, and with little enterprise or ambition to excel, I was not really good for anything outside of my trade, and so I had delved along, spending as I earned, and cherishing no hope of rising above the life of a journeyman.

The example of John Glum, once a "poor tool" of a bookbinder, but now gathering in money like dirt, had set my thoughts going in a new direction, but I shrunk back with an inner feeling of repulsion at the idea of standing behind a counter and serving out liquor when that way of bettering myself was clearly presented.

It was not reputable, and for all that Lloyd said and I tried to think, I could not make it out so. I had always felt that a man must lose self-respect, be very low in his instinct or have an utter disregard of others' well-being when he consented to be a bar-tender or keep a drinking-saloon. I had never seen any good come of the business, but knew of a great deal of harm.

Drawing a deep breath in an effort to throw off the weight a conflict of feeling had produced, I said, in answer to Lloyd's last remark, "One is as bad as the other. Your Hartleys and your Logans are all in the same boat—all engaged in the work of making men worse instead of better."

"Pshaw!" exclaimed my companion, with a good deal of contempt in his voice. "Men will drink, and if they do so to excess, they have nobody but themselves to blame. The saloon-keeper only supplies a common want. His business is just as honest and respectable as his neighbor's. No one is obliged to buy his wares. If I get thirsty on a hot day like this, the man who sells me a cool glass of ale is my benefactor. He has done me good. It is no fault of his if I should drink at a dozen different places and make a beast of myself."

"No, of course not," I replied, backing away from my view of the case, and falling in with what he said. Indeed, I felt a little ashamed of myself for the decided way in which I had spoken of liquor-sellers, classing them as I had with evil-doers.

"It's just as fair and honest a way of getting a living as any other," reiterated my companion.

"Maybe it is," I answered, trying to push back all thoughts to the contrary.

"I know it is;" and Lloyd clenched his fist and threw it out before him violently. It was a way he had of emphasizing his words. "Anyhow," he added, in a cold, half-sneering tone, " it's the easiest way to get along in the world for such poor devils as you and me, and if I had a hundred or two dollars to begin with, I'd follow suit to-morrow. As to the right or wrong of the matter, it wouldn't trouble me a bit."

"If a man doesn't look out for himself," said I, "he'll not find any one to do it for him."

"Of course not," answered Lloyd; "every man for himself in this world."

"Yes, and if every man took care of himself," I rejoined, "the world would be a very different affair to-day from what it is."

"Exactly. And now let us see if we cannot take better care of ourselves than we have done in days gone by. What say you?"

"I'm ready for almost anything," I replied, "except stealing."

"How much can you raise?" asked my companion.

"Toward setting up a grog-shop?" I could not help betraying in my voice something of the contempt I felt for the thing I named.

"Yes, a grog-shop, if you will; I am not particular as to what you call it. How much can you raise?"

"Haven't a dollar ahead," said I.

Lloyd shrugged his shoulders and looked disappointed.

"Can't you borrow a hundred dollars?" he asked.

"Will a hundred dollars be enough?" I queried.

"I don't believe John Glum had twenty. But then we couldn't afford to begin on a keg of beer and a quart of whisky, as he did. I have six mouths to feed, you know. If we go into the business, it must be in a larger way."

"How many saloons and whisky-shops do you think there are in this city?" I asked.

"I have heard it set down as from five to six thousand," he replied.

"Great guns! Can that be really so?"

"I wouldn't wonder. You find them everywhere."

"I'm afraid there's no room for another. Where is our custom to come from?" I said, with an involuntary depression of voice that betrayed the interest I was taking in the new scheme for bettering our fortunes.

"I was just thinking of that," Lloyd replied.

"Well? What are your thoughts worth?"

"A great deal. You get the money to start with, and I'll find the custom."

"Where?"

"There are from fifty to sixty men and boys, all told, in our bindery and printing-office, and there is not a respectable saloon within a block of the building. More than half the men take from two to three glasses a day now, some going out for it, as we do, and some sending the boys to bring them lager or ale on the sly. Now, if we can find a house close to the building—closer than anything else—and fit it up nicely, we will have two advantages—a nearer and more attractive place and the good-will of all the men."

"Capital! you've hit the nail!" I responded, quite lifted up by this view of the case. "We ought to sell two or three hundred glasses a day to the bindery and printing-office alone."

"And two or three hundred more every evening to the printers who are on at night, and to our friends in the bindery who would drop in to pass away time, to say nothing of transient custom. There never was a better opening than this."

"Splendid!" I rejoined, entering warmly into the scheme. "And we'll do it."

"You can get the money?"

"That isn't so clear; and besides, a hundred dollars won't be enough. It will cost more than that for counters, shelves, signs, furniture and the like, to say nothing of the stock of liquors. But 'where there's a will there's a way.'"

CHAPTER IV.

WE had arrived by this time at Lloyd's house. I went in and stayed to tea, as I often did on Sunday evenings.

There were four children in the family. The oldest was a daughter named Maggy, then just turned of seventeen. She was a fair-haired, blue-eyed girl, and very pretty, but peculiar. I say peculiar, meaning that she was unlike the ordinary run of girls in her station. Her manners were reserved and quiet. She talked but little, and you never heard her say a weak or foolish thing. Always when she spoke you saw just a little mounting of the blood to her face, and sometimes a flashing change in her eyes. She had entered the normal school a year before, and was perfecting herself for a teacher.

Thomas, a very fine boy a little over fourteen, came next. He had just gone into the bindery as an apprentice, and was earning three dollars a week, which was a great help. Harvey and Willy, the two younger children, were aged respectively eight and five.

There was a visitor at Lloyd's whom I had never seen there before—a well-dressed, clean, bright-looking young man, who had called to see Maggy. I saw her color rise and her eyes quiver and brighten as she introduced the young man to her father as Mr. Watson. Lloyd met him with a coldness of manner that I scarcely understood, and I could see that Maggy was hurt and disappointed. The young man felt the coldness, and showed a little embarrassment. He did not stay long after we came in. Maggy went to the door with him, and stood talking on the step for several minutes. On her return her father said, a little roughly, at which I was surprised, for he was usually very tender and considerate in his way of speaking to Maggy,

"Who is that fellow?"

A deep color came into Maggy's face, and her eyes filled with tears. She answered with a stifled tremor in her voice,

"He's one of the teachers in our school."

"Indeed!" Lloyd did not conceal the surprise this gave him. "One of your teachers, ha?"

"Yes, sir."

"He's a young-looking chap to be a teacher."

No reply was made to this, and we all sat silent for some time. I was looking at Lloyd, and saw a shadow creeping over his face, and I don't think I was wrong in my guess at the cause. If so respectable a person as a teacher in the normal school should take a fancy to Maggy, there would come trouble in the household about the new business, should Lloyd conclude to go into it. Maggy would feel it to be a disgrace, and the young man, if he were really taking a fancy to her, would hardly continue his attentions after it became known that her father kept a drinking-house.

Maggy and her mother soon went out of the little front room or parlor, as they called it sometimes, to look after the supper, and Lloyd and I drew together to talk in undertones about the matter uppermost in both of our minds. Thomas, the oldest boy, was reading in a Sunday-school library book brought home that day, and we talked low, so that he might not be attracted to what we were saying.

"I'm in dead earnest about this thing," said Lloyd as soon as we were enough alone to be able to talk freely. There was a kind of relief in his voice, as if he had been restraining himself. I noticed a hardness in his face not usual in its expression, and a fierce, half-defiant look in his eye—a sort of eager, awaking cruelty—that was altogether new to me. "The more I think of it, the more it grows on me," he added.

"Just the way I am feeling about it," was my reply.

"Do you know what a glass of ale or a drink of spirits costs?" he asked.

I did not, but I was very sure the profit was large.

"It's nearly all profit, or I'm mistaken," said Lloyd. "Let's see. How shall we find out? Ah!

It's just come to me. There's Perry Flint. He kept bar once."

"Who is Perry Flint?" I asked.

"Don't you know old Perry? He's been a hard case in his time. Used to drink like a fish. He was in a good business down on the wharf some years ago, I'm told, and right well off, but got broken up somehow, and was never able to get on his feet again. He works around, doing most anything. Everybody knows 'Old Perry.'"

"Where does he live?" I inquired.

"Round in Bell's court."

"Very well. Let's hunt him up."

So round to Perry Flint's we went as soon as tea was over. He was a gray-haired old man, with a worn-down look, such as you see in persons who take no care of themselves. His face bore the marks of long dissipation, and his voice was deep and husky, as though he were suffering from a cold. Any one who has heard that peculiar voice knows it as the sure sign of a hard drinker.

"Why, bless us, Mr. Lloyd, is that you?" he exclaimed as we entered the poor-looking room in which he lived.

"Yes, it's me, Perry, and this is my friend Jones. We work in the same place," returned Lloyd.

"Oh! ah! At the bindery round in Harvey street?"

"Yes, at the bindery. Where's the old lady?"

"Gone into one of the neighbor's. Here, take

seats, gentlemen. Not much of a place for company, but it's the best I have;" and the old man bustled round, handing us each a chair.

"We've called to have a talk with you, Perry," said Lloyd, coming at once to the subject of our visit.

The old man's eyes brightened, and a pleased expression drifted into his face.

"At your service, gentlemen," he replied, and then waited for Lloyd to open his mind.

"You've kept bar?" Lloyd was in no mood to beat around the bush, and so put direct the question he wished answered.

"Yes, a little in my time," answered Flint.

"So I thought. How long did you keep bar?"

"Off and on, a good while."

"In the city?"

"Yes; I kept bar at the Eagle Hotel more than a year."

"Then you're our man," said Lloyd, "and we want to have a good talk. But this is not just the place, you see; the old lady might drop in upon us."

"It wouldn't do to say 'bar' if she were around," answered Flint, giving his shoulders a shrug.

Just as this was said a hand pushed the outside door open gently, and an old woman entered. She was small and had a thin, pale face, mild, almost tender, gray eyes, and a sad, sweet mouth. I had seen such faces in pictures, but never before just such a living face. Her dress was a rusty black bombazine or alpaca, I don't know which, but it was clean and fitted her neatly. A white handkerchief, folded corner-wise, was drawn around her neck, and she wore a plain white cap. Poor and old and humble as she was, you felt that she was a lady and out of her place.

A look of surprise came into her face when she saw us—surprise mingled with uneasiness.

"Mr. Lloyd and Mr. Jones, Mrs. Flint," said the old man, introducing us.

"Good-evening, gentlemen." She spoke in a low, soft voice and with a grace of manner such as you do not often meet. But I could see a questioning disquiet in her eyes, that were reading Lloyd's face and mine with a penetrating scrutiny. I began to feel embarrassed and ill at ease.

"A pleasant evening," I remarked.

"Pleasant, but warm," she replied. What a sweet old voice it was! The tender gray eyes looked at me with a steadiness that I could not endure. I had to drop my own to the floor; when I lifted them again, I found that she was still reading my countenance, and the shadow that was stealing over hers told me that she was not satisfied with what she found there.

We did not remain long after Mrs. Flint came in, nor ventured, while we stayed, to make even the remotest allusion to the purport of our visit. When we left, Flint, without putting on his hat, walked with us to the end of the court.

"Come round to the 'Shades,'" said Lloyd as we parted.

"This evening?" queried Flint.

"Yes; you'll find us there."

"All right; I'll soon be on hand."

We waited at the "Shades," a tavern close by, for over fifteen minutes before the old man came in. His step was slow and his face grave. A change had passed over him.

"I'm here, gentlemen, as I promised," he said. "Perry Flint always keeps his word."

"Why, what's the matter, old boy? You look as sober as if you'd just come out of a prayer-meeting;" and Lloyd put his hand familiarly on Flint's shoulder.

"Maybe I have," was the response, made without a change of countenance.

"Oh!" returned Lloyd, with a covert sneer; "the old lady—"

"Take care now!" A fire seemed to blaze out of the old man's eyes. "Keep your hands off of her."

I saw Lloyd's mistake, and tried to correct it.

"Yes," I broke in warmly, "keep your hands off of her. A dearer old lady than your wife, Mr. Flint, I have never seen. I don't wonder that you say, 'Keep your hands off of her.'"

"You are right, my boy," Flint responded, turning to me with a look of pleasure in his marred face. "She is a dear old lady—yes, a *lady!*—and too good for me. Oh dear! the trouble I've brought on her!"

There was genuine regret in the deep, rattling voice of the old man, that sunk and trembled as he spoke.

"Come," said Lloyd, taking hold of Flint's arm; "let's go over to that corner, where we can be more alone."

Flint went passively, and we took our places at a table.

"Three glasses of ale," Lloyd said to a waiter who came up as we sat down.

"No, thank you; none for me," said Flint, with an upward side motion of the hand, like one trying to ward off something. I looked at him, and saw a struggle in his face.

"Nonsense! Three glasses, waiter," spoke out Lloyd.

And the waiter left us to fill the order.

"I tell you, Mr. Lloyd, I don't want anything," said the old man; "I didn't come here to drink. I said I wouldn't touch a drop, and I won't. So there, now!"

His manner was nervous.

"Oh, well, never mind." I spoke soothingly. "You needn't take anything if you don't want to. This is a free country, you know."

"Of course it is. I haven't taken a drop for nigh on to three weeks. You see, I've sworn off."

"Haven't taken the pledge?" There was just enough of a sneer in Lloyd's voice to be annoying.

"No, but I 'most wish I had."

I was struck by the tone in which this was uttered. It was that of one who felt himself in danger.

Three foaming glasses of ale were set down upon the table. The old man turned his face away. I took up one of them, and Lloyd another. After we had each of us taken a deep drink, Lloyd, as he removed the glass from his lips, said,

"That's splendid liquor; don't know when I've tasted so fine a glass of ale."

Flint sat very still, with his eyes turned away from the glass, which had been placed right before him on the table. I saw that a struggle was going on between appetite and resolution, and I had little doubt as to which would conquer. I could not but feel pity for the poor old man, and regret for having brought him into temptation.

"Don't let that glass of good liquor spoil," said Lloyd. "See, the bead is going off. Take it, man, quick, or it will be as flat as dish-water."

The smell of hops and malt was in the old man's nostrils. His morbid thirst, irrepressible in its craving, was too strong for one so weak in moral force.

There was a pause, a silence, a waiting. I don't know why I felt as I did, but there came a heavy pressure on my breast; I could hardly draw in air enough in breathing, it was so heavy. Then I saw the weak old man reach out and take the glass. He raised it to his lips slowly, but drank with the full draughts of a man long athirst. I was sorry for him; I could not help it. But I have seen sadder things than that since then without a touch of pity.

"I thought you'd come to it," said Lloyd, with a low, ill-sounding laugh, as Flint set down the glass, which he had emptied before taking it from his lips. "Good liquor, that!"

The old man did not reply, but sat very still, as if in a maze. I watched his face, as I had done before. It was half a puzzle to me.

"Yes," he said, like one coming out of a dream—"yes, it is good liquor."

"And you pretended you didn't want it. But I knew better."

"Well, gentlemen, it's done, and can't be helped. And now, what can I do for you? What is in the wind?" His manner changed entirely. The ale had worked a revolution.

"How much do you suppose that glass of ale cost the landlord?" asked Lloyd.

"About two cents and a half—maybe three cents," replied Flint.

"I guessed as much," was returned. "Three cents, and the landlord gets ten."

"Yes; they make money hand over fist, these chaps," said Flint.

"Seven cents a glass will do, Hiram." Lloyd spoke with a chuckle of satisfaction in his voice. "A hundred glasses, seven dollars. That isn't bad, is it?"

"Oh, they make that easy," spoke out Flint, his

hoarse, deep, rattling voice sounding out into the bar-room.

"Hu-s-h!" and Lloyd put his finger to his lips. "'Tisn't none of their business what we're talking about."

"Beg pardon," said Flint; "didn't mean to talk so loud, but my old shaky voice runs off with me sometimes."

"Do they make as much on spirits?" now asked Lloyd.

"That's according to how they do it. Some of 'em make a good deal more. We used to sell, at the Eagle, a tip-top brandy at fifteen cents a glass that didn't cost much, if anything, over three or four."

"You don't say so!" exclaimed Lloyd.

"Fact! We made it ourselves."

"Made it?"

"Certain. You can make any kind—gin, brandy, rum or just what you please. We had a book at the Eagle that told all about it."

"How did you make the brandy you sold at fifteen cents a glass?" I inquired.

"Well, you see, we got four gallons of sweet liquor—"

"What is sweet liquor?" I asked.

"Sweet liquor? It's what they call rectified spirits, I believe."

"Well, go on."

"We took four gallons of sweet liquor that cost

us a dollar and three-quarters a gallon. That is seven dollars. Then we bought a gallon of brandy for eight dollars, and mixed them all together, adding something to make the color rich and bring out the flavor. So we had five gallons of liquor that few men could tell from genuine cognac, and all for about fifteen dollars."

"I see, I see!" returned Lloyd, a pleased interest in his face. "And now can you tell how many drinks there are in a gallon?"

"Somewhere from sixty to seventy. We always called it sixty, so as to be on the safe side."

I took out an old stump of a pencil that happened to be in my pocket and began figuring on the margin of a newspaper which lay on the table, talking aloud as I did so:

"Five times sixty are three hundred. Three hundred drinks at fifteen cents. Three times five are fifteen; three times one are three, and one makes four. Forty-five dollars for fifteen. That's how much on each glass? Three into fifteen goes five times. Just five cents a glass, which gives ten cents profit."

"Splendid!" ejaculated Lloyd. "No wonder they pile up money."

"Most of the taverns charge twenty-five cents a glass for brandy, and at some of the tip-top places they charge fifty cents for liquor just like ours. We hadn't a great run of brandy customers at the Eagle, and so only charged fifteen, to draw 'em on. We got the same for all other spirits, and none of them cost us any more than the brandy. According to your figures, we made ten cents a glass on the brandy, but it was nearer eleven or twelve, I guess. There was always some doctoring done that I didn't see, and, whatever it was, you may be sure it didn't add anything to the cost."

As the old man talked, his eyes growing brighter and his manner more free, I noticed his hand reach out for the empty glass in a mechanical sort of way. He took it up, as if not conscious of what he was doing, turned it round and round in both of his hands, and then, while still talking, raised it to his mouth and sipped the few drops that had collected at the bottom. Seeing this, Lloyd made a sign to one of the waiters, who took our glasses and filled them again.

There was no hesitation on the part of Flint when the second foaming glass of ale was set before him. He lifted it from the table in a pleased kind of way, and holding it up, said, as he examined it with a knowing look,

"They've got the knack of it, I see."

"The knack of what?" I asked.

"They know how to draw a glass of beer high up and low down, as we used to say at the Eagle. There's a great deal in it. A chap that understands his business can get ten or twenty glasses more out of a keg than a greenhorn."

"Possible?"

"Yes, sir. You must know how to put a good strong froth on the top that will last. Just like this."

He could wait no longer, but raised the glass to his lips, and poured down most of the contents before removing it.

"There wasn't much over two-thirds of solid liquor in that glass," he said, smacking his mouth. "All the rest was froth. They know just how to do it here. I've watched 'em many a time. It's high up and low down," lifting his glass and then drawing it steadily down a distance of several inches.

"You have the knack of doing it, I suppose?" said Lloyd.

"Me? You'd better say so! I can draw a glass of beer just right, and that is more than ten in a hundred can do—just right for the profit, I mean, and not too low down to spoil your customers. They won't stand too much froth, you know."

"What will it cost to fit up a pretty fair sort of a place?—not so large as this—say half as large? Have you any idea?"

I put the question to Flint.

"That's according to how you do it, gentlemen. The nicer the better, you know. And so this is what you are driving at? I kind of guessed as much;" and his watery eyes twinkled. "But take Perry Flint's advice, and don't do it. Stick to honest work. Bookbinding is a great deal more respectable than rumselling, and pays better in the end."

"Thank you for your advice, daddy," replied Lloyd, a little impatiently.

"No thanks required, sir. I'm an old man, and have seen a good deal of the world in my time, and a good many ups and downs among all sorts of people, and I say to you now, gentlemen, what I've said a hundred times before, and it's this: I never knew a man who got better off by selling liquor—better off in the end, I mean. Somehow, a curse always goes with it. I could count you a dozen names on my fingers to-night of men who got tired of honest work, and went into the liquor business, and there is not one of them that has not rued the day he did it. They all made money for a while. Some made a good deal, and kept it. But, oh dear! all the money in the world wouldn't buy what most of them lost."

"There! there! That will do, my friend," said I, breaking in upon his untimely speech. "We don't care about a temperance lecture to-night."

Lloyd rose to his feet suddenly; there was a heavy frown on his face.

"All right, gentlemen, all right!" muttered the old man. "I've said my say. Perry Flint hasn't lived sixty-five years for nothing. Go ahead! But it won't come out right. It never does."

"Oh, shut up!" exclaimed Lloyd, unable to restrain himself.

"Never did that in my life at any man's word," answered Flint, growing angry, "and don't mean to do it now. *You* tell *me* to shut up!" His voice was full of contempt for the man he addressed. "And who are you, I wonder?"

The weak, almost tottering, old man drew himself up into a firm, dignified attitude, and fixed his eyes in scorn and rebuke on Lloyd.

"Come," said the latter, addressing me. I went out with him, leaving Flint in the tavern.

We walked nearly half a square before either of us spoke. Lloyd was the first to break silence.

"It's well I got out as quickly as I did," he said, speaking like one from whose feelings some great pressure was but half removed. "I don't know what devil got into me, but it was as much as I could do to keep my hands off of that cursed old wretch."

"Why, Tom Lloyd!" I exclaimed, not concealing the surprise I felt. "The poor old man didn't mean any harm; he wanted to do us a service."

"Yes, I suppose he did, and I was a fool to let it anger me so. But I couldn't help it; my mind was setting all one way, you see, and when that is the case, anything like opposition ruffles me."

We did not return to Lloyd's house, but went into another saloon, that we might sit together and talk further on what was uppermost in both of our minds, and also to take note of what went on therein. We had seen and heard and thought enough on that Sunday afternoon and evening to satisfy us that the difference between bookbinding and liquor-selling was the difference between hard work and poor pay and ease and competence.

During the hour that we sat there thirty-two glasses of ale and beer and sixteen of spirits in one form or another were drank, and we counted the profit on an hour's business at not less than four dollars.

Before separating we had agreed, if it were possible to raise enough money to furnish and stock a small saloon, to open one as near the bindery as it was possible to get, for it was from the bindery and printing-office that we counted on getting the chief part of our custom.

"What will Mrs. Lloyd say?" I asked as we sat together.

The question sent a dark shadow over my companion's face.

"There'll be trouble," he answered, fretfully. "She'll set herself against it like a rock."

"What will you do?"

"Go ahead!" He shut his teeth, looking hard and resolute. "It will be all plain sailing with you, Hiram, but I shall have the devil to pay," he added, in a troubled voice. "Between Maggy and her mother, I expect to have a lively time. But I shall do it; you may count on that. It may be uphill work for a while, but when the silk dresses and fine ribbons come, everything will run as easy and smooth as oil. Money works wonders, you know, Hiram, and we're going to make money like dirt."

CHAPTER V.

ON the next morning, while on my way to the bindery—I was an hour late—I saw a crowd around Bell's court, and stopped to see what was the matter.

"There's been a murder," I heard some one say.

"Who is it?" I asked.

"Don't know," was replied. "They say a man has killed his wife."

I passed through the crowd that blocked up the entrance to the court, and threaded the narrow way packed with people, until I came in front of one of the small houses. The crowd stood a little back from the half-open door. I felt a strange suspense, a half-defined terror. I knew that Flint lived in the court, but having been there only once, I could not recognize his house.

In a blind, desperate sort of way I pushed open the door and went in, closing it behind me. There were, maybe, a dozen persons in the room, two of them police officers. But I saw them only obscurely. One object instantly fixed my gaze. It was the white face of Mrs. Flint. She was lying on a settee that stood opposite the door. There was no mistaking what was written on that finely-cut, peaceful, sweet old face. It was death! Lying on the floor, just in front of the settee, face down, was Flint, motionless as the dead form above him, his white, abundant hair shining like silver in the few rays of sunshine that came in through a corner of the window where the shade was broken, and fell just where his head was resting.

I lost my breath for several moments, my head swam, I felt as if about to fall from some great height. As I stood thus spellbound I saw the still form on the floor stir. Then a strong shiver ran through it, and then slowly and heavily the prostrate old man rose upon one elbow and looked at the face of his dead wife.

"God help me!" he groaned, falling back upon the floor with a heavy thud. The sorrow and despair in his voice were terrible.

One of the policemen now bent over him, and grasping his arm, said, not roughly, but almost tenderly,

"Come." He did not move.

"Come!" The policeman repeated his command, pulling on his arm as he did so, and raising him partly up by main force. At this, Flint seemed to comprehend what was meant, and yielded passively when another of the policemen took hold of him. As he stood erect I saw his face for the first time. It was so haggard and pinched and awfully wretched that I scarcely knew it.

The policeman drew the miserable old man toward

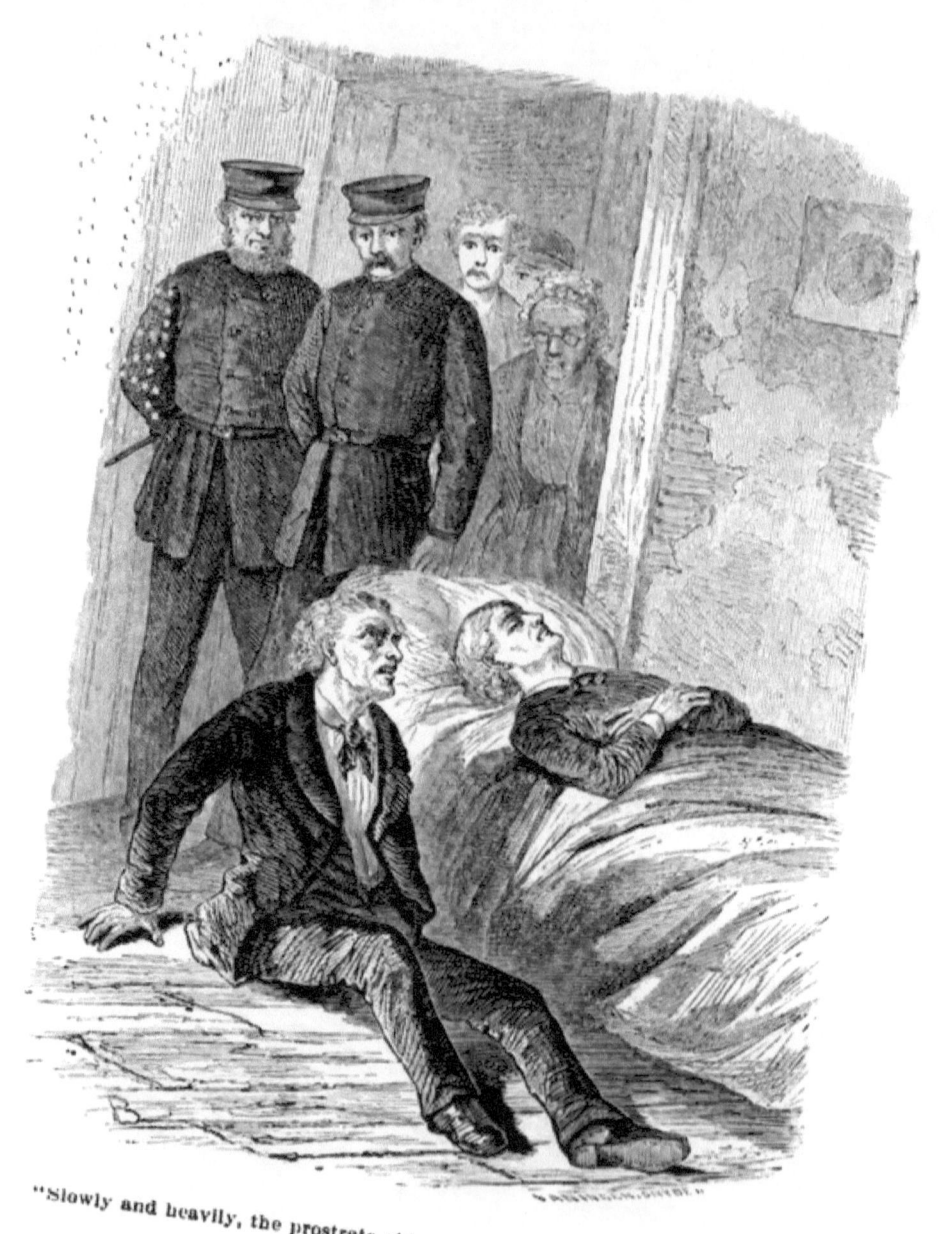

"Slowly and heavily, the prostrate old man rose and looked at the face of his dead wife."

the door. He held back, turning his head all the while and looking at the form of his dead wife. At the door he stood still in partial resistance.

"Come on, sir!" cried one of the men, with some impatience.

"Let me go back just for a minute," pleaded Flint, with a tone and manner that were irresistible.

The policeman released him. He returned slowly to the settee, and sunk forward on his knees and bent down over the quiet, dead face, looking at it, oh so lovingly and so sorrowfully. Then he laid his lips softly on the white forehead, and then his old heart broke. Such a wail of agony as rung out from his lips I hope never to hear again. He fell forward, then slipped heavily to the floor. When we lifted him, he was dead.

I went to my work in the bindery like one in a dream. I spoke to no person of the dreadful tragedy I had witnessed, not even to Lloyd. How could I, with the stain of murder on my own garments? I say here squarely what I felt, but would not acknowledge then. Yes, the conviction that at my door and Lloyd's was the guilt of this fearful work haunted me like a ghost. But I kept it all in my own heart.

"What's come over you, man?" asked Lloyd, who worked beside me. He had tried in vain to get me to talk, but could only draw "Yes" and "No" out of me.

"Nothing," I replied, evasively.

"You needn't say that. What's gone wrong?"

"Nothing;" and that was all he could get from me. So we worked on in silence for most of the day, standing side by side.

I was anxious to see an afternoon paper, and got one as soon as issued. It contained an account of the scene I had witnessed in the morning, under the head of "A DOUBLE TRAGEDY—MORE OF RUM'S DOINGS," and ran thus:

"A fearful tragedy took place at No. 6 Bell's court some time early this morning. An old man named Perry Flint killed his wife in a drunken fit, and then, in horror at the deed, fell dead as the policeman laid hands on him. Many of our citizens remember Flint very well. His father was Aubrey Flint, a highly-respected merchant in this city, who accumulated considerable property, all of which was left to Perry, who was his only child. The son carried on the business for several years, but fell into habits of dissipation, and at last became bankrupt. His wife was widely known in her younger days as a woman of rare culture.

"After Flint's failure in business he became very poor, and his accomplished wife was no longer seen in fashionable circles. They had two or three children, but all died when they were young. In his poverty and degradation Flint's wife, it is said, steadily clung to him, doing all in her power to hold him back from dissipation, and to make his hard, self-imposed lot as comfortable as possible. Flint, like most drunkards, often tried to reform, and sometimes kept away from drink for weeks at a time. But there is little or no hope for poor wretches like him when every block has its one or a dozen taverns.

"For a longer period than usual Flint had been abstaining from drink, and things were beginning to look more comfortable in his poor little home, and the pale, thin face of his patient, long-suffering wife to wear a more hopeful aspect, when, it is said, two men called to see him on Sunday evening and tempted him away to a tavern. Some of the neighbors heard him coming home about midnight. He was noisy, as was apt to be the case when he had been drinking.

"About seven o'clock this morning the people living up stairs heard voices in the 'old couple's' room. Flint cried out angrily several times, and they could hear his wife trying to coax him, as they thought, not to go out. But he did go, staying away perhaps half an hour. 'Oh, Perry, Perry!' his poor wife was heard to exclaim as he came in at the end of that time. Then he cursed her, using fearful oaths. There was silence for a little while. His wife's voice was again heard. In a moment after, a savage imprecation broke from his lips, and then a heavy fall was heard. A death-like silence followed, broken in a few moments by a cry of terror from the old man. He had struck his wife in his blind fury, and had killed her.

"He was found lying on the floor beside her as

she had fallen. The blow had been given by his clenched fist just under the right ear, and death had been instant. There was no wound, but a dark and wide discoloration.

"The deadly effect of the fearful blow dealt in his drunken frenzy sobered the unhappy man. The scene that followed was touching in the extreme. When they lifted the dead woman from the floor and turned her face upward, no eye could look upon it without tears. It is long since we have seen a face in death so calm and soft and beautiful, thin and white and marked by the death-angel as it was. All the fear and pain, if they had marred it when the mad blow was given, had faded out, leaving only the signs of a spiritual beauty which a long-tried, patient and religious soul had cut thereon.

"But the tragedy was not over. That blow had a fatal rebound, killing twice."

I folded the paper quietly, slipped it into my pocket and went on with my work.

"Heaven and earth!" exclaimed a journeyman near me, in a startled voice. "More doings of the rum fiend. Old Perry Flint has killed his wife."

"What?" eagerly inquired many voices, and a little group came round the journeyman, who read aloud the account I have just given.

I watched Lloyd stealthily. He did not once raise his eyes from the floor, nor, when the reading was over, make any comment. As for myself, I had no heart to say a word.

"You are not one of the men who called for old Perry yesterday?" said a journeyman near me, speaking in banter to another.

"No, thank God!" was the quick reply. "I'd about as soon be in the hangman's shoes."

"You'd deserve to be in the other man's shoes."

"What other man? Oh, the one to be hung, you mean?"

"Exactly."

"Just my sentiments. No punishment is too severe for a man who would draw a poor old wretch, making a feeble effort to save himself, back into the horrible pit of drunkenness from which he had escaped. It's a pity the names of the two men had not been given."

"A great pity. Maybe the inquest has or will put the public in possession of their names."

I felt a shiver of alarm pass through me. Various comments were made by the men, none of which were very pleasant to hear. Several times I was on the eve of joining in, lest my steady silence should attract attention, but I was afraid to trust my voice. It might betray the uneasiness I felt.

"Bad business, that," said I to Lloyd as we came out of the bindery together that evening.

"Oh, well, it's done and can't be helped," he replied, with more indifference of manner than I had expected. "I'm sorry we had any hand in it, but how did we know the old sot was going to make a beast of himself and kill his wife? When a man gets so far gone that he can't take a glass of beer without getting drunk, it's time he was dead."

I did not feel so very greatly shocked at this. Indeed, Lloyd's view of the case acted as a kind of relief to my feelings, and my spirits began to return.

Harvey street, in which our bindery and printing-office were, was a narrow street running between two of the larger ones in our city. Another narrow street crossed it at the distance of only two or three houses from our establishment. In these streets were a great many small houses occupied by poor families. There were, as is always the case in such localities, a number of drinking-shops, but none at all respectable or attractive in appearance.

As Lloyd and I walked away from the bindery that evening we noticed a bill on one of the houses only a little way off. It stood three or four doors from the corner of the two narrow streets, and entirely out of sight of the main entrance to our establishment, but close to one of the rear entrances. It was an old two-story house, with garrets and dormer windows, and had been used as a shop of some kind. There were two entrances, one into the shop and one into a narrow hall leading to the dwelling part of the house.

"That's the very place," exclaimed Lloyd as his eyes rested on the bill bearing the words "To Let." We crossed over and read on the bill, "Key next door."

"What is the rent?" we asked on getting the key.

"Five hundred dollars."

Five hundred dollars! It seemed to me a frightfully large sum.

"We can never stand that," I said as we returned to the street.

"It won't be anything at all," answered my companion, "after we get once started—only ten dollars a week, and we can make more than double that every day."

"Just the thing," said Lloyd, after we had gone over the house. "It will just suit my family. We pay two hundred and forty now, and by moving in here that much will be saved."

"But what is your wife going to say about it?" I asked.

A shadow dropped over his face, his brow fell, his mouth grew hard and resolute.

"There'll be trouble, I suppose," he replied. "There always is when women are concerned. But it won't last long. I've been master in my own house so far, and intend continuing so for a while yet. So, you see, it will be what I say about it."

"It is not a very nice place to bring your children," I remarked.

"Necessity knows no law. If I was able to pay two rents they might stay where they are, but as I am not, they will have to come here—that is, if we conclude to take the house. But we won't talk of outside matters now. The thing to decide is,, Can we raise the wherewithal to fit up a decent saloon?

This is the place; there is no doubt of that. We can get enough out of the bindery and printing-office to live like nabobs. I've figured it over half a dozen times."

"The men don't all drink," I said. "We can only count on a certain number."

"There's a way to bring most of them along," answered Lloyd, in a satisfied tone. "We've got to make things attractive. We'll have free lunches and music, and all that sort of thing. You see, I'm not going in after any dull, sleepy fashion. We must be wide awake. There are plenty of fish in the water, but they will stay there if you don't drop a hook or draw a net."

We met again that evening in one of the many taverns to be found in the neighborhood where we lived, and spent a couple of hours in talking over the question of ways and means. We had seen the owner of the vacant house, who was rather pleased than otherwise at the prospect of having it nicely fitted up as a saloon. He knew very well that after a good run of custom was obtained he could add from one to three hundred dollars to the rent. As a dwelling or small shop for retailing provisions and groceries a permanent tenant could not be found at the rent he asked, but as a first-class drinking-house the rent would be sure, and might be increased. So he entertained our proposal favorably.

But how were we to get the money necessary to fit the place up? It would take from six to eight hundred dollars, for the whole of the first story front would have to be changed. There must be a new door of some handsome pattern, ingrained wood, signs and a fancy gas-lamp. Inside, there must be counters and shelves and showy furniture, and last, but not least, a good stock of liquors. We must have not less than a thousand dollars. As I looked the matter squarely in the face I could not help saying,

"It's all folly, Lloyd; we can't do it."

"We can do it if we will," he replied, resolutely. "Now, it's my belief that if we offer the landlord six hundred for the first year and seven hundred for the second, he'll fit the place up for us."

I shook my head doubtfully.

"I mean to try him, anyhow," my companion said. "If he is satisfied that we are all right—and I reckon we can get as good characters as the next man—I believe he will do it. I saw that he was mighty well pleased when he talked of the handsome manner in which we meant to do the thing, and the way in which we expected to draw customers. He sees as well as we do that the stand is a splendid one, and that as we are journeymen in the bindery and know all the men, we can control the custom better than any one else. It's a splendid chance for him, and he knows it. Once get a good house started here, and his property will pay him forty per cent. more than he has ever received from it. All right, Hiram. The thing's done."

And he slapped my shoulder in a sudden rise of spirits.

"I wish I could see it," was my doubtful response.

"You will see it before a month goes over your head, or my name isn't Tom Lloyd. I read that old chap like a book. I saw the pleased, eager light in his half-shut eyes. He knows where dollars are, and how to get them. Let me alone for managing him."

"And you really think he will do the fitting up?" I said.

"I'm sure of it, if we cut our cards right. Nothing will pay him so well as a good tavern, and all he cares for is the money his house will bring. We can't get a thousand dollars to spend on the house, nor five hundred either, as to that matter. But we can make the thing a grand success if once started. Our advantage over outsiders will lie in the fact that we can control a large custom. I shall put this to him squarely. Then, after I get him warmed up, I shall quite coolly say, 'But there is one thing you will have to do, if we take your house.' I think I see his dull gray eyes coming wide open;" and Lloyd laughed to himself. "'What is that?' he asks. 'We are only two journeymen bookbinders, with nothing ahead,' I reply, 'and cannot stand the expense of fitting up a saloon. Now, if you will put this improvement on your house, we will give you six hundred a year instead of five.'"

"And he'll say, 'I'll do nothing of the kind,'" I responded.

"Of course he will," said Lloyd.

"Well? What then?"

"'All right,' I shall say. 'That ends it, as far as your house is concerned. We like its location best of any in the neighborhood, but shall have to take the next best. We already hold the refusal of two places in the square, and the landlords are anxious to fit them up nicely for us. They see that it will be the making of their property. Your house is just in the right spot, and we would rather have it. But that will be as you say. We were about closing for one of the others when we saw the bill on yours.'"

"You'll do, old chap," was my laughing reply. "Didn't know before that you had such a gift for lying."

"Lying? Psha! It's management. Well, that will bring him, you may bet."

And that or something else did bring him, for in less than a week carpenters and bricklayers were at work on the old house, and we were in possession of a lease for two years at seven hundred dollars a year.

We found no difficulty in arranging for a stock of liquors. Brewers and wholesale dealers in spirits were ready to give us a start. The more retail shops, the better for them, and so they made it very easy for us.

CHAPTER VI.

AMID all our plannings and preparations for the new business in which we were to make money "hand over fist"—my companion's favorite expression—I could never think of Lloyd's family without an uncomfortable feeling. In a mild way I had made objections several times to the plan of moving them over our saloon, but Lloyd always said positively that he couldn't and wouldn't pay two rents—that what was good enough for him was good enough for them. His feeling toward his wife and children was growing strangely cold and hard, and every time I referred to them he showed more or less irritation and annoyance.

Trouble was brewing—I felt sure of that. I had ceased to call on Sunday afternoons, preferring to meet Lloyd at some tavern where we could talk over our plans freely; besides, I had a sort of guilty feeling when I looked Mrs. Lloyd and Maggy in the face. I saw that their suspicions were awake, and that my intimacy with the husband and father was a source of uneasiness to them.

Soon after the carpenters got to work we let it be known in the bindery that we were going into a new enterprise. It created considerable stir among the men. Some approved and some condemned. One young man named Hargrave indulged in some strong language, and there had like to have been trouble between him and Lloyd.

"Better turn pirate or highwayman at once," he said, a stinging contempt in his voice that was irritating beyond measure.

I saw an instant pallor in Lloyd's face and a fiery devil in his eye. Putting my hand on him, I spoke in a low voice, and for his ear alone:

"Don't mind him, Tom; he's one of your pious chaps."

Lloyd curbed his passion. He saw, as I did, that just the worst thing we could do would be to get up a quarrel.

Hargrave said no more, but his remark turned the tide against us in a good many minds, and threw a blur on the respectability of our new enterprise.

"Too many grog-shops now," remarked another of the journeymen. "If I had my way, I'd suppress the whole of them."

"Do you think that would stop drinking?" asked a man at work near him. His name was Wilson.

"No, not while the present army of poor tipplers are alive," was answered. "But a few years would finish them up. In the mean time the business of drunkard-making as a profession would stop, and the trade, being confined to lady-and-gentleman amateurs in their homes, would languish, and year by year the product would be less. If no other good came of it, your son and mine would not be tempted at every corner."

I saw a pained look in Wilson's face, and knew what it meant. He had a son in the printing-office down stairs who was not over twenty years of age, but who had already fallen into intemperate habits. The argument went home, and Wilson leaned over his work and said no more.

Running remarks were kept up by the men for some time, and both Lloyd and myself were not a little chagrined and disappointed at what we heard. We had, besides, to stand a good deal of rough banter that chafed more than skin deep.

"I'd like to have a word with you, Mr. Jones," said the foreman of our bindery as I was going away that evening. His name was Ashley. Some of us did not like him very much, but I will say this of him: he was never unjust or arbitrary, though strict in his requirements with every one. If a man shirked his work or was off duty, there was no escape when pay-day came. He had to stand in his own shoes, and I guess that was all right. Well, I felt rather uncomfortable when he said, "I'd like to have a word with you, Mr. Jones."

I dropped behind, and Mr. Ashley drew me into his little office in a corner of the building.

"Jones," said he, when we were by ourselves—and he spoke in a kind but serious way and with a doubt in his voice—"it can't be true what I hear?"

"That will depend on what it is," I returned, dropping my gaze from his steady eyes.

"It is said that you and Thomas Lloyd are going to open a drinking-saloon in the house now being fitted up round the corner."

"We are," I replied as firmly as I could speak.

"I'm sorry to hear it," he answered, gravely. "It's all wrong, and will lead to no good."

"I can't see where the wrong is, Mr. Ashley," I replied. "It's as fair and honest a business as any other, and sanctioned by law."

He shook his head in a half-sorrowful way, saying,

"It's a business that hurts all who touch it. Crime, beggary, vice, idleness, sorrow, disease and suffering are its only fruits. Neither you nor any other man can point to a case where it has given to society a single benefit."

I thought rapidly, trying to find the case, but memory was at fault. I was not able to answer him. He went on:

"Are you, then, ready to go over to the side of what is evil?—to become a hurt and a hindrance in society, instead of a helper and benefactor? As a bookbinder every day's work is a good service to your neighbor, but as a liquor-seller every day's work will be a curse. Think it over, my friend. Look things squarely in the face and call them by their right names."

He was very earnest, but kind and pleading.

"I am much obliged for the interest you take, Mr. Ashley," I returned, trying to speak with firmness, "but it's too late to talk about it now; we've signed a lease for the place, and can't back down."

He looked baffled and distressed, then said,

"I'm sorry you didn't go somewhere else. I have trouble enough with too many of our men as it is. With a saloon next door, it will be worse than ever. I wonder at your doing this. Don't you know that there are more than twenty men in the establishment —good workmen, and right in all but one thing— who will fall over the stumbling-block you put in their way and go to ruin in the end?"

"If there was no other saloon in the neighborhood or in the city," I replied, "I might feel the force of what you say, Mr. Ashley, but as it is, I do not. Men who want to drink will go after it, near or far. If we are near to any of them, we will stand the best chance of getting their custom, that is all."

"But there are lads and young men in the establishment—some of them easily drawn aside, I fear," said Mr. Ashley, the troubled look still in his face. "You will put temptation in their way, and some of them will fall. It will be a terrible thing, sir, to have the guilt of ruined human souls and the curse of broken-hearted wives and mothers on your conscience. I speak plainly because I feel strongly, and because I see that what I deprecate will surely come."

As further talk was useless, I went away, expecting to find Lloyd in the street waiting for me, but was disappointed. He had gone home. So after tea I called at his house, but rather unwillingly, for I did not care to meet his wife and Maggy. If they had not known of our plans before, Thomas, who worked at the bindery, had of course brought home the unwelcome news.

I rang the bell, hoping that Lloyd would come to the door. Instead, Maggy opened it. I did not know her at first, though she stood in the strong light of a street-lamp, her face was so changed. It was pale and suffering, and her eyes were red and full of tears.

"Is your father at home?" I asked.

"No; he has gone out," she replied, in a voice so low and choked that I scarcely caught the words.

I was turning away, when she put out her hand and grasped my arm, saying, in a wild, tremulous manner,

"It isn't true, Mr. Jones! It can't be true!"

"What?" I asked.

"That you and father are going to—to—"

"Pshaw, child!" I answered, as lightly as I could speak; "what's the use of worrying yourself for nothing? You'll have silks and satins and a carriage to ride in before a year goes over your head."

"I'd rather live in a garret than have him do it, Mr. Jones," she said, wringing her hands and crying. Oh, it's something awful!"

"What a weak little fool you are, Maggy!" I replied, feeling half angry with the girl. "It's just as good and respectable a business as any other. There are thousands of better people than we are in it."

"It's wicked and disgraceful, Mr. Jones," she answered, speaking in a calmer voice, "and I'd rather see father dead than go into it."

"Good-evening," I said, turning away, for I didn't want to bandy words with the girl, and besides, I had a mean, guilty sort of feeling as I stood before her.

"Oh dear!" was my exclamation, speaking to myself, as I walked from the door. "It's first one thing and then another. What fools some people are!—always worrying themselves for nothing. To have Maggy set herself up like this! But it's no concern of mine. Tom Lloyd must take care of his own cattle;" and I tried to shake off the weight this short interview had laid upon my feelings.

I found Lloyd in one of the taverns where we had been in the habit of meeting. He was sitting at a table with a glass of beer before him, and ordered one for me as I sat down at the opposite side. I saw at a glance that he was unusually disturbed and out of humor.

"What's up now?" I asked, looking at him across the table.

"Oh, the devil to pay at home," he replied, angrily, knitting his brows and setting his teeth. "Tom got home before I did, and blowed the whole thing. Such a hornet's nest as I found! I'd half a mind to thrash him."

"I don't see that Tom is so much to blame," I returned, for I liked the boy. "It had to come out sooner or later."

"Of course it had, and I was going to speak with my wife about it this very evening. But Tom's report of that rough talk in the bindery has thrown all my fat into the fire. If you had seen the way they all came down on me! A charge of cavalry was nothing to it." He gave a low, sullen kind of laugh, but there was no touch of humor in his eyes nor on his lips. He was angry and bitter.

"If you'll take my advice," I said, "you'll not push this matter too far."

"What do you mean?" he asked.

"I mean that, if I were in your place, I wouldn't put my family over the saloon. It's pushing them a little too hard, and besides, the neighborhood is not the best in the world for children."

"And pay two rents? Not if Tom Lloyd knows himself."

"Don't be a fool, Tom," I replied. "There are two sides to this matter. In the first place, we don't know but what we may want the whole house ourselves, and in the second place, if we should not, it will be easy enough to get a tenant who will not be as much in the way as your family might be."

"Want it ourselves? What do you mean by that?" he asked.

"Young men like to have little suppers and champagne parties now and then, and we ought to have a room or two to accommodate them."

"Blamed if you ain't right there, Hiram," Lloyd answered, striking his hand on the table. "Never thought of that."

"Besides," I argued, "things get loose sometimes in taverns when parties go it a little too strong and raise a row."

"Fact!" responded my companion, with the manner of one into whose head some new idea was coming.

"And the farther away your wife and children are on such occasions, the better for your comfort and theirs."

"Something in that too, and I guess you're right about it," returned Lloyd. "Anyhow, we'll get in first, and see how the cat jumps."

I felt relieved at this ready acquiescence. My notion of keeping the rooms up stairs for suppers and drinking-parties was a new thought, coming at the moment, and the more I considered it, the more sure I was that in this way we could turn them to best account.

"Then," I said as I talked it over with Lloyd, "we shall have no women about to trouble us—nobody spying around. We shall be a great deal more independent. If I was in your place, I'd rather have my wife and children a mile away than under my nose."

"Guess you're right about it, Hiram;" and my friend took a deep breath like one who felt relieved.

"It will make it a great deal easier for you," I remarked. "You will have a hard row to hoe, as it is, or I'm mistaken. I saw Maggy a little while ago."

"You did?"

"Yes. I called round at your house before I came here, and Maggy opened the door for me. She looked dreadfully. I hardly knew her at first."

Lloyd made no reply.

"Ashley pitched into me as I was coming out this evening," I then remarked.

"He did? What about?"

"He wanted to know if it was true that you and I were going to set up a tavern close by the bindery."

"I wonder what business that is of Ashley's?" said Lloyd, with quick irritation.

"I wanted to say as much, but then, you see, it isn't our game to quarrel with anybody in the place."

"No, of course not, if we can help it. But human nature can't stand everything. What had he to say?"

"Oh, he gassed a spell over the harm we might do among the men."

"Harm!" Lloyd chuckled. "He thinks we're in the right place to catch them."

Catch them! Yes, that was it. He had never said it out before, and I had never thought it.

When a boy, living in the country, I had often seen little conical-shaped holes in the ground, with smooth sides formed of light sand. At the bottom of each of these holes, covered up from view, lay an ugly creature that we called an ant-bear. Often and often have I watched by these holes to see the ants fall in. The moment they passed over the sides the light sand would begin to give way under their feet, and they would commence falling to the bottom. Then up would poke the ugly head of the ant-bear, and his cruel claws would seize and drag the little creature out of sight into his murderous den below. I never saw one poor ant escape.

Strangely enough, when Lloyd spoke of our catching the men, my thoughts went back to the little round holes in the woods, and an ant-bear lying in wait for prey at the bottom of each of them. It made me feel uncomfortable, to say the least.

The next thing to be done was to give our place a name. While discussing this matter, considering and rejecting first one name and then another, I said in half banter and half bitterness—for since I had come to look this thing of keeping a drinking-house more closely in the face, and to consider all that it involved, I had begun to have sundry misgivings, and to wish I had never consented to go into the business—"Let us call it 'The Trap.'"

"What do you mean?" asked Lloyd, firing up and looking at me angrily.

"Pshaw! you're getting to be a perfect tinder-box," I replied, laughing. "Every spark sets you on fire. Can't a man have his joke?"

He growled a little about not being in a humor for joking. "Business was his word."

"Then," said I, "let's call it 'The Retreat.' One name is about as good as another, after it gets to be known."

He shook his head. "The Retreat" was too common and too tame.

"We want something new and striking."

"Better have something that suggests rest and comfort for tired men—that will make them think of pleasant evenings," I replied.

"How would 'The Rest' do?" asked Lloyd, falling in with my notion.

"Very well, besides being novel. Still, 'RETREAT' has in it something more than 'REST.' It makes you think of a place into which you can go and be away from common observation. There are a great many men who don't care about everybody knowing where or how they spend their evenings."

"I see," returned Lloyd. "Yes, 'RETREAT' is best. Suppose we fix on that, and be done with it?"

"Agreed." And so our saloon was called "THE RETREAT."

CHAPTER VII.

WE opened "THE RETREAT" with a grand flourish. There was a free lunch and free liquor for our friends from ten until two o'clock, and the number who found us out during these four hours was remarkable. I never knew that I had a tithe as many. Out of the sixty men and boys in the establishment, not less than forty paid us the compliment of eating our lunch and drinking our liquor. Among the rest came John Ashley, the son of our foreman, a nice lad of sixteen. He dropped in for a few moments when his father happened to be away, and took some lunch and a glass of beer.

I must say that when I saw John come in I had a feeling of regret. He was, as I have said, a mere lad, kind-hearted, social and easily influenced. His father was a little strict with him—too strict, some of us thought.

"How elegantly you are fitted up!" he said, in a pleased way, as he stood at the bar eating his lunch and washing down the mouthfuls with beer. "I guess you'll do well."

"That will be as our friends say," replied Lloyd. "I hope we shall see you now and then?"

"Oh yes; I'll look in once in a while for old

acquaintance' sake, if for nothing else. But it won't do to let the old gentleman know anything about it."

Poor boy! He came oftener than "once in a while," and a great deal oftener than was good for him.

On the next day we had a large placard hung out bearing the words, "Free lunch from ten till twelve o'clock." It consisted of fried liver cut into little pieces, and we gave each one who came in a small plate of this and a piece of bread, costing about a cent. Of course every one who took the lunch was expected to call for a glass of something to drink. One after another the men from the bindery and printing-office came in for the lunch, and some came twice within the two hours that we kept lunch on the counter, drinking both times. Boys came as well as men. The sight of these lads, some of them as young as twelve years, drinking beer with a satisfied air, was not pleasant to me. I wished they would stay away.

Soon after eleven o'clock, John Ashley made his appearance. He came in almost stealthily.

"Ah! Good-day, John," said Lloyd, putting on a pleasant air. "I've been looking for you all the morning. Let me make you up a nice lunch;" and he filled a plate heaping full and gave it to him, adding a large piece of bread.

"Thank you! That's splendid. I'm pretty sharp this morning. You see, I was a little late getting down to breakfast, and the old gentleman hurried me off to work before I was half through. A glass of beer, if you please."

Lloyd drew the beer and set it before him. John ate and drank hastily, so as to get back before his father missed him.

"He'd give me fits if he caught me here," was his remark as he set down his empty glass and paid his ten cents.

"Call round in the evening some time," said Lloyd, in his blandest way. "We had some nice people here last night."

"Thank you! Maybe I will;" and the lad hurried off.

In the evening he came in a little after eight o'clock. Lloyd was very gracious to him, and John was pleased and flattered by the attention.

"How are you getting on?" he asked.

"Elegantly," was replied. "Our friends have rallied about us strong. We count you among the number, of course."

"Thank you," said John. "Oh yes, you may count on me, only, as you know, Lloyd, I shall have to fight a little shy. A glass of ale, if you please. It wouldn't just do for the old gentleman to know I come here. 'Where are you going, John?' he asked to-night, and he looked at me sharply. I said, 'Only round to Mr. Oram's.' I don't think he half believed me."

"Bully for you!" cried a journeyman printer who

was standing near, and he slapped John familiarly on the shoulder.

"He's a brick," chimed in another.

Lloyd smiled approvingly, and the weak lad, pleased at their rough compliments, drank off his ale with as manly an air as he could assume.

"Your friend Joe Wilson's up stairs," said Lloyd as John, after drinking his ale, stood leaning on the counter.

"Is he?" a pleased expression lighting up his face. "Which way do you go?"

"I'll show you;" and Lloyd took him through a door that led into the entry and up to the second-story back-building, where we had two rooms fitted up for little parties of two, three or four who liked to have a social hour to themselves and be out of common observation. There was a private entrance to these, so that any person who did not wish to be seen coming through the bar could get in without attracting notice.

Joe Wilson, mentioned incidentally before, was about twenty years of age. Both he and his father worked in Harvey st., and both of them drank too much. The father was one of your old, regular drinkers who has to keep his nerves well strung with beer or spirits daily in order to hold them steady enough for work. Twice within a year had these over-stimulated nerves refused to come up to time, and then mania seized him. His last attack had been unusually severe, and wellnigh finished him. We did not see him at the bindery for over a week.

He and old Jacobs the pressman were drinking cronies, and both of them had been pretty mellow on the night before—our opening night—not going home until after eleven o'clock. Joe had come in soon after his father. When the old man saw him, his countenance fell. I was looking at him just then, and noticed the change. He got up, and crossing the room, met his son not far from the door. They stood for a little while talking in low tones. Once or twice I heard an impatient word from Joe, and then this sentence:

"'Tisn't any use to talk, father! I can't stay home, and if I don't come here, I'll go somewhere else."

The argument ended. Wilson came back and sat down with Jacobs, and Joe asked a fellow-workman standing near the bar to drink with him, spending twenty cents.

"It isn't just the thing for you, Joe," said Jacobs, who was a great talker, and not over-particular about what he said. "If I had a boy—which, thank God, I have not now!—I'd tie him up at home rather than let him come out to a place like this o nights."

"Easier said than done," answered Joe with a laugh.

"I'd soon show you that, my hearty," said Jacobs.

"Would you? Don't think you'd try it on

twice," returned Joe, a faint tinge of anger coming over his face.

"Leave that to me," now put in Wilson, laying his hand on the arm of Jacobs. "I'll settle it."

"Hope you will," returned the pressman. "If you don't, it will settle him."

We all heard the talk, and it caused a silence in the bar-room for some moments. This was broken by one of the guests striking up a song and singing through two comic verses, which had a good effect, causing Jacobs, who was getting a little merry with drink, to join in with a will.

"I wish Jacobs wasn't a fool," said Lloyd, with much irritation, speaking for my ear alone.

"He's peculiar," I returned, "but we can't choose our customers, you know. His money is as good as anybody's, and if he wants to talk, let him."

"I'm not as cool as you are," he replied. "I don't like to be insulted in my own house, and it will come to that, I'm afraid, before a week goes over our heads."

"Who will do it?" I asked.

"Jacobs."

"Oh, I guess not."

As I said this, the voice of Jacobs again broke out in a high key, answering to some remark of Wilson's.

"It'll be a curse to our whole establishment, mark my word for it," he said, striking his hand upon the table.

"And to you among the rest," answered a printer who worked in the office with Jacobs.

"Oh, you can't hurt me," returned the pressman. "I'm like stale fish—past spoiling. But there are a good many chaps about our place who can be hurt, and who will be."

And he cast a meaning glance about the room, letting it rest on one and another of the inmates, most of whom he knew.

"There's Harry Glenn, for instance," calling a journeyman printer by name. "I wonder what his wife would say if she knew just where he was this evening? I'm afraid, Harry, you're falling from grace."

Glenn colored deeply. I had always thought him a strictly temperate man, and was gratified and a little surprised when I saw him come in to the morning lunch and take something to drink with the rest. He had looked pleased and was quite social, saying some complimentary things about the way in which "The Retreat" was fitted up.

Lloyd was getting very nervous, and gave vent to his feelings by swearing at Jacobs under his breath. But the old man didn't hear him, and it wouldn't have made much difference if he had.

Before anything further that was unpleasant could be said, three hard-looking young men came in noisily. They were strangers, and of the class known as roughs—ugly customers to have, always, and never very welcome.

"Hi!" exclaimed one of them as he stepped into the room and looked boldly around. "Shiny as a new pin."

"Bully!" responded one of the others, throwing a half-approving, half-sinister gaze around.

Then they walked to the bar, the first speaker saying, "What'll ye take, Jack, and you, Jerry?"

"Anything, so it's good and strong," was the answer.

"Well, hand out the whisky," said the one who had just spoken.

I set a decanter and glasses on the counter, and he took up the bottle and poured the glasses more than half full. A little water was added by each, and the liquor drank. The one who had ordered the drinks laid twenty-five cents on the counter, and was moving away.

"It's thirty cents," said I.

"The —— it is!" he responded, turning upon me with an ugly gleam in his eyes.

"Yes, sir. Ten cents a glass."

"And don't you wish you may get it?" He leaned over, grinning in my face, while his two companions ranged themselves by his side, looking ripe for a row.

"It's our price," I answered as quietly as I could speak. "But no matter, gentlemen; have it your own way. It isn't worth quarreling about."

"It's a swindling price, by ——!" and he swore savagely.

"If you don't like our prices, you needn't come again," I returned, betraying a little anger. "It's a free country."

"—— you, and your prices too!" was the loud, menacing retort. The three men meant mischief. They had come in for no other purpose than to get up a row, incited, no doubt, by some low tavern-keeper in the neighborhood who was afraid our attractive place would draw away custom.

Six or seven men, our friends from the bindery and printing-office, came forward instantly and confronted the three fellows.

"And what in —— have you to say?" demanded one of the roughs.

"That will depend on circumstances," was coolly answered.

As quick as a flash three murderous knives gleamed in the gaslight, and the three men put themselves in an attitude of defiance.

The blood went back to my heart. A feeling of terror crept over me. I was not educated to anything like this. The cruel murder I saw in the men's faces, and the glitter and flash of their knives, caused me to shiver. I was a coward, and could not help it. I would have run if there had been a way open for me.

"Go for the police, Harvey," I called to a man near the door.

He opened it and went out quickly.

Three chairs, in the hands of strong men, were in

the air above the heads of the three roughs in an instant after their knives were drawn.

"Hold, hold, gentlemen!" cried Lloyd. "Don't strike! Put up your knives, and go."

For the space of half a minute, I gazed on this tableau of three savage-looking men holding ugly knives, and three others, stern and resolute, with chairs lifted ready to strike, in a maze of suspense.

"Put up your knives!" was sternly commanded.

"Put down your chairs!" was answered, accompanied by a volley of oaths.

Slowly the knives were returned to their places of concealment, and slowly the lifted chairs dropped toward the floor. I drew a long breath of relief.

Two policemen, summoned by Harvey, now came in hastily.

"What's up?" asked one of them as he stepped across the floor and looked keenly at the group of men surrounding the three roughs.

"Oh, it's you, Jack!" and he confronted one of the fellows. "What's the row? Do you want to get down below again?"

"Not over-anxious," was replied, in a dogged sort of growl.

"Very well; then you'd better make off with yourselves;" and he nodded his head toward the door. "If you can't behave decently, keep out of decent places."

Jack, as he was called, did not hesitate, but left at once, his two companions going with him.

"Ugly customers," said the policeman who had ordered them out. "What did they do?"

"Refused to pay the price of their drinks, and then tried to get up a row."

"Exactly! The devil himself goes into these fellows with whisky, and there's scarcely a night that we don't have trouble with some of them. That Jack Thompson—or Fighting Jack, the name he is best known by—is one of the worst of them all He was in the State's prison for manslaughter—it was an out-and-out murder, and he should have been hung—and served five years. His sentence was for ten, but—pardoned, you see!"

"What are we to do?" I asked, betraying my disturbed state of mind both in voice and countenance.

"The best you can," answered the policeman, rather roughly, I thought. "Every business has its customers, and these are some of yours;" and he gave his head a twist and his shoulders a shrug.

"Exactly, captain!" chimed in old Jacobs—"exactly! You never see 'em at the bakers' and butchers'"

"Not often, I guess. They let other people do their marketing," was replied.

The old man now came forward, ready to talk and glad of a new listener.

"Guess our friends here will see such chaps pretty often."

"Shouldn't wonder. There's a large lot of 'em about, and plenty more coming on. Six or seven thousand places like this in our city breed such vermin fast. They make lots of work for us. If it wasn't for rum, our force might be cut down one-half, and even then we'd have an easy time of it."

"Don't doubt it," said Jacobs.

"Rum don't make thieves and housebreakers," said one of our company, who felt that this kind of talk was rather out of place.

"It makes poor thoughtless, shiftless, desperate men," answered the policeman, "and from this great army come most of your criminals. I happen to know."

"And your paupers, too," chimed in Jacobs. "It's a great curse, and you can't make anything else out of it."

The policeman looked at Jacobs curiously, and then said,

"I wonder at your coming here, seeing that you understand the case so well."

"Don't wonder that you do," was answered, a low gurgle in the old man's throat that was meant for a laugh. "But I'm one of the cursed, you see. Got a-going, and can't stop. All down hill."

"Take something," I said now to the policemen, recollecting myself.

"Don't care if I do," was answered by each. They drank like men who were used to it.

"Take my advice," said one of them as he turned to go, "and keep out of a quarrel with these roughs. They'll look in upon you now and then, sure, and get up a fight if they can. Drink makes them little better than devils incarnate. It was only last week that a party of them went into a tavern down town, and after smashing up things cut the tavern-keeper with a knife shockingly. They're a desperate set, and think no more of putting a knife into a man than they would into a pig."

I didn't feel very cheerful after this. We shut up at twelve o'clock that night, having taken in over forty dollars for drinks. It was a good beginning, more than coming up to our expectations. I felt that our new enterprise was an assured success.

But I could not get to sleep until near morning. I dreamed of being chased by devilish-looking men who wanted to murder me, of fighting in the bar-room and a jumble of other dreadfully disagreeable things. I awoke as the sun shone into my window with a feverish feeling and a dull headache, and as the scenes of the previous night rose vividly before me I felt a strange depression of spirits. The shadow of some great evil seemed upon me.

It came very distinctly to my mind that from the very beginning of this business matters somehow or other got at cross purposes both with Lloyd and myself. Every day I grew less and less comfortable and at ease in my feelings. The death of Perry Flint and his wife gave me a shock that it seemed as if I would never get over. I was troubled, too, in spite of myself, about Mrs. Lloyd and her daughter Maggy, who were distressed beyond measure because of this new business. They felt it as a sore disgrace, and saw nothing in it but shame and evil. Lloyd was angry and rough with them, as he had never been before.

Then, I did not feel right about Mr. Ashley's son and two or three others in the bindery—weak lads whom we would be almost sure to lead into temptation, perhaps ruin. I had not been able to get the father's strong sentences out of my mind. Last but not least of the depressing influences that now shadowed my spirits was that visit of those roughs. I had not counted on customers like them.

"Old Jacobs may be right, after all," I said, "and the whole business be accursed."

In this not very pleasant frame of mind I entered on my second day's business of saloon-keeping.

CHAPTER VIII.

MY story got mixed a little in the last chapter. I was speaking of John Ashley's visit on the second evening, when the mention of Joe Wilson as being up stairs in one of the rooms led me to refer more particularly to him and his father, and then to give a history of what took place on the night that followed our opening.

When Lloyd came back into the bar-room after taking young Ashley up stairs, as mentioned in the preceding chapter, I said to him, with something of the concern and uneasiness I felt in my voice,

"Look here, Tom: I don't just like this thing. I wish John Ashley and two or three other young fellows from the bindery and printing-office would keep away from here. It is not good for them."

He laughed in my face, answering,

"Oh, you'll soon get over this sort of squeamishness. If they don't come here, they'll go somewhere else. And there are worse places, you know."

"Yes," I said, weakly giving up the opposition I had intended to make.

"As for Joe Wilson," remarked Lloyd, "he's stepping in his father's tracks, and needs no help from us. He's bound to spend nearly all he gets in liquor, and the money might as well come to us as to anybody else."

"Joe's a hard case for one so young," I returned. "But I don't care for him so much. He's spoiled already. It's on young Ashley's account that I feel troubled. Joe's not a good leader for him."

"What a white-livered chap you are, Hiram!" exclaimed Lloyd, with undisguised contempt. "Take my advice and sell out. I'll find half a dozen men any one of whom will give a handsome bonus to change places with you. You never had such an opportunity in your life, and now, just as Fortune meets you with a smile, you begin to chaffer with her. Out on you! Be a man, not a whining woman."

There was no further opportunity for talk. Our friends were beginning to come in freely, and we had other things to do. Somehow, every time I saw the door begin to open I had a feeling of unpleasant suspense, and looked keenly to see who the newcomer might be. I dreaded another visit from the roughs—dreaded lest Mr. Ashley should come in seeking for his son—dreaded vaguely I knew not what. I was exceedingly uncomfortable—foolishly so, I said to myself—and did not get over this feeling until I had taken a stiff glass or two of brandy and water. After that I was all right, and drew and poured and mixed liquors with as ready a will as my partner and without a care for the good or evil of any one.

Among our visitors from the bindery and printing-office this evening was Harry Glenn, the young printer mentioned in the preceding chapter. He had a wife and one child.

"Why, Harry! Glad to see you!" I heard one of the men exclaim as he came in.

Glenn returned the greeting cordially, and then said,

"Take a glass of beer with me?"

"Don't care if I do," was answered, and they stepped forward to the bar.

"Thought of your nice, cozy place after supper, Hiram," said Glenn as he stood with glass in hand, "and couldn't stay away. I declare! You and Lloyd have done the thing up elegantly. And then one can meet the fellows here, and it's pleasant to see people. Don't know when I was in a tavern before last night."

"Always glad to have you come in," I replied.

"I wonder what his wife would say if she knew where he was?" remarked a fellow-journeyman as Glenn crossed to the other side of the bar-room.

"Growl, like some other women I know, instead of trying to make home comfortable," was answered by a man who was leaning on the bar. He had been drinking before he came in, and was considerably in liquor.

"I don't know about her growling," said another. "She isn't that kind."

"Who was she?" asked the first speaker.

"Henry Lawrence's daughter."

"Katy Lawrence?"

"Yes."

"Oh! I knew Katy very well. She was a pretty, gay little thing. I'd forgotten about her marrying Glenn. I wonder what sort of a wife she makes?"

"So-so-ish," was answered with a lifting of the speaker's brows and a meaning shrug of his shoulders. "It was very nice to get married. Most girls think so, but I have my guess about the housekeeping and all that. Men about to marry are apt, you know, to draw fancy pictures of home-life—the cozy room, the warm evening fire, the dressing-gown and slippers, and, above all, the smiling young wife daintily attired, with, maybe, a white rosebud in her hair, to crown her husband's blessings. But he doesn't always find it so. The young wife has her fancies too. She may be fonder of social life than her husband, may have a love of dress and admiration, may have no taste for household affairs, may be weak, vain, selfish, self-indulgent and slovenly at home. The more of them we have, friend Hiram, the better for you."

And the man laughed, but not heartily. There was an undertone of pain in his voice.

"Then we're likely to see Glenn once in a while?" I remarked.

"Treat him well, and you'll see him often," was the reply.

"We expect to do that to every one," said I.

"Of course. You know your business;" and the man turned and went away.

There were now in the room four boys who worked in the bindery. They were between the ages of fourteen and seventeen. Only two of them had, so far, come to the bar for liquor. The others had not yet acquired an appetite for drink, and merely dropped in to meet each other and pass the time away. Two were the sons of widowed mothers and another the son of a poor clergyman, all of whom would have been in great trouble of mind if they had known into what associations and peril their sons were drifting.

"Let's have some beer, Ned Allen," I heard one of these lads say to the clergyman's son.

The boy shook his head, at the same time laying his hand against his empty pocket.

"Oh, I'll stand treat. Come along!" urged the other, and the two boys came up. Small glasses of beer were called for, and I drew and set them on the counter. They were minors; it was against the law to sell them intoxicating drinks, and punishable with fine and imprisonment. I knew this, and thought of it as I handed them the beer, but I was reckless now. The brandy I had taken made it all right with my conscience, and I silently cursed the law.

The boys emptied their glasses, young Allen in a half-shy way, as if conscious that he was out of place and doing wrong.

When I next took notice of the lads, they were listening, with evident satisfaction, to some very dirty and obscene talk that was going on among two or three men of the coarser sort, joining in the laugh when anything witty was said, the wit always turning on something grossly indelicate. So their minds were filled with lewd ideas and their imaginations corrupted.

"I wonder if John Ashley has gone home yet?" I remarked to Lloyd, about half-past ten o'clock that evening.

"I guess so," he replied.

"Haven't seen him come down," I said.

"Went out at the side door, most likely."

I ran up stairs to see if this were so, and found him leaning on a table fast asleep. I aroused him with some difficulty. To my great relief, he was not drunk. He was tired, having been at work all day, and, after spending an hour or two in talking and playing cards, bent down over the table at which he was sitting, and fell asleep.

As soon as he came fairly to his senses he looked scared and hurried away. I said to him as he was going,

"Mind, John, it won't do to say you were here."

"Oh no. Trust me for that," he answered, promptly. Then, with a sly, comical look, "Been to the reading club. That's the go! All right!" and away he went, taking the side door instead of passing through the bar.

CHAPTER IX.

WE could not have asked a better beginning. Our customers were at our very door, and came without invitation. We needed no drummers nor travelers, no advertising nor expensive ways of drawing attention to our wares. Men's appetites were all on our side, and brought us into favor.

For the first two or three months scarcely a day went over that I was not surprised at the character of some of our customers. Men from all grades of life came in to drink, among them citizens of high social and even religious standing. Old gray-headed men and youngsters in their teens often stood side by side at the bar drinking. The father would come in, get his glass and go, and soon after the son would stand in his place, just missing each other. Now and then a father and his son would come face to face, each surprised—maybe pained and shocked—at the encounter. Clerks and employers would have like meetings, often to the chagrin and uneasiness of the former.

"This isn't the place for you," I have heard said hundreds of times by the old to the young, by the merchant to his clerk, by the father to his son, by the old tippler to some junior friend met unexpectedly in our bar-room. I could not help noting it as remarkable that, with few exceptions, the old warned the young, and the toper the moderate man, to keep away from bar-rooms and let drink alone.

"If you don't look out, it will catch you!" "I don't like to see you here so often, my young friend!" "'Tisn't safe, John!" "Take care, my boy!" "You'll go to the devil faster than a horse will carry you if you don't keep out of these places!"

Words of warning like these, spoken in all seriousness and by men who were free drinkers themselves, I have heard more times than I can count. Most of these men felt safe from excess themselves, but saw and feared the danger to others. How many of them have I seen pass the line of self-control and become the slaves of appetite!

I soon came to understand that, with few exceptions, our business was not regarded as good for the people, that it was attended with evils of the worst kind, and that our best customers were often strongest in reprobation and warning.

A few weak young men who were flattered by our familiarity and pleased with our attentions—idle young men of bad habits and loose principles—professed to think it all right. But, somehow, I never had any real respect for them. There was another class, regular hard cases, bold and bad, who never talked anything but obscenity and coarse blackguardism—tavern-loungers by day and by night, except when engaged in schemes of money-getting understood only by themselves. These were out and out on our side.

There was no getting away from this fact. It became more and more apparent every day. Our business was hurtful, and in low esteem by all for whose good opinion any one cared.

But I gradually grew hardened and indifferent to what others might say or think.

"Who cares for me?" I would sometimes say, crushing down little emotions of shame that stirred in my better nature. "If I wanted a dollar, who would offer it to me? I might die as a dog in the street, and nobody give me anything but a kick. It's every man for himself, and the devil take the hindmost."

So I stifled all better feelings, and threw myself with a will into this business of getting gain by ministering to an appetite that hurts or depraves all who indulge in it. I shut my eyes to all consequences, and determined to go ahead.

Lloyd had not been troubled from the first by any weakness or scruples. He dropped down at once to the cold depths of indifference for others. He went in to make money, and make it he would. If any one was fool enough to drink more than was good for him, the sin and shame lay at his own door, not at ours. So he felt, and so he talked if the subject came up. He was apt to be rough on your regular old bruisers, and wouldn't let a drunken man stay long in the bar if he could help it.

In less than six months we found ourselves in a highly-flourishing condition—lots of good custom, and money flowing in by a hundred little streams.

"But what of Lloyd's family? of Maggy and her mother?" is asked. "Have they become reconciled to the new order of things? Have the silks and ribbons prevailed?"

Let us see. One day—it was only a few weeks after we opened "The Retreat"—Thomas Lloyd's oldest boy, who had been sent away from the bindery by the foreman for taking a mug of beer to one of the men, which was against the rule, came in from the street and said something to his father. Lloyd looked disturbed, and putting on his hat, went out, and was gone for over an hour.

"Anything the matter?" I asked, on his return.

"Yes. Maggy came home sick. She fainted in school," he answered, anger and concern struggling, I could see, in his mind.

"Nothing serious, I hope?"

"I don't exactly make it out," he said, "but I've my guess. It's something to do with that Watson you saw at our house one Sunday evening. He's a teacher in the school where she goes."

"Has he been to see her since that evening?" I inquired.

"Oh yes. He called for her on the next Sunday evening, and they went to church together. I had a mind to tell her she couldn't go, but, somehow, hadn't the heart. But I knew well enough that if a chap like Watson took a fancy to Maggy, and she got a fancy for him, there'd be trouble in the camp when the saloon question came up."

"Has he been to see her since we opened this place?" I asked.

"Yes, 'most every Sunday evening. But he's stopped coming, I believe. He couldn't stand our new business, I fancy."

"Then she's well rid of him," said I. "If he had any true feeling for her, a trifle like that wouldn't throw him off."

"Curse him!" Lloyd answered, bitterly. "She's as good as he is, any day, and a thousand times better."

"How did she seem when you came away?" I asked.

"I left her in bed looking as white as a sheet, and with something so strange in her face that it made me sick to look at her."

"What did she say?"

"Nothing. You can't get a word out of her."

"Did anybody come home with her from school?"

"One of the girls, but she couldn't tell anything, except that Maggy fainted in her seat, and that it took a long time to bring her to."

"I think," said I, "that it will be best for her not to go back to the normal school."

Lloyd did not reply, and I made no guess at what

was in his thoughts. After an hour or so he put on his hat to go out. We were quite busy, it being near noon, the men coming in freely from the bindery and printing-office for lunch and a drink.

"I'm going home for a little while, Hiram," he said, "and you must get along the best you can. I'll send Thomas down to help in my place until the throng is over. He isn't doing anything just now, and might as well make himself useful. Besides, it will keep him out of mischief."

Thomas made his appearance in half an hour, and took his place behind the bar with a ready will. He evinced no shrinking or shame. I looked at him as he handled the glasses with the air of an adept, and felt sorry for the boy. If he had been mine, I would about as soon have seen him dead as behind our bar.

Poor Maggy! I must talk about her now. As I have already said, she was not like the ordinary run of girls, but in most things unlike them. There was a refinement and maidenly reserve about her, as she grew into young womanhood, in marked contrast with the jaunty, half-indelicate freedom too often seen. Her face was fair and very attractive, her eyes blue and tender, her manners quiet and reserved, almost to shyness. She was refined and sensitive by nature, with a clear mind and quick feelings. As remarked before, you never heard her say a weak or foolish thing.

She entered the normal school, about a year before the time of her introduction to the reader, with the purpose of qualifying herself for a teacher, and was making good progress in her studies. Lloyd had been very proud as well as fond of Maggy, and often talked with a kind of tender warmth of her goodness as a child and her smartness as a scholar. The first time I ever heard him speak to her in anything but a gentle way was on the occasion of Watson's visit that Sunday afternoon. If it had not been for the tavern scheme, he would have been pleased and flattered by the young teacher's attention to his daughter. But under this new state of things it was like a stone dropped suddenly into a shallow stream, causing it to fret and ripple.

Mark Watson, the young man referred to, was a teacher of mathematics in the normal school. He was well connected in the city, his family moving in some of its best circles. At the death of his father, a well-known merchant, it was found that an estate supposed to be very large would not yield over fifteen or twenty thousand dollars. There were two sons and one daughter. The young men were at college, but had to come home and look the new condition of things in the face. There was no will, but the young men left everything in the hands of their mother and sister, threw themselves out into the world to fight the battle of life.

Mark, the elder, who was nearest the end of college work, stood high in his class in almost everything, but especially excelled in mathematics. Soon after he came home he succeeded, through the aid of friends, in getting an appointment in the normal school as teacher. Here he met Maggy Lloyd, and was attracted by the rare beauty of her face, but more by the charm of her mind and manners. There was something so fresh and sweet and artless about her, and yet so grave and womanly, that he found the interest at first awakened deepening into admiration, and then into a warmer sentiment.

As for Maggy, her heart soon began to beat quicker at the sound of his voice, and it was not long before she was deeply in love with him. How could she well help it? He was handsome, cultivated and refined, superior in most things to any of the young men she had met in her humble sphere—a real man embodying her heart's ideal.

Mark was sincere in his admiration. The more he saw of Maggy, the better he liked her. There was a struggle with pride when he learned that her father was only a journeyman bookbinder, but the beauty and sweetness of her character were influences stronger than any considerations of family or position. So the young man let his heart lead him whither it would.

As for Maggy, she was one of the kind that never love by halves and never love twice. I have read of such in stories, but never saw a case in real life before.

Well, things went on between them until Maggy was too deeply in love ever to get out. I don't know that there was an actual engagement, but looks and tones and actions all spoke of love, and they understood each other.

For several weeks after our saloon was opened young Watson called regularly every Sunday evening for Maggy, and they went to church together. He also came to see her at least once during the week, but one Sunday evening he failed to appear as usual. Maggy was ready waiting for him, feeling nervous and troubled, as she always did now. A great evil somewhere in the not far distant future had cast its baleful shadow upon her. She felt it coming with the sure tread of relentless fate, and was holding her breath for the shock that was to destroy hope if not life. Watson could not accept the disgrace of her lot; she felt and knew it, but had not the strength to free him by a word. She must wait, suffering and in suspense, until the truth came to him, as sooner or later it must come, and then bear as best she could the desertion and heart-break that would surely follow.

As I was saying, the young man did not call for Maggy one Sunday evening a few weeks after our tavern was opened. She waited for him, dressed for church, until half an hour after the usual time of his arrival, and then went quietly up to her room, not coming down again. In the morning she looked so changed on meeting the family that her father and mother became anxious, fearing she was ill. Mrs. Lloyd understood the case a great deal better than her husband. He had been too much interested in his new business of liquor-selling—which occupied him on Sundays as well as week-days—to notice or care for anything else. His wife had told him of Watson's Sunday-evening calls for Maggy, but it went into one ear and out at the other. What was a matter of beaux and church-going to him now? He had more important matters on hand. If Maggy liked it, he was satisfied. In fact, it pleased him at the moment to know that his new vocation had not hurt Maggy in the young teacher's estimation, as he had every reason to fear that it would.

The girl could not eat anything at breakfast, and both her father and mother were a little troubled about her, and insisted that she should stay at home from school, but neither argument nor persuasion had any influence with Maggy. To school she would go. What occurred there I was never able to learn. In some way the young man let her know that he had discovered the new occupation of her father, and that, in consequence, there must be an end to their intimacy. It was for this assurance, if it was to come, that she had gone to school, nerved for the shock, and vainly trusting in her strength to bear it.

And so the sweet and tender flower was struck down, the loving heart broken, the beautiful life that might have been a happy one marred and hurt beyond repair. It was the first blighted fruit the hand of Thomas Lloyd plucked from the evil tree he had planted.

Poor Maggy never went back to school. For nearly a week she lay in a dull, half-conscious condition, answering no questions and taking scarcely any food. It was feared that she might lose her reason. Her father was alarmed and distressed, and went back and forth from his home and our tavern several times each day.

Business steadily increased. The fame of our cozy "Retreat" widened. It was becoming a favorite resort for quite a number of respectable men who didn't like to be seen going into more public places. They could pass into Harvey street as if on business, and then slip round into our house, the chances being as one in ten that nobody would suspect where they were going.

So Lloyd and I were kept very busy, and he could not be spared unless some one took his place. For this reason, on the first day of Maggy's illness Thomas had been sent to help me, and as she continued in what seemed a critical condition, Lloyd went home several times each day, and so the need for Thomas remained, and the boy continued to assist at the bar.

After the first day, I saw him help himself to beer with his lunch, imitating those who came in from ten to twelve in the morning.

"I guess you'd better let that alone," I said.

He was not pleased with this interference, and in looks, if not in words, told me to mind my own business.

"You can go to the devil, for all I care," was my unspoken thought, for his manner irritated me. And I didn't care then, and tried not to care afterward.

"It's none of my business," I said to myself. "Lloyd must look after his own. If he can afford to have Tom here, I can."

It was amazing to see how that boy changed in a week. In the bindery he had been noted for industry and a quiet, good behavior. We all liked him, and it was often said that he would make a good and substantial man.

But a single week amid the associations of a bar-room transformed the modest, retiring boy into a free-talking, incipient rowdy, who could not only laugh at an obscene jest, but utter one himself. When his father was present, he kept quiet and aloof from the men who lounged in the bar-room and talked about things no boy could hear of without being corrupted, but as soon as Lloyd went out Tom drifted into the society of those present. It seemed to have a fascination for him.

At the end of a week Maggy rallied a little from the shock which had so broken her down, and Lloyd no longer absented himself from business. I expected Tom to be kept at home after this, but he came as usual, and assisted at the bar.

His father had never seen Tom drink anything, but one day, coming on him unexpectedly, he found him with a glass of beer at his lips. Lloyd was very angry, and rated the boy soundly, threatening to thrash him if ever he caught him at that work again.

"I don't see what else you could expect," I said to him on the first opportunity. "If you put temptation in the boy's way, what is to hinder him from falling?"

"Have you seen him drink before?" he asked.

"Yes," I replied; "every day."

"Why did you let him?"

"I said what I could, but it was of no use. The fact is, Tom," I added, "this is no place for your son. It will be his ruin. If he were my boy, I'd rather see him dead than to run the chances of such an education as he will get here."

A look of trouble came into Lloyd's face.

"What am I to do with him?" he asked. "That Ashley sent him away from the bindery out of spite to me, I know, and, curse him! I'll pay him off. I'll make him sorry till the day of his death."

"Let Tom go to school," I replied; "you can afford it now."

"School? He's got schooling enough. I'm sick of schools," he answered. "No, he must find another place."

"There are other binderies in the city."

"Yes, but I don't want him to learn a trade. I'd rather get him into a store where he can learn clerking and business. I don't always mean to stand behind a bar and get money selling liquor by the glass. After I've laid up my pile I'm going into something bigger."

"By the gallon, the case and barrel," I remarked.

"Exactly so, and it will be just the thing for Tom to have a good knowledge of business, to understand trade and be able to keep books."

I smiled to myself, but made no answer.

"He'll see water run up hill before that comes to pass," I said in my thought.

Tom's services in the bar were dispensed with from that time. But as he had nothing to do, and as his father was too much occupied in the saloon day and night to look after him, he spent most of his time idly roaming about, and in the company of lads whose society did him harm instead of good. A few feeble efforts to get him a place in some store were made, but without success. To one business-man after another who came in to drink Lloyd mentioned his son.

"He's a smart, likely lad," he would say, "and the making of a first-rate business-man."

But none of them had an opening for him. I think I was not mistaken in the reason. They did not see much hope for anything good in a saloon-keeper's son.

At last a wholesale dealer in wines and liquors, to whom Lloyd mentioned his wish to get a place for his son, said he was in want of a lad, and would take him.

There was considerable opposition on the mother's part, but Lloyd said it was a great deal better than to have him running the street. So he went into the store of the liquor-dealer.

CHAPTER X.

SO many things have crowded on my memory since I began to tell this story of three years' experience in liquor-selling that I have brought the reader's mind, I fear, into some confusion. There is so much that I have seen and heard, so many life-tragedies that re-enact themselves before me, so much that is like a troubled dream in my consciousness, so many persons and incidents mixed together, that I find it almost impossible to make a clear and coherent record of what I wish to tell.

So the reader must bear with me, and keep the thread of my story as best he can. It will not run in the channel at first marked out, but keep breaking away on this side and on that, now turning back in dark caves, or leaping down sudden falls, or rushing into foamy rapids, or hiding itself in stagnant marshes amid things ugly and venomous. It is an evil story, and deals with evil things. A hundred times, up to this point, have I been on the eve of burning what I have written and letting all die, but something I cannot resist impels me to go on and write it out to the end.

I move forward a year. That first year! What a history it made! I could not have believed that in two men of so little account in the world as we were lay such a marvelous power to do harm. I have thought it over many times since, and wondered. We were nothing of ourselves—two obscure mechanics, without name or influence — but the moment we ranged ourselves on the side of what was hurtful to our fellow-men, all hell seemed working through us.

We had prospered in that first year. If I were to tell how much we made, it would scarcely be credited. Lloyd had removed his family into a good-sized house up town, and furnished it handsomely. I had money in bank, wore a diamond pin, and had a gold watch for which I paid two hundred dollars, but, on the other side, there were more than a hundred men, women and children who were poorer for our prosperity. I do not care to think of the wives and children who went meaner clad and ate poorer food that year in order that I might have a gold watch, a diamond pin and a balance to my account in bank. It was a sorry business.

We had many new attractions now in our place, for we had spent several hundred dollars in mirrors and pictures, bits of statuary and other things to please the taste of our customers and make our saloon pleasanter to them, if possible, than their homes.

One evening, about this time, as I stood at my post answering the calls of customers, the larger part of whom were old fellow-workmen, I noticed young Harry Glenn, the printer I have mentioned before, come in. He had been drinking rather freely all day—much freer than usual—and seemed to be all out of sorts. Something had evidently gone wrong with him. He came up to the bar and called for liquor. I gave him what he wanted, and he drank in an eager sort of way. For the last three or four months Harry had been running down fast, and frequently went home at night from "The Retreat" more drunk than sober.

After drinking he turned from the bar, and going to the opposite side of the room, sat down. He looked worried and kept aloof from the rest.

"What's the trouble with Glenn?" I asked of a printer who knew him.

"Haven't you heard?"

"No," I replied.

"There's been a lively time at his house."

"Indeed! what about?"

"Well, you see, Harry's been going down hill terribly during the last few months, spending his money in drink, neglecting his wife and running in debt to everybody—butcher, baker, grocer, milkman, and all the rest. I've talked to him about it several times, and he's promised to let liquor alone. But his love for it has grown too strong, and besides, you made it so much pleasanter for him to come here than to stay at home with his wife that he couldn't resist the temptation."

I was more gratified with the compliment than

troubled about Harry, for I had got over caring much about who went to the dogs.

"Mrs. Glenn kept it all to herself, and tried her best to bring Harry round again. But it was too late. Prevention might have held him safe, but there was small hope in the effort to cure. It is said that she didn't make home as attractive as it should have been. He married her for her pretty face and lively manner, but she had no taste for domestic affairs, and made for her young husband, I am told, a sorry sort of a home."

I remembered having heard this before.

"Well, you see," ran on the speaker, "it all came out last night. Harry went home from here as tipsy as a fool and abused his little wife—beat her, they say —and she took her baby at eleven o'clock and went home to her father. I tell you there was a row! It put the poor old mother in bed, and set her father, Mr. Lawrence—you know him—almost beside himself with anger. Look! By George! There's her brother, Fred Lawrence, now."

I followed the direction of his eyes, and saw a young man apparently about twenty-five just stepping in from the street door. He had been drinking, I could see.

His face was pale, his lips closely set together, his eyes intense and angry. He glanced quickly about. He did not see Glenn at first, but the instant he caught sight of him he drew a cowhide from under his coat, and, springing across the room, brought it down over his head and shoulders in heavy blows, cursing him at every stroke.

Glenn was not able to recover himself from this fierce assault, being more than half intoxicated, but fell forward upon the floor in his attempt to rise from the chair in which he was sitting. As he did so his assailant lifted his foot in a blind and savage fury, and would have kicked him in the face if he had not been caught hold of and dragged away by two or three men who rushed upon him as soon as they could recover from the bewilderment this sudden attack on Glenn had occasioned.

Struggling, panting, swearing, and accusing, in broken and incoherent sentences, the prostrate man with outrages on his sister, Lawrence vainly tried to free himself. A policeman happened to be in the neighborhood, and hearing the noise, came in. Both the young men were arrested and carried off to the station-house, where they remained all night. In the morning they were taken before an alderman and required to give bail for their future good behavior. A report of the affair, omitting names, got into the newspapers. It was as follows:

SAD AFFAIR.—A young man, respectably connected, made an assault last night, while under the influence of liquor, on his brother-in-law. It took place in a drinking-saloon in the neighborhood of Harvey street. He cut him over the face with a cowhide, wounding one cheek severely, but was prevented from doing him further injury. They were both lodged in the station-house, and this morning each gave bail to keep the peace.

"As far as we were able to learn, this case is a sad one, and stands as another instance of the terrible demoralization of drink. It is not over two years since a beautiful girl in our city became the wife of a steady, industrious young man. Everything looked bright before them. They were fond of each other, and happy. But in an evil hour the young man commenced going to a drinking-saloon for a midday lunch. He met pleasant people, the taste for liquor grew upon him, evenings were dull sometimes, and so it came about that he drifted away from his home and fell into dissipation. He went down fast. His story is that of thousands. He neglected his wife, got in debt, drank deeper and deeper, and at last, in a drunken fit, abused her so badly that she left him and went back to her father's house, broken hearted, with her baby in her arms.

"Her brother, stung to madness by his sister's story, and made blind and reckless by a glass of liquor, assaulted the poor debased husband, as we have seen, and so made all things worse. It is a sad story, and has its moral."

Glenn did not even make an effort to recover himself. The disgrace put upon him by the brother of his wife seemed to break down all the manliness left in him. He did not return to the printing-office, but got work somewhere else. It was a long time ere I saw him again.

One night, a few months before this occurrence, we had in a jolly company, who were talking, singing, drinking and in other ways enjoying themselves. All at once the noise and merriment ceased. A woman, tall and slender, but closely veiled, had come in silently, and now stood a few steps from the door, motionless as a piece of marble, but evidently searching through the room with her keen glances.

For a few moments you could have heard a pin drop, the stillness was so perfect. There was a spell on every one, and it was not broken until the strange figure turned slowly and passed out with noiseless feet.

"Was that a ghost?" asked one as the door closed behind her.

"Who is she?" queried another.

But no one could tell. The veil was drawn so closely that not a feature was visible.

"Somebody's wife," said old Jacobs, who was nearly always on hand.

"Does anybody here own her?" inquired Lloyd, trying to make light of the visitation and give the incident a humorous turn.

"I wouldn't care to be in his shoes," returned one of the company. "That woman knows tragedy."

"And is playing it now," said Jacobs, "and will go on playing it after the curtain falls and the lights are out."

Our guests were less noisy after that. There were some present who were evidently made uncomfortable by the incident—some who could not help thinking of a lonely wife at home. Two men, one a handsome, rather stylish-looking person whose name I did not know, but who dropped in occasionally, went out quietly soon after.

"I shouldn't wonder if they knew her," was remarked.

"If they do," spoke out Lloyd, "I hope they'll put a strait-jacket on her. No woman of delicacy or with any respect for her husband would go spying around of nights in taverns and saloons. Suppose she'd found him here. Would it have helped matters any to disgrace him in our eyes? These women are the very devil."

No one answered him. The fine hilarity of the evening did not return. Our guests were human, and could not shake off the influence of that weird-looking visitant.

A month afterward she came in, veiled, noiseless and ghost-like. I looked at her closely as she stood a little way inside of the door, with her eyes, that shone through her veil, searching about the room. I saw her bosom rise and fall like one trying to repress strong feelings.

Again the silence of death was on the company. She stood a little while, as on her first visit, then turned with what seemed a weary and disappointed air, and vanished through the door.

"There's a little too much of this!" exclaimed old Jacobs, in a mock serious tone. "And, anyhow, it isn't in the play. Look here, Hiram"—addressing me—"you've got to suppress that woman. She mustn't be coming on the stage every night after this fashion, or else you must put her in the bill. Then we'll know what's coming, and get our nerves ready."

A laugh greeted this sally, but it wasn't very hearty.

"I'll tell you what I think about it," said another.

"Well, what's your guess?" inquired Jacobs.

"She's after some fellow."

"No doubt, and that fine fellow's her husband," was replied.

"Don't believe it. Didn't you notice one hand in her pocket?"

"No, no," went round the room.

"Well, I did—noticed it both times."

"And what does it signify if she had?"

"It's my guess that there was a pistol in her pocket."

"By George! I believe you've hit the nail on the head!" exclaimed two or three in a breath. "I've seen women looking round after their husbands," added one of them, "but never a critter of her kind. She's one on 'em as knows how that a man isn't going to be reformed by such doings. There's a gay deceiver running round who'd better say his prayers in double quick when she gets her eyes on him."

"All afloat, gentlemen—all afloat," sang out Jacobs, in a high key. "I know what she's after; it's just come to me. She's going to shoot a saloon-keeper. So look out, Masters Lloyd and Jones."

This was greeted with a laugh from the company, and an oath from Lloyd.

"Oh, you needn't swear about it," retorted the old pressman; "it can't help the matter any. But it's plain to see that she's got wound up for a strike, and it's my guess, if she finds somebody she knows here, there'll be a dead rum-seller to put under ground. She'll be a dead shot. Them kind always are. So take my advice, Tom Lloyd, and make your will."

Lloyd became very angry at this, and swore fiercely at the old pressman.

"If you can't keep a civil tongue in your head, you'd better stay away," he added, cooling down a little. "I won't put up with these insults in my own house."

"Insults!" retorted Jacobs; "I'd like to know where the insult lies? What did I say to insult you, ha, old chap? Insult! Bah! you're growing mighty thin-skinned. But getting mad won't save you when she comes round, if somebody happens to be here. So, as I just said, get your will ready."

"Women grow very desperate sometimes, and do desperate things," remarked a person who had been silent until now. He spoke quietly, but soberly. "They are made up of passions and impulses—are soft as summer breezes when all goes pleasantly with them, but fierce and reckless as the wildest storm if crossed and thwarted. It's a dangerous experiment to drive a woman to the wall, to rob her of what is dearest in life, to rouse in her the sleeping lion."

The man spoke in a deep, musical voice, and in a style of language not often heard in our saloon. He was a stranger among us, and had rather a seedy look. Every one turned to him. He went on:

"Home is a woman's world, and its inmates her most precious things. Her life is bound up in her husband and children. If a maiden, and she have a lover, it is bound up in him. Touch any of these, and you touch her life. Hurt them, and you hurt her. Some women are weak, and some saintly, and some are strong-willed and desperate; when annoyed and threatened, a tiger. The weak fall, the saintly find strength in religion, but the strong-willed get a new vitality when the evil days come. You saw one of these latter just now. One that she loves is, I take it, drifting away from her on the river of inebriation, else why seek him here? If she lose him, she loses all she has in life. It is a fearful thing for her. She will save him if she can, and if any one stand in her way, he must go down.

"I don't think," he continued, his tone softening, but every word coming clear and emphatic, "that you gentlemen"—and he looked at Lloyd and myself—"count the cost of your work—really comprehend what flows from it; if you did, you would be little better than devils incarnate."

The hot blood rushed to Tom Lloyd's face, and I felt like throwing a tumbler. But there was a fascination about the speaker's voice and manner that completely won our company, and I saw with angry annoyance that his hard thrust at us was enjoyed.

"But I know," he went on, "that you have shut your eyes to all this. It is none of your business, you say. Men will drink, and you only give them what they want. I'm sorry—sorry for you, sorry for myself and sorry for every man here who feels as I do the almost irrepressible cravings of an appetite grown too strong for him. And if there be any among you not over on the wrong side, be warned in time. Let this thing alone. Keep away from places where drink is sold."

"Bravo!" cried old Jacobs; "them's my sentiments. I've been preaching 'em here from the beginning. I've told the boys over and over again that it wasn't the thing to be coming here night after night. 'Just look at me,' I've said, 'and take warning.' But it doesn't seem to be of any use. They come and come, and drink and tipple, and will all go to the devil, I'm afraid, in spite of everything I can say."

All this, Lloyd and I were compelled to hear and yet keep silence, for the general feeling was for the time against us.

"It is a bad business, take it as you will," said the stranger, in a depressed voice; and rising, he commenced buttoning his coat. He moved toward the door, but hesitated after a few steps, and then came round to the bar and called for a glass of brandy.

"I preach and practice both, you see," was his remark as he poured out the brandy. "You mustn't be offended. I have to talk sometimes, but I guess all I say will not do you much hurt—not half so much," he added as he set down his glass, his voice changing and his eyes flashing a little, "as you will do yourselves in this wretched business. Curses, like chickens, always come home to roost. Keep that in mind, gentlemen. Good-night;" and he went away.

CHAPTER XI.

THE work of a year was very apparent even to my eye, that cared not to see. Of the thirty or forty men and boys in the bindery and printing office who patronized "The Retreat"—our fellow workmen against whom we had conspired—nearly every one was worse off in something. Two or three once steady journeymen, who hardly ever lost a day, had become idle bar-room loungers for a third of their time. Among all I noticed a steady increase from month to month of the daily number of drinks and a lowering of the standard of health. Rheumatism troubled a great many. Dyspepsia was a common complaint. I don't think any were free from some ailment. One was bilious, another had a torpid liver and another's head was out of order, and the worse they felt, the more liquor they generally drank. It was a common thing to hear the question, "How are you to-day?" answered by, "Only so-so. Stiff with rheumatism;" or, "Miserable;" or, "Head terribly out of sorts—no appetite—can't sleep;" or, "Nothing to brag of—running down somehow—don't know what's the matter." As I recall in mind the men who drank with us regularly, I am not able to remember one who was in vigorous health. All were ailing in something.

Mr. Ashley, the foreman of the bindery, took the matter seriously to heart, and gave positive orders that no liquor should be brought into the establishment, on penalty of an instant dismissal of the offender. A great deal was smuggled in, however. Lloyd's son had been caught in the act, as before mentioned, and summarily sent away. The foreman saw the evil work going on, the hurt and hindrance occasioned by the daily tippling and diminished product of his men, and set himself at last to the business of "rooting us out," to use his own words. We heard of it, for he uttered his threat openly.

"Let him try it on," was our derisive response to those who repeated his threat.

"He's bound to catch you if it can be done, for Ashley isn't a man that does things by halves," they said.

"How will he catch us?" we asked. "We've got a license."

"There's a law against selling to minors, and he's going to trip you there. So look out."

"Oh, is he? Give him our compliments and tell him to go ahead."

There were from eight to ten persons in the establishment under legal age who often came in for beer. If it could be clearly proved in court that we had sold intoxicating liquors to one of these, there was danger of a fine and sixty days' imprisonment. The trouble would lie in getting the evidence, and even then the jury might not agree.

Forewarned, we felt safe enough. It was easy to make a show of not selling to the boys, yet have an understanding with them that if they went up stairs, where no one could see them receive the liquor or drink it, they could have all they wanted.

Ashley dropped in upon us half a dozen times, now in the day and now in the evening. Once or twice he found minors whom he knew in the bar-room, but that wasn't enough; he must see them drink. He tried to get some of the sober men in his employment to help him by visiting our place and spying around, but none of them cared to engage in that sort of business. He then tried the constables of the ward, giving them the names of every minor in the establishment and urging them to do their duty, but the constables laughed in their sleeves and gave us warning of our danger.

It all came to nothing. Ashley, after worrying himself for two or three weeks to no purpose, gave it up. He found out, by that time, that the law regulating the sale of liquors had been very carefully framed, and that, while it appeared to be very stringent and against us, had essential defects that made it little more than a dead letter.

I believe he was successful in getting the proof of sale to two minors, and consulted a lawyer about having us arrested and tried, but the lawyer told him that the chances were all against a conviction; that the liquor-sellers would combine the moment one of their number was brought up and spend any amount of money to defeat the ends of justice; that there were shrewd and unscrupulous lawyers, known to these men, who understood all the ins and outs of court practice, and who could make a case of this kind go almost any way they pleased.

"You'd better let it alone," said the lawyer, in conclusion, "unless you have a good deal of money to spend and a good deal of time on your hands. It will certainly take both of these to make success anything like probable, for all these are on the other side."

I learned this much from one of the men, who heard it from Ashley, and who also heard him say that our saloon had, in a single year, lessened the average product of the establishment at least ten per cent. The aggregate of that was a very heavy discount on the productive labor of this one establishment, and could not have been less than from eight to ten thousand dollars.

The loss of wages by the men in consequence of diminished health, idleness and demoralization could not have been less than two-thirds of this sum. Add what they spent for the liquor that worked all this loss and demoralization, and it is easy to see what lessening of personal and home comfort among them must follow—what deprivation, suffering, want, discouragement and sorrow in their families.

No wonder that Ashley desired to "root us out."

But he was not able. There were cunningly devised laws on our side, and we felt that we were safe.

I have mentioned that among the apprentices in the bindery were two sons of widowed mothers and one lad, the son of a poor clergyman, named Allen.

I remember when Ned Allen came first to the bindery. He was a fresh, bright, innocent boy. I do not believe he had ever been inside of a tavern until after we opened "The Retreat." Then it became easy and natural for him to drift in among us. Our new place was the talk of the bindery, and our tempting lunches, varied from day to day, had an enticement about them strong to young and keen appetites. Ned came one forenoon, about a week after we opened, in company with a journeyman who had asked him to come and get a lunch. The boy looked shy and not quite at ease, but he ate a slice of cold ham and a piece of bread and drank a glass of beer with the relish a good appetite gives. The journeyman paid for both drinks. Then, after lingering and talking for a little while, they went out.

I did not see him again for several days. When he next came, it was by himself, and at lunch-time. He was little better at ease than on the first occasion, and only drank a part of the beer I gave him with his lunch. He took a few pennies from his pocket, and selecting five, paid for the first glass of beer he ever bought. It might have been fancy, but I thought his hand trembled a little as he reached me the five small coins. His face looked very sober.

It was clear that he felt conscious of doing something wrong.

It was a week before the boy came again, and then it was in company with John Ashley, who treated him.

"Ned and I are coming round to-night," said John as they were going out.

"All right! Glad to see you," Lloyd answered, cheerily. "Nice place up stairs to meet the boys and play dominoes or backgammon."

Sure enough, after supper John and Ned came in. John treated, as in the morning. After lingering a while in the bar-room among the men they knew, and listening to their not very proper talk, the two lads went up stairs, and I did not see them again.

"Isn't that Rev. Mr. Allen's son?" inquired a man who had been looking pretty closely at Ned.

Some one who knew answered that it was.

He shook his head gravely, remarking, "I'm sorry to see *him* here."

"Why?" asked Lloyd. "Is he any better than John Ashley?"

"Perhaps not," the man replied, "but neither of them has any business here."

A retort was on Lloyd's tongue, but I touched him in warning, and he kept silent.

"Let him have his say." I spoke in an undertone. "It doesn't hurt anybody."

Young Allen did not come very often at first, but after some months he became a regular visitor, and spent two or three evenings with us every week, enjoying himself. He learned fast after the change began—could swear glibly and talk "smutty" talk as easily as the next one.

This change in the boy could not take place without it being noticed at home, and I heard, incidentally, that his father and mother were getting very much troubled about him. I had some knowledge of his father—a g od man, but not very highly gifted as a preacher. He was not in charge of any church, but was employed by a religious society in looking after the spiritual needs of certain poor people. He was a kind of city missionary, and was kept by those who employed him as close to starvation as was safe. He was a seedy-looking man, but with a countenance so placid and resigned that you felt he was working in his hard, thankless office from a love of doing good.

I had some knowledge of him, I said. It was a year or two before, and while I worked at my trade. One of our men who was very intemperate and spent half of his wages in drink was taken ill, and as he had worn out his constitution, there was little for nature to go and come on, and so he died. His poor forlorn-looking wife called at the bindery to say that he was very sick, and some of us felt that we were called upon to see after him. We made up a little collection, and I took charge of the sum thus raised.

I found everything poor and wretched enough.

The man lived with his wife and three helpless children in two rooms on the second floor of a miserable house in a narrow, dirty street. There was little furniture in the rooms. The sick man lay on a hard straw bed. His children, half clad and with pinched faces, looked at me hungrily out of their large eyes.

It made me sick. I gave them what money I had brought, and promising to come again in a day or two, got off as quickly as I could.

At the door I met the pale, tender, wasted face of Mr. Allen the preacher.

"How is Mr. Hollis?" he asked, in a sweet, earnest voice that was full of interest for the sick man he had called to visit.

"In rather a bad way," I replied.

"Do you know him?" he asked.

"Yes," I returned. "We have worked together for a year or two."

"Oh! Then I hope his fellow-workmen will look to it that his poor wife and children don't suffer while he is sick."

"I have just left them some money," I answered. "We will see that they don't want for anything."

"Oh, that is right. I am so glad of it," he said, with as much pleasure in his voice as if a favor had been done to himself.

I met him two or three times afterward on my visits to the sick journeyman, and was more and more impressed with the simple beauty of his character and the unselfishness of his devotion to the poor and suffering.

"This is thankless work for you, sir," I remember having said to him at one of our meetings, and I didn't soon forget his reply, nor the look and tone with which it was given. My first thought when he began to speak was of cant. But it did not linger an instant in my mind. I felt that he was sincere.

"If I looked for thanks or gain, my friend, I would look somewhere else. I am only God's servant, trying to do his will. He went about doing good while upon earth, and I am trying humbly to walk in his footsteps. That is all, my friend. And I have my reward."

A faint smile, but very sweet and tender, broke into his wasted face.

"But, oh dear!" he added, and a shadow of pain swept across his countenance. "If men would not give themselves to this dreadful work of destroying souls and bodies just for gain! It is drink, drink, drink, that makes nearly all of this suffering and poverty and crime that I have to meet and minister to, help and hinder, every day. It is drink that has impoverished this poor workman's family and made the father's death almost certain. It is drink that is cursing the poor. A deep and bitter cry has gone up, and still goes up, but the cry is yet in vain. God help the poor women and children, for there seems to be none in man!"

He was strongly agitated now. The great con

cern he evidently felt for the poor and wretched among whom he labored seemed to shake his very soul. The beaded sweat stood on his pale, pure forehead, and for a little while he trembled.

But he grew calm in a few moments, saying,

"We must work and be patient, my friend. God has his own good time, and he will bring it to pass. 'I have seen the wicked in great power, and spreading himself like a green bay tree. Yet he passed away, and, lo, he was not. I sought him, but he could not be found.' God is good and wise and strong, and his judgment sure. He will recompense evil."

I saw him again, after our fellow-workman died, trying as best he could to comfort the stricken ones who had been left in utter destitution, and once again when he came to the bindery to solicit help for the widow and orphans. And this was the man whose only son we were corrupting and depraving!

Very fast the evil work went on. Before the year was out, Ned Allen had fallen far away from the pure life he had known at the beginning. At first he had very little money, and oftener drank his glass of beer at another's expense. John Ashley and he were very thick, and the former nearly always stood treat when they came to the bar together. But after a few months Ned had more pocket-money, and spent, to my knowledge, in drinking, theatre-going and in other ways, not less than three or four dollars a week. I wondered to myself sometimes where it all came from, but then it was none of my business, and I didn't trouble my head about it.

We kept open on Sundays, of course; these were among our best days. There was a law against selling liquor on that day, but it was as much a dead letter as the law against selling to minors, or to persons known as common drunkards. There must be proof of the selling and drinking, and, as things were, this was not so easily done as might be thought. At any rate, there were from five to seven thousand places for selling liquor open every Sunday, and no one was called to account. The law lay dead upon the statute-book.

Among our Sunday visitors we were pretty sure to have some of the boys. Ned got to coming in about church-time and staying until service was over, when he would go home, and pretend that he had been to church.

The first time he came, one of our regular Sunday drinkers, who knew him and his father's calling, said, half in surprise and half in reproof,

"What brings you here, Ned Allen?"

"Came to Sunday-school," answered the boy, promptly, giving his questioner a knowing wink.

At this, a loud laugh went through the bar-room.

"He'll do," said one.

"Didn't take him long to graduate," added another.

"Go it while you're young, Ned," put in a third, slapping the boy on the shoulder as he spoke.

Ned looked pleased at these compliments, and then said, nodding toward the door leading into the entry,

"Has the class begun?"

"Yes," replied Lloyd. "The boys are in their places, and only waiting for their teacher."

"All right: he's on hand;" and he went up stairs to join young Ashley and three or four others who had already come in.

After that, scarcely a Sunday went over that Ned Allen did not visit us, sometimes spending hours in playing at cards, bagatelle or some other game, and drinking a glass or two of beer. He was always careful to go home just about the time church was out, and in this way managed to deceive his mother. His father had missionary work to do on Sundays that usually kept him away from home all day.

So it went on for a good while, Ned running his downward course with unusual rapidity. He always seemed to have a good supply of money, at which I wondered.

One afternoon, near the close of our first year, I sat reading a newspaper, no customers being in. Hearing the door open, I looked up and saw Ned Allen. His face was pale, and he had a scared look in his eyes.

"What's the matter?" I asked.

"I feel kind of sick, Hiram," he answered, in a low, mumbling voice. "I'm going up stairs to lie down on the settee."

"I'm sorry to hear it. Hadn't you better take a little whisky or gin first?" I said. "It may make you feel better."

"No, thank you; I'd rather not. I'll just go up and lie down."

"Very well, and if you want anything ring the bell."

So he went up stairs, walking so silently that I scarcely heard the sound of his feet. I felt that there was something more than bodily sickness the matter.

After a while a man came in from the bindery, and as he stood drinking, said,

"Bad business in there."

"What?" I asked.

"They've caught Ned Allen stealing."

"Oh no! That can't be," I returned.

"Fact! Ashley has suspected it for some time, but the young rascal was cunning as a fox, and kept him off the scent. It all came out to-day—the proof so plain that there's no getting over it. Mr. Ashley has sent for his father."

"Where is Ned?" I inquired.

"Mr. Ashley sent him home, I believe; for his father's sake, he won't let the matter come into court. Poor old man! It will go very hard with him. And he's such a good man, and so kind to the poor."

I had it on my tongue to say, "The young villain!" but could not get out the words, for the feeling came strong upon me that I had helped to make the wretched boy what he was.

"He's up stairs," I said.

"He is? What is he doing there?"

"He came in a short time ago, saying that he was sick and would like to lie down."

"Sick! I should think he would be!" returned the man. "He'd better hang himself and be done with it."

I went up stairs half an hour afterward to see what had become of young Allen, and found him lying face down upon a settee in one of the rooms. He lifted his head, turning it partly around as I opened the door. His face was still pale, and his eyes had the same scared look I had noticed when he came in. He did not speak, but looked at me anxiously.

"I'm sorry to hear this about you," I said, not harshly, but with something of pity in my voice.

He made no reply, but turned his face downward again, hiding it from me. I stood looking at him for a few moments, utterly at a loss what to say, and then went back to the bar-room.

Ned remained up stairs until toward evening. At six o'clock work ceased, and the men called in larger numbers than usual to get a drink before going home. Old Jacobs the pressman was among the first. The talk was all about young Allen. In the midst of it there came a hush, and I heard a person standing close to the bar say in a suppressed voice,

"As I live, there's his father!"

It seemed as if I had been struck. There was not a man, dead or alive, that I wouldn't rather have seen than Mr. Allen.

I looked, and there he was, a step or two inside of the bar-room. Mr. Ashley was with him. It was nearly two years since I last saw the pure but wasted countenance of this good old man. The sweetness and tenderness, the patience and submission, I had marked before as something beautiful and touching, were all gone now. There was a look of suppressed anguish in his white face—white almost as his hair—that seemed to hurt my eyes as they rested upon it. He came up to where I stood behind the bar, and said, huskily—how clear and sweet his voice was the last time it fell on my ears !—

"Is there a lad here named Edward Allen?"

"You will find him up stairs," I replied, turning my face partly away, lest he should recognize me. But there was not much danger of that.

"Which way?" he asked.

I came from behind the bar, and led the way for Ned's father and Mr. Ashley up to the room where the unhappy boy still lay on his face in a kind of dumb despair. Mr. Allen went over to the settee, and bending above him, said, in a voice strangely calm, but oh, so full of tenderness and pity,

"My son!"

I saw a start and quiver in the prostrate boy. That was all.

The father then knelt down, and clasping his thin

hands tightly together, turned upward his pale face and eyes wet with tears.

"O Lord!" he said, hushing his voice to keep it steady, yet not able to repress the heartache that was killing him—"O Lord! have mercy on my poor boy!"

No further word could he say. There was a moment or two of silence, and then, with a sob and cry of anguish, he fell forward upon his son.

"Oh, father! Don't! Don't! I can't bear it! Oh, I wish I was dead!" cried the poor boy, in a wild, helpless way, as he endeavored to get up. But his father lay heavy upon him.

"Father! Dear father! Oh, I've killed my father!" and Ned struggled up.

Mr. Allen was still on his knees, bowed over on the settee. He seemed to have lost all strength.

"Father! Oh, father!" the boy cried again, and then I saw him get his arms about his father's neck and lay his pale face down softly on the white head bowed so low. "Dear father! dear father!" he sobbed.

Tears were running down Mr. Ashley's face, and my eyes were dim.

I began to be alarmed for Mr. Allen, as he did not stir, nor in any way respond to his son's sorrowful appeals. But in a little while I saw him slowly lift his bowed head, yet not rise from his knees. As Ned's arm fell away from his father's neck, the father's arm was drawn about him. Then they knelt side by side, and were very still for a few moments, after which Mr. Allen again clasped his hands together in prayer, lifting his face upward.

Again he said, "O Lord! have mercy on my poor boy! Pity him, and cause him to repent and turn away from sin. I have tried to nurture him for thee, but the devices of the wicked have been too strong. They have snared him and brought his soul into great peril. I am weak and broken and helpless, but in thee, O Lord! is strength, and in thee is forgiveness."

Then he got up, and taking his boy by the hand, went out with him, Mr. Ashley going at the same time.

CHAPTER XII.

ON returning to the bar-room I was beset with inquiries as to what had happened up stairs. I would rather have kept it all to myself, but this could not well be, so I told just what had taken place.

"I wouldn't have the ruin of that boy on my conscience for all the world," said one of the men who had come in from the bindery. He spoke with much feeling.

"If he hadn't been a thief at heart, he wouldn't have stolen," retorted Lloyd, who felt that the remark was aimed at us.

"Let him that is without sin cast the first stone," answered the other, with much bitterness of tone, and he looked steadily at Lloyd.

"What do you mean by that?" demanded Lloyd, a flash in his eyes.

"There are many ways of stealing besides taking a man's goods or putting your hand in his pocket," was replied with a calm impressiveness that gave force to the speaker's words. "If you deliberately corrupt and deprave a man, in order that you may get his money, by what name, I pray, do you call the act? Is it a fair and honorable and honest deed? That poor boy, I take it, was no more a thief at heart than you or I when he first began coming to this place."

"I guess you're right there," came in old Jacobs, who never lost an opportunity to have his say.

"He deserves our pity more than our execration," continued the other. "We should consider all the circumstances of the case."

"Gammon!" retorted Lloyd. "As if a few glasses of beer were going to make a thief out of an honest person! You must all feel very much complimented."

"You can't turn it off in that way," said Jacobs, driving up against Lloyd, as he always did when a chance offered. "When Ned Allen came here first, he was as nice a boy as you could find in a hundred: I know that. But beer and bad talk hurt him in body and mind, and beer and games, the theatre, and maybe worse places, couldn't be enjoyed without money. The boy was not strong enough to swim against the stream on which he was floating, and so went down with the current. It is sad enough and bad enough. I am not trying to excuse him, but don't let all the blame and all the curses fall on his poor head. There are a good many dollars of the money he took from his employers in your till, and you can't make it out any other way."

I shut my teeth hard and kept silent. Lloyd boiled over and swore roundly at Jacobs, but it wasn't of any use. The old pressman had the sympathy as well as the convictions of nearly all on his side. What he said had the effect of softening every one toward Ned Allen and turning harshness into pity.

"If I was his father," was remarked on that same evening, but later—the men from the bindery and printing-office could not get done talking about the affair—"I'd send him to the house of refuge at once. It's the only way to save him."

"Of whom are you speaking?" asked one of two well-dressed men who had come in a few minutes before and were standing at the bar.

"Of a boy in ——'s bindery who was caught stealing to-day," was answered.

"Did you say his name was Allen?"

"Yes, sir—Ned Allen. He's the son of Rev. Mr. Allen, more's the pity."

The man started, a look of surprise and pain settling over his face.

"Oh, that can't be, surely!" he said.

"It's too true, sir. The thing's been going on for some time, and to-day it all came out. They'll probably hush it up for his father's sake. But that won't save the poor boy from ruin, I'm afraid."

The man then asked a great many questions, and drew out the whole story, which was related even to the scene that had occurred up stairs between Ned and his father. He seemed very much concerned about it, and he and the friend who was with him talked the matter over together for a good while.

Once I heard him say, with a great deal of earnestness,

"I'll do it for his father's sake, if for nothing else. Dear, good old man! My heart aches for him."

"When a boy gets so far gone as that, there isn't much hope for him," the other replied. "And then it's a great risk to take a person whom you know to be dishonest."

"I'd rather run the risk of losing a few dollars than see him go to destruction without an effort being made to save him," was the firm answer. "Poor old Mr. Allen!"

Then the two men went out together. One was a merchant, and the other was agent for an eastern insurance company doing a large business in the city. It was the latter who had expressed so deep an interest in Mr. Allen's son.

Mr. Ashley was very much excited over the matter, and even went so far as to go before the grand jury and try to get us indicted for something or other. But he was not able to put them in possession of any facts sufficiently well authenticated to warrant their finding a bill against us.

One morning, about a week after the occurrence just related, I was reading a newspaper, when I came upon the following:

"A GOOD MAN GONE TO HIS REWARD.—In the record of deaths this morning will be found that of the Rev. Edward Allen, who died yesterday. The poor and humble, among whom he has worked for so many years, will sadly miss his gentle face, his tender voice and loving ministrations. Death will be his gain, but their irreparable loss. Like the Master in whose footsteps he walked, he went about doing good. Peace to his memory! It will be precious to hundreds."

I then turned to the list of deaths and read,

"On the fourth instant, after a brief illness, Rev. Edward Allen, in his sixty-third year."

And just below,

"On the evening of the fourth instant, Jane Allen, wife of Rev. Edward Allen, in her fifty-eighth year.

"He giveth his beloved sleep."

For some minutes I seemed to be in a kind of maze.

"Dead! That good old man dead!" I said this in my thoughts, and kept on repeating it over and over. "It can't be possible!" I answered back, and lifting the paper, read again. I did not speak of it to any one, and tried to banish it from my mind, but that was not to be done.

I missed from the bar-room, after this trouble with Ned Allen, several familiar faces. Among them was that of John Ashley. Most of the boys had kept away, at which I was better pleased than otherwise. We got considerable out of them one week with another, but there was a law against selling to minors, and here was about our only danger of getting tripped. Besides, Ned Allen's fall had caused a great deal of talking among the men, and one or two of them more than hinted that if we did not stop selling liquor to the lads complaint would be made.

On the evening after a notice of the death of Mr. Allen and his wife appeared in the newspapers, we had in an unusual number of workmen from the bindery and printing-office. They came to talk about the matter, and to learn what they could about it from each other. It had caused, I found, a good deal of stir. Putting this and that together as it came out, I learned that when Mr. Allen got home with his son, and the mother came to know of their sorrow and disgrace, the poor old lady was stricken down as if dead, and did not come to for a long time. Adding the shock and alarm of this to the crushing weight under which he was trying to hold himself up was too much for the heart-broken father to bear, and nature kindly gave him ease in unconsciousness.

Out of this he came at length, but in mind and body so weak that he seemed almost gone. He rallied but little—never sufficient to leave his bed. So he lingered on for a week. His wife came up better. Anxiety for her husband caused her strength to return, and she kept about him night and day, doing all in her power to save him. But in vain. Body, heart and brain had all been overworked too long, and there was not enough vitality left to meet the sudden and large demand this terrible shock had occasioned. And so he passed to his rest. It was said that up to the moment of his death his wife showed no signs of breaking down, but that when all was over, and friends tried to lift her face away from the dead face of her husband, her life seemed to be going out with his. She never spoke to any one afterward, nor seemed to hear any voice that called to her, but was like one heavy with sleep. In a few hours her pulses too were still and her heart cold.

My thoughts troubled me that night. A heavy weight lay on my feelings which I tried vainly to shake off. Was I not guilty of the death of this good old man? The anguish of spirit, too bitter for human strength to bear, that had occasioned it, I helped to lay on his stooping and overburdened shoulders. And the unhappy boy I had assisted to snare and ruin, what was to become of him? what was to be his fate?

I tossed through the night, haunted by thoughts like these, unable to sleep and longing for the day to come. But with the day I went back to my work, and pushed them all aside. What had I to do with consequences? If men or boys chose to drink, steal, rob or commit murder, that was their own affair, not mine, and they must reap as they sowed. I was sorry if any one suffered, but the blame was with him alone.

For a while after this things went on in the usual way, and the death of Mr. Allen became an incident of the past, and was rarely mentioned. No one seemed to know anything about Ned Allen, but it was a common impression that he would come to no good. John Ashley and other minors from the establishment next door drifted back among us and enjoyed themselves as before.

But in the nature of things, we could not be long at peace. Affairs would not run smoothly. An element of discord was continually showing itself, fretting and disturbing us. We were making money, but not really enjoying our gains. It was a rare thing for me to lie down at night with a tranquil mind and peaceful thoughts. Scarcely a day went by without some unpleasant incident. Now it would be an angry dispute among two half-tipsy customers; now a bar-room row, with a show of knives or pistols, and sometimes their use; now the appearance of a father in search of his son, or of a poor forlorn-looking mother after her wandering boy; and now the irritating ordeal of being compelled to listen to a general discussion about the character of our business and the evil we were doing. Hundreds of times have I wished myself well out of it.

Several months had passed since our last visit from the strange woman closely veiled who had come in with the silent step and movement of a ghost, and then, after glancing through the bar-room, as silently retired, and we did not expect to see her again. But one night—it was nearly eleven o'clock—as a gentleman named L——, well known in the city and eminent in his profession, stood at the bar drinking, I saw her enter. The gentleman's back was turned toward the door, and he did not notice her. She was closely veiled, as before. Her dress was of some dark but fine material, and fell in graceful folds about her tall figure. A rich, dark shawl was drawn closely around her shoulders, and I saw the sparkle of a brilliant solitaire on one of her ungloved hands. Her other was thrust into the pocket of her dress. She stood for a moment or two in that statue-like way before mentioned, and then came swiftly but silently across the room, and laid a hand on the gentleman's arm, at the same time drawing back a portion of her veil, so that on turning, as he did quickly, he could see her face.

I saw it first, of course. It was the face of a woman past thirty—a face strongly marked, but beautiful, the complexion a light brunette and the eyes large, black and brilliant. Every look and flash of her great eyes showed intense but repressed passion.

Mr. L——, on feeling the touch on his arm, turned with a start. As he did so, I saw the hand of the woman that still rested in the pocket of her dress move as if about to be withdrawn. For an instant they looked at each other, while I stood scared and breathless, for I had seen murder in the woman's eyes.

But only for an instant did she look at Mr. L——. I saw her catch her breath, while a baffled and disappointed expression swept over her face. Then with a swift movement her veil was drawn, and before the astonished Mr. L—— could utter a word she had vanished from the room.

"Do you know that woman?" he asked, in unfeigned astonishment, and with considerable excitement of manner.

"I do not," I replied.

"Has she been here before?"

"Two or three times, but not for several months until to-night."

"What does she want?"

"I do not know. This is the first time she has seemed to recognize any one."

"Indeed!"

"Yes. When she came in before, she merely took a glance through the bar-room, keeping her veil down, and then went out quietly. Some called her a ghost, her movements were so gliding and noiseless. I never saw her face before to-night."

"And you have no idea who she is?"

"None in the world," I answered. "But let her be whom she may, she has deadly designs on somebody, and it's my guess that you made a narrow escape just now."

"You think so?"

"I'm sure of it. Each time she's been here it has been noticed that she kept one hand in her pocket, and to-night I saw her move that hand as you turned in a way that could not be mistaken. She certainly held a pistol or dagger, and when she came springing across the room with the eager motions of a wild animal, I believe it was in her heart to kill you."

I saw him shudder.

"Why did she not do it?" he asked, after a few moments. And he looked at me curiously.

"Because," I said, "you were not her man."

"Humph! Maybe not." It was his only reply. Then he walked the floor of the bar-room for a good while, his eyes bent down.

"She's an ugly customer to be about," he remarked, at length, buttoning up his coat, "and if she does meet 'her man,' as you say, society will have a new sensation."

"Do you know her, Mr. L——?" I asked as I saw him make a movement to go away. I put the question abruptly, and watched his face. I did not make much out of it.

He only shook his head in reply. I did not believe him.

"She mistook you for some one else," I said, trying to lead him on.

"Of course. If I'd been 'her man,' as you say, I don't know what might have happened."

"She's a splendid-looking woman," I remarked.

"Splendid!"

"I never saw such eyes."

"Nor anybody else," he returned, a little off his guard, I thought. "At least," he added, "judging from the single glimpse I got of them. But I must go. I don't just like the kind of customers you have. They're dangerous. Good-night;" and he went away.

CHAPTER XIII.

I HEARD of the woman next day as having visited over a dozen drinking-saloons on the night she called on us. It was said that she lived in New York and was connected with a good family there, and that she had become partially deranged in consequence of an unhappy love affair. Others said that she belonged to our own city, and that Mr. L—— knew all about her, while others affirmed that she was an actress from New Orleans, and was after a certain gambler well known in all our principal seaboard towns.

I had often seen this man, and, now that he was mentioned, I recalled his face as bearing some resemblance to that of Mr. L——. And, what was a little singular, they had the same name, and for aught I knew to the contrary might be relatives. But L—— the gambler was a man of notoriously bad character, while L—— the lawyer stood high in the community as a man of honor and integrity.

On the next afternoon, a little to my surprise, I saw L—— come in with two other well-dressed men. He had never before been at "The Retreat" in the daytime. I noticed a magnificent diamond pin on his bosom, and he wore, besides, a heavy gold chain and other jewelry. I did not remember to have seen these on the night before. His companions had also a good deal of jewelry about their persons.

In looking at L—— as he stood drinking with his companions, I was struck with something a little strange in his appearance. His face seemed fuller and coarser, I thought, and the eyes less clear and calm, and not just like the eyes I remembered. Then I seemed to lose the old likeness, and to doubt if it were really Mr. L——, after all.

The three men, after drinking, walked away from the bar, and stood talking together in undertones about something which appeared to both interest and disturb them. They looked excited and annoyed, I thought. After a while, L—— came back to the bar and handed me a bill to pay for the three drinks. As I gave him the change, I said, venturing to be a little familiar,

"Hope that little affair didn't keep you awake last night?"

"What little affair?" he asked, with a half-angry flash lighting up his eyes.

"Oh, you know—the veiled lady," I answered, keeping my voice low and for his ears alone.

I saw him start. A heavy frown darkened his face. He almost glared at me, a hell of passion burning in his eyes. And then I knew him. It was L—— the gambler.

I drew quickly back from him, half afraid of what I saw in his countenance, saying,

"Oh, pray excuse me. I mistook you for another person."

"You did, ha? What other person?" he demanded.

"I thought you were Mr. L——," I returned. "You look so much alike."

"I am Mr. L——. And now, sir, I want you to explain yourself." He had been drinking a good deal, I could see, and was growing more excited. His two companions, seeing that something had gone wrong between us, came up to the bar and looked at me curiously.

"See here, my young friend," said L——, taking out a revolver as he spoke and laying the barrel across the railing of the bar, "I never permit fellows like you to meddle in my affairs."

He looked like a devil incarnate, and I don't wonder that I turned pale.

"Put up that thing, Harry," exclaimed one of his friends. "He isn't the sort of game to deal with in this fashion. If he's insulted you, spit in his face, knock him down."

As soon as I could speak, I said,

"Beg pardon, sir. I thought you were Mr. L—— the lawyer."

"The devil you did!" fell in tones of surprise from the gambler's lips. "And what had he to do with the veiled lady?"

"She came in last night when he was here, and

gave him a little start," I replied, not stopping to choose my words.

The three men looked at each other in silence for some moments. Then L——, speaking in a different tone, but with repressed excitement, asked,

"What sort of a person was this veiled lady?"

I described her as minutely as I could, and while I did so I saw the men exchange glances and nod intelligently to each other.

"What did she do?" the gambler asked.

I described the way in which she almost leaped across the room when she saw L——, the expression of her face when she drew aside her veil, and the movement of the hand thrust down into the pocket of her dress.

I saw his countenance darken and his lips draw tightly together.

"A perfect she-devil!" one of the men said, in an undertone.

"Was she ever here before?" asked L——.

"Not lately. A few months ago she came in two or three times."

"What did she do?"

"Only stood for a moment or two, with her veil down, and then went out."

"You mistook me for Mr. L—— the lawyer, who resides in the city?" said the gambler.

"I did."

"Do we look so much alike?"

"The resemblance is strong," I replied.

"Humph!" he ejaculated, and then stood musing for a while.

"You mustn't mind me," he said as he recollected himself. "I was a little rough, but it's my way when things get crosswise. I thought you were meddling in a matter that did not concern you."

Without further remark he turned away and went out with his friends, but in a little while came back alone, looking, I thought, pale and flurried.

"Have you a private room," he asked, in a nervous sort of way.

"Yes," I answered.

"I want it!" He spoke in a quick, imperative tone of voice.

I was coming from behind the bar to show him up stairs, when a hand pushed open the street door suddenly and with force. I turned, and our lady visitor of the night before, with her veil drawn aside, looked at us with her large, dark, passion-lighted eyes.

I saw the gambler blanch. He stood as if paralyzed. With a bound the woman sprang upon him, and ere he had time to gain an attitude of defence had flung one hand spitefully in his face, and with the other stabbed him in the throat.

I saw the blood gush over the woman's hand. At sight of it she dropped the dagger with which she had wounded L—— and vanished through the door. All passed so quickly that it seemed the work of an instant. No attempt was made to follow her.

An exclamation of horror fell from the gambler's

lips as he drew his hand from his throat and saw that it was covered with blood. Almost at the same moment his two friends came in from the street.

"She's done it for me," he gasped as they came up to where he stood. And then he cursed her with a foul profanity such as I had rarely if ever heard.

No attempt was made to follow the woman. L—— was taken up stairs, and the nearest surgeon sent for. In the mean time every possible effort was made to stanch the flow of blood.

The wound proved dangerous, but not fatal. After it was closed and dressed by the surgeon, his friends took him away in a carriage. An effort was made to keep the matter out of the newspapers, but the reporters got hold of it, and made it the sensation of the hour, at least among the flash and professionals. I don't know that people generally gave it more than a passing thought, but readers of the *Police Gazette* and kindred papers had an appetizing morceau served up with quite a variety of sensational pictures, not one of which gave the stabbing incident correctly.

Few men can look at blood without a shudder—human blood, I mean—and I am not of the number. A thrill of horror ran through me as I saw the glitter of steel in the woman's hand, the quick, flashing stroke and the gush of blood. I was so paralyzed for the moment that I could not stir, and L—— stood with his hands dabbling about his throat until his two friends came in from the street. They had met the woman just outside of the door, but not knowing what she had done, made no attempt to stop her.

Only a week before, there had been a fight in the bar-room, during which a man had been badly cut, and now we had another stabbing affair. I could not get used to such things. They shocked my nerves terribly. If bad-looking fellows came in—and we saw them pretty often—I felt uneasy until they went away. If two men who had been drinking freely got to arguing with each other in voices raised to a higher pitch than usual, I was in a state of uncomfortable suspense until the battle of words was over. I had seen these little disputes over trifles run too often into quarrels that ended in blows. There was no counting on men after a glass or two. The most quiet were sometimes the most quarrelsome after drinking. Over and over again have I seen men who had come in with a good-humored face and a pleasant word for every one, change in half an hour to ill-natured, snarling curs. It kept one on the tenter-hooks of anxiety and fear all the while.

It took me a good while to get over this affair. I have not seen the gambler L—— in our city since, nor have I heard anything of the woman who made the attempt on his life. As for the gentleman whose resemblance to the gambler came near costing him his life, he did not make another call at "The Retreat," wherever else he may have gone.

CHAPTER XIV.

THE weeks and months passed on, and we gathered in our harvests. "Were they bountiful?" Yes. "But as a man soweth, so shall he reap." We had full harvests, but I do not think either Lloyd or I carried our sheaves with rejoicing.

As for me, I had no one to care for or think about but myself. I had no wife or children to set themselves in opposition to my schemes, or to feel disgraced by my business. I went and came, and did as I pleased. It was different with my partner, Tom Lloyd. The harvest I reaped was not all grain and sweet-scented clover—no, not by any means—but as he gathered in he found more of juiceless brambles and stinging-nettles than wheat or hay. His harvest was indeed accursed.

I had long since ceased to visit in his family. The opposition of his wife and daughter Maggy was so strong and unyielding that I found it unpleasant from the beginning to meet them. Maggy, as I have already said, was unusually attractive, of a sensitive mental organization, and superior to most girls in her condition. Lloyd had been very fond and proud of her, as well he might be.

My readers will remember the incident of her fainting in school, and the utter prostration of mind and body that followed. The young teacher Mark Watson never called to see her again, and Maggy never went back to school. A gulf had opened suddenly between them, and it did not close.

It was two or three months before Maggy showed interest in anything. During most of this time she suffered from physical as well as nervous prostration. For a whole week after she had the fainting spell at school she lay in a dull, half-unconscious state, answering no questions and showing no interest in anything. Lloyd was very much alarmed and anxious about her. His old tender love for her came back, and I know the thought that he had really brought her to this haunted him like a spectre and hurt him like a throbbing sore.

"How is Maggy?" I asked, one morning, several days after her trouble at school. Lloyd had come in at a much later hour than usual. His face wore an anxious expression.

He merely shook his head in reply, and shut his lips tightly.

"Not worse?" I ventured to say.

"Don't know. Can't make it out," he replied, gloomily.

"Hasn't she rallied any within a day or two?"

"A little, maybe. She's more restless, and starts and moans in her sleep."

"Does she answer when you speak to her?"

"No. This morning I sat down by her bed, and

taking her hand, squeezed it tightly, saying, 'Maggy dear—'"

His voice broke a little, and I saw his lips work nervously. But he recovered his self-possession, and went on.

"'Maggy dear,' I said, 'is there nothing I can do for you?' But for all I could see in her face—her eyes were shut—my voice made no impression. I tried again and again. I said, 'If you love me, Maggy, just press my hand.' But she did not seem to hear. Oh, Hiram, it's dreadful to see her so. I'm frightened about it. I haven't an instant's peace of mind."

He went back and forth between his home and the saloon several times each day. All his old love, which had seemed under the excitement and cross purposes attendant on the starting of our new business wellnigh crushed out, stirred once more in his heart and regained its old power.

After about two weeks, Maggy began to recover from the shock she had received. To my question as to how she was, Lloyd answered, with a troubled look on his face,

"I don't know what to think about her, Hiram. I'm sometimes afraid her mind's gone. I'd give almost anything to know just what happened at school—if that teacher said anything wrong to her. Blast his heart! If I was sure he'd done or said anything out of the way, I'd murder him."

"That wouldn't mend matters," I replied.

"It would teach him a lesson, confound him!" he answered.

A few days after, he seemed a little more cheerful, and to my question about Maggy said,

"I hope she'll come all right. Yesterday she sat up for an hour or two and talked a little. But her face is so sad, Hiram. I never saw anything like it. It makes the tears come into my eyes to look at her."

Slowly her life-pulses came beating back, but never with the old strength and fullness. After a few weeks she began to take some interest in household matters, and to care for her two younger brothers, Harvey and Willy, the latter not yet six years old. But she remained weak in body, and tired easily if she made any unusual effort. Often, for a whole hour at a time if not disturbed, she would sit with her hands laid across each other on her lap and her eyes fixed in an absent way. If spoken to at these times, she would give a low sigh, and drift back to what was around her like one coming out of a dream. Sometimes she would try to force a smile to her lips as you disturbed her reverie, but it was so faint and fugitive that you scarcely saw it.

So it went on, month after month, Maggy gaining a little all the while, but so little that both father and mother gave up all hope of ever seeing the old sweet light in her face. Six months passed without her foot going over the threshold of her father's house, and no persuasion could draw her out. If urged too strongly, the answer of her wet eyes and trembling lips always closed the argument. Several times her father brought a carriage to the door, hoping she might consent to ride out with him, but she could not be induced to go. If he lost patience with her, as he did now and then, particularly after he had been drinking a little more than usual, she would break into a fit of sobbing and crying, and so end the contest. He bought her handsome dresses, but she did not wear them; he gave her a watch; he gave her earrings and breastpins and one pretty trifle after another, but they were all laid away in her drawers. Her heart was not in them.

Lloyd was baffled, worried and unhappy. He could not understand the case. He did not know a woman's heart. I wonder if any man does?

"I shall have to make a change at home," he said after we had been in business six months and were beginning to get ahead. "Maggy won't go out, and she'll die or get beside herself if there isn't some break in her life. You'd hardly know her, Hiram, she's so altered. No more color in her face than there is in a snowbank. It used to do my heart good to hear her laughing and singing about the house, and to meet her smiling face when I came home. She would put her arm about my neck sometimes and kiss me when I came in, saying, 'Poor, dear father, you look so tired.'"

Lloyd stopped and turned his head away. I knew what it meant, for I heard a choke in his voice on the last word. In a little while he went on, dropping his voice to a lower key:

"But there's nothing of that now. She hardly looks up when I come in, doesn't seem to hear my step, never smiles when I speak to her, and looks at me sometimes in such a strange way that it sends a kind of creep to my heart."

"What kind of a change do you think of making?" I asked.

"I must move out of that little house into a larger and better one, and buy new furniture: I can afford it now."

"I have been wondering that you did not do this before," I replied.

"I have thought of it, but when I did move, I wanted to make a sort of dash, and I'm not just able to do that yet."

"Never mind about the dash. Get a nice new house somewhere in a pleasant neighborhood, and set Maggy and her mother at work to furnish it. Let them have their own say and gratify their own taste. I don't know anything more likely to bring Maggy round."

"Glad you think so, Hiram," he answered, brightening. "I don't see what else I can do."

"It will work like a charm; you may count on that," said I, confidently.

But it didn't. They could not even get Maggy out to look at the new house. But after it was taken she assisted her mother in moving and arranging their new home to the utmost of her strength. After that she fell back into her old sluggish state.

"How are you getting on at home?" I asked of Lloyd after he had been two or three months in his new house.

The question sent a cloud over his face.

"Isn't Maggy coming round all right?"

He shook his head gloomily.

"I had hoped for a better report by this time."

"So had I, but I seem to have lost my reckoning in this world, and don't know that I shall ever find it again. Things don't come out as they used to. If I got a little wrong or out of sorts or troubled in my mind, home generally brought me right again. I could count on the pleasant faces there, on the rest and peace and comfort of my little nook, poor as it was. But now I feel a shadow settling down on my feelings as I get nearer and nearer my home, and an icy chill sometimes when I enter it. Nobody smiles there, nobody talks cheerfully and lovingly, nobody is happy. Even little Harry and Willy have lost their old wild playfulness."

"How is Thomas getting along?" I asked.

The gloomy lines on his forehead deepened.

"Badly," he answered.

"Hasn't left his place, I hope?"

"Yes."

"How came that?"

"Don't know all the ins and outs of it, but he's at home. That much is clear."

"Wouldn't it be better to try and get him into some bindery again? He's worked at the trade, and it will be safer for him than a place like the one he left."

"Easier said than done. If Ashley wasn't such a spiteful dog, he'd let him come back again. But there's no use trying him; besides, Tom's been away from regular and close employment for six months, and got idle habits, I'm afraid. Don't believe he could be made to stick to work."

"So much the worse," I replied.

"I know, and it's worrying me dreadfully. The boy'll go to ruin if he's left on the street, as he now is. His mother can't do anything with him, and I've got my hands full here."

I had no clear advice to give, and so said nothing more. But in my heart I was thankful that I had neither wife nor children.

I knew but little of what went on in Lloyd's family after that, but I could see from his countenance and state of mind when he came each morning that he was still "out of his reckoning," as he had said—that he had lost his home and was not able to find it. The better house and the new furniture had not done all that he had expected. They did not ease the heartache, nor allay anxiety, nor take away the sense of shame and disgrace. They were accepted and used, not enjoyed.

But for one thing, I believe Lloyd would have absented himself almost entirely from his home. He was making some rather dangerous friends—sporting men, most of them—and was beginning to find in their society a refuge from the disquiet he so often felt. He would frequently ride out with some of them, and be away from the saloon in their company for hours at a time. But there was one thing that ever drew him back to his home, and that was his love for his daughter—a love that seemed to grow stronger every day. I wondered at this sometimes, seeing how she had turned herself from him, and how utterly irresponsive to his affection she had become. After a year, Maggy's coldness toward her father began to give way. Her heart responded, feebly at first, to the tender care and unfailing interest he had never ceased to show. She would welcome his coming home with a little faint smile, and when he kissed her show that she was pleased. Then he began to lavish things upon her, buying now a bit of jewelry, now a handsome scarf, now a fan or some pretty article for the toilette.

"It isn't worth while, father," she would say, when he brought such presents. "I've got more now than I know what to do with."

Even that response was grateful to the father's heart, hungering as it was for the lost love of his child. She gave him what she could, and tried to give more from a growing sense of filial duty. Little as it was in outward sign, Lloyd took it as a sweet morsel.

One day he said to me, with a new pleasure in his face,

"I shall not be back this afternoon—not before night. Going to drive in the park with Maggy and her mother."

I did not express surprise, but looked the pleasure I felt.

"Glad to hear it," I returned. "Hope you'll have a nice time."

"Guess I will. Mean to have an elegant turnout. Ordered a phaeton and pair of the handsomest horses in R——'s stables."

He was in high spirits all the morning, and went home early to dinner. It was near eight o'clock before he came back. The moment he entered the door I saw that something had gone wrong. He did not look at me as he came to the bar, but reached for a decanter of brandy and filled a glass nearly half full; adding some water to this, he drank off the liquor at a single draught.

I did not deem it best to say anything to him then, for I saw that from some cause he was suffering deeply, and understood his peculiarities well enough to know that I had better let him alone. After remaining half an hour he went out, and did not return again that night.

He looked careworn and troubled when he appeared next morning.

"I hope no one is sick," I remarked.

He did not answer me, so I let him alone.

Something very serious had occurred, that was plain. I watched his face when he did not observe me, and saw that pain, not anger, was below. He drank more freely than usual, and was irritable.

"I shall not be back to-night," he said as he was going away, a little after six o'clock.

"All right," I returned, pleasantly. "We can get along."

CHAPTER XV.

IT all came out on the next day. When Lloyd made his appearance in the morning, some of the shadows had fallen away from his face, though it still wore an anxious look.

"You haven't told me about your drive in the park," I said when a good opportunity offered.

It was as if I had touched him with a probe. I saw the quick flushes of pain break into his face.

"What has happened, Tom? There was no accident, I hope?"

"No—oh no," he answered.

"But something went wrong. What was it, Tom? I hope Maggy didn't get frightened, or take cold, or—"

"No, nothing of that," he replied.

"What then? I feel anxious to know." Then he told me.

"I had a splendid turnout," he began — "as handsome a team as you could find on the road. Maggy looked sweet. There was just a little color in her face, and her eyes were so large and bright! She was dressed like any lady in the land. I did feel so proud of her, Hiram. It would have done your heart good to see how everybody gazed at her. I heard it said, 'Who is she?' a dozen times.

"Every little while I turned to look at Maggy or to say something pleasant. Now I pointed out some pretty view as we rolled through the park, now tried to amuse her by making sport of some of the funny turnouts and queer-looking people we met, and now asked if she were not enjoying the ride. Her interest in things did not come up to my expectations. Still, she was pleased. It was doing her good; that I saw plainly.

"We had driven through the western park, across the river at the Falls, up and down the Wissahickon, and were coming back by the river-road. Maggy was getting tired, and when I turned, as I did every little while, to say something, I noticed that her face had lost its color and looked pale and weary. The old sad expression I saw, too, settling about her mouth.

"'You are feeling tired, Maggy?' I said.

"'Yes,' she answered.

"'I'm sorry I drove so far. But we'll soon get home;' and I touched the horses to quicken their speed. They sprung forward with a sudden bound, startling Maggy and sending the color again into her cheeks. Just then, a little way in front, I saw a handsome buggy coming toward us. It contained a young gentleman and lady. They were talking familiarly, leaning toward each other, while the horse, left almost to himself, walked leisurely. They were in the middle of the road. We were dashing along at a rapid rate. I drew in my horses with a sudden pull, and just in time to prevent an accident. For a moment our teams stood nearly side by side, and both parties, now only a few feet distant, looked into each other's faces.

"Something in the young man's countenance struck me as familiar, and to my surprise I saw from its expression that Maggy was recognized. In the next instant we were dashing forward again.

"When I turned to Maggy, she was leaning back against the cushions with her eyes shut and her face as white as marble.

"'Look at Maggy!' I cried to her mother. 'She's fainted.'

"Jane caught hold of her in alarm, and called to her.

"'It's nothing, mother. I only feel a little faint,' Maggy answered, without opening her eyes.

"'She was frightened,' Jane said.

"But I knew better. She didn't open her eyes all the way home, and only answered to our questions that she felt a little faint.

"When we got back, she was so weak that I had almost to carry her across the pavement and into the house. She lay on the sofa in the parlor until I drove the carriage home. On my return I lifted her in my arms and took her to her room.

"'I'm sorry to be so much trouble to you, father,' she said as I laid her upon her bed. She did not open her eyes as she spoke. But I saw the lids quiver and the shine of tears under them.

"I could not ask what ailed her. I knew that too well, and dared not put the question.

"All her strength seemed suddenly to have died out. Her mother brought her some tea, but she pushed the hand that offered it gently away, saying in a weak voice,

"'Not now, mother. After a while. Let me lie here just as I am. I'll feel better soon—maybe.'

"That maybe, spoken to herself—oh, Hiram, it had in it a longing for death! I never so felt the meaning in a tone of voice before.

"She lay all night in a still, half-waking sleep. I could not go to bed. I was afraid she might die. In the morning there was little change. If we roused her, she would answer feebly, and then sink away, breathing softly like an infant. She made an effort to eat when food was brought by her mother, swallowing a few mouthfuls. But there was no relish. She did not want it, and only took a little of what was offered from a desire to allay our concern.

"'Don't be troubled about me, father,' she said, in reply to my anxious questions as to how she felt. 'I'll come all right again. I'm sorry to give you so much trouble, but I'm very weak, and can't help it.'

"All that day she remained in bed, lying with her face to the wall, and looking, oh so pale and sad. She seemed more like herself last evening, and once, as I sat holding her hand, she raised mine to her lips and kissed it.

"'Like a faithful dog,' I could not help saying to myself, 'that kisses the hand of his master after it has struck him a death-blow.' It was a strange thing for me to say in my thought, but the speech was from an impulse hardly my own.

"She seems better this morning," Lloyd continued—"sat up in bed and took some breakfast. She even tried to dress herself, but was too weak."

It is hardly necessary to tell the reader that the young man seen in the park was Maggy's old lover, Mark Watson. That meeting him under the circumstances should have had such an effect upon her is one of the heart mysteries I do not pretend to understand. All this dying of love and breaking of hearts I had never believed in. It was pretty stuff to put in books for young girls to read, but I had no idea that it ever happened in real life— certainly not in the kind of real life I had come across.

The case of Maggy puzzled me. I had seen Watson a few times. He was a fair sort of a young man, and tolerably good-looking, but I can't say that I liked his face altogether, and saw nothing in it to set a young girl crazy. As for Maggy, she was lovable and no mistake. There was something about her that made her seem different from any other girl I had ever met. Her manners were those of a born lady, and she had always appeared like one lifted up somehow above the people with whom she associated—one very tender and sensitive cast in among the coarse and the common, with whom she could have but little in kind, and who hurt her always when they touched her.

This incident of meeting Watson in the park had the effect to throw Maggy away back. All she had gained in months was lost.

"I feel so troubled about her," Lloyd remarked to me some weeks later. "She used to be so strong and bright, and had such a happy heart. But now she has scarcely the strength of a child, and her pale face is a picture of sadness. She wants change. The doctor says I must take her to the seashore."

"The very thing for her," I replied.

"Yes, but she will not go," he answered.

"You will have to use authority," I suggested. "She is sick in mind as well as body, and not capable of judging for herself. Take my advice, and insist on her going. Say that the doctor has positively ordered her to be taken to the shore."

"Suppose she were to meet Watson there?" said Lloyd. "It's as likely a thing as not."

"She's got to get over that somehow," I rejoined, "and the sooner the better. A second meeting will not be half so bad as the first. A scary horse is cured by making him look again and again at the thing that frightened him. I don't believe she'd be half as much disturbed if she were to meet him face to face to-day as she was when she saw him for the first time in over a year. Two or three meetings will make it an old story."

Lloyd was inclined to take my view of the case. He saw the doctor, and got him to give a positive order to take Maggy down to the seashore. Finding that her father's heart was set upon it, Maggy ceased to offer any opposition.

"It will be of no use," she said. "But if you wish it, I will go."

She stayed a couple of weeks, and came back stronger and brighter. Her father was much elated by the result, and wanted to go with her to the mountains. But she begged so not to be taken away again that he had not the heart to compel her.

After that she led a quiet, dreamy sort of life. She read but little. Books seemed to disturb her. Of her two younger brothers she was very fond, and had them with her a great deal.

So it went on for another year. Then a new life began to awaken in her. She had become interested in some poor people living near by, and in her visits to their houses met one day a lady who was drawn toward her at once. This lady, a member of one of the churches, was devoting herself to works of charity among the poor. She saw in Maggy all the qualities of mind and heart needed for a companion and helper, while Maggy found in her a friend and guide who could lead her into new paths of life and lift her mind into more peaceful regions than it had ever been able alone to reach.

Through the influence of this lady, Maggy was led to join the church and to become a Sunday-school teacher.

Lloyd told me about it one day with a pleased manner, at which I could not but wonder, seeing that our interests were all on the other side.

"It won't work well," I answered.

"Why not?" he asked.

"Can't you see? It won't be a month before every teacher and every scholar in the school will know that her father keeps a liquor-saloon."

"Confound you, Hiram! Haven't you anything else to say?" An angry flush reddened Lloyd's face as he spoke. "And suppose they do know it, what then?"

"It won't be long before some good Christian among them will draw back the skirts of her garment as she passes, lest the touch be pollution."

"Christian! Faugh! Better say Pharisee!"

"Christian or Pharisee, it will be all the same to Maggy," I returned.

I had troubled the waters of his spirit. The light went out of his face; he looked very sober.

"And then," I continued, "it won't be a great while after that before some other good and wise Christian brother or sister will feel moved to talk with her about the iniquity of your business, and urge her to use her influence to get you to abandon it."

"Good heavens!" Lloyd ejaculated, beginning to

walk about and show considerable agitation. "No, no, Hiram. I don't believe any one would be so thoughtless and cruel. Why, it would almost kill the poor child. She'd never hold up her head among people again."

"I'm sorry she's got into this thing, Tom," I replied, speaking seriously. "It can't go on long. You must look for a break at any time, and be prepared for it. Sunday-schools and churches are not in our line, and Sunday-school and church people don't tolerate us. They're down on us in every way —set us over to the devil's side—and there is nothing too bad for them to say about us. No, Tom. It isn't the place for one like Maggy. She isn't strong enough to bear what will surely come upon her. Just imagine some cur of a boy looking up into her face and saying,

"'Doesn't your father sell rum?'"

Lloyd fairly caught his breath and seemed to stagger back as I said this, while he grew dark with anger and pain.

"But I see no help for it," I went on. "Poor thing! It's gone hard with her ever since we went into this business, and it is sure to get no better. I'm beginning to think, with our temperance friends, that it's under a curse. You can make money, and money's about everything in this world—at least you and I thought so once. But peace of mind and a good conscience, if they are of any account, don't come, I'm thinking, in this way. If my pile was large enough, I'd shut up shop or sell out to-morrow."

"Yes, if the pile were large enough, Hiram," Lloyd answered, moodily, "but it isn't, you see. We can't afford to shut up shop: what would you and I be worth as bookbinders? Not much, I take it. My hand's out, and I couldn't make my salt."

"I don't intend trying," I returned. "In for a penny, in for a pound. Going to get my pile, and so be able to snap my fingers in the world's face. After that—the gentleman!"

The trouble for poor Maggy was not in the far distance. She was a liquor-seller's daughter, and in a Sunday-school and among religious and charitable people out of place. The needy and suffering poor whose miseries she sought to alleviate were in most cases made poor and miserable through the very traffic that she was aware gave her a pleasant home, good food and fine clothing.

One day she went to visit a poor woman who she learned was sick and unable to work. She took food to her hungry children, and did all in her power to comfort and help her. But the woman seemed hard and unthankful, and had a look in her face that hurt Maggy.

Just as she was going away, this woman, whose drunken husband spent most of his earnings in dram-shops, took hold of Maggy's dress, which was

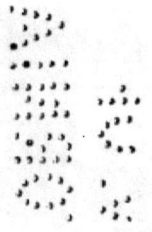

"I wonder how many children went starving that you might wear this?"
Page 183.

of some fine material, and said, with a bitter sneer in her voice,

"I wonder how many children went starving that you might wear this?"

Lloyd found her in bed when he got home that day, with her white face turned to the wall. All he could learn from her mother was that she had come home from one of her visits to the poor and gone quietly to her room. To all their questions she gave no answers as to the cause of her trouble, but her father had his guess, and it was not far out of the way.

After a few days Maggy was about again, but the sweet, tender patience that made her face heavenly was gone. Instead of saintly peace you saw the martyr's calm endurance. She went back to her work self-compelled, treading on thorns, but sustained by a pious trust in God. It was her duty to do what in her lay to help and comfort the poor and wretched, most of whom were in need because of the evil wrought among them by just such work as her father was doing daily.

One Sunday a temperance lecture was given to the children of the Sabbath-school where she taught, and the lecturer was very severe on men who sold liquor, classing them among the worst in the community. His strong denunciations sent the hot blood to her thin cheeks, and though she held down her head in shame, keeping her eyes on the floor, she was conscious that many eyes looked often toward her. She felt them striking her with the pain of arrows.

On coming home she went to her room, and as she did not appear at tea-time, her mother, going to see what was the matter, found her again with her white face to the wall. She had learned to let her alone when such states fell upon her, and quietly left the room.

"What can have happened?" the father asked as they gathered about the table.

"It was that man who talked to us in school," said little Harvey.

"In Sunday-school?" inquired Lloyd.

"Yes, sir. And I don't like to go there. The boys call me 'rummy,' and say that my daddy keeps a whisky-mill, so they do."

A dead silence fell upon the little group sitting at the tea-table. Mrs. Lloyd did not venture to look at her husband. He was dumb for a while.

"What did the man say?" he asked, at length, anxious to know the truth.

"It was about temperance," answered Harvey.

"Well, what did he say?"

"Oh, he talked ever so much about rum-sellers, and called them dreadful bad names."

"He did?"

"Yes, sir. And it made Maggy turn red and then white, and she held down her head, and the teachers and children looked at her. And Tom Grant, he punched me and said, 'Your daddy's one of 'em.' I don't want to go to that Sunday-school any more, I don't. Can't I stay home, father?"

Lloyd pushed back his chair with a bitter exclamation and flung himself out of the room. He was angry beyond measure, yet with an anger so blended with pain that he was in torture.

CHAPTER XVI.

"PROPHET of evil!" Lloyd said to me in a strange rasping voice as he came in that Sunday evening to help in the bar. His eyes had a wild, desperate expression, and he looked something like an animal at bay.

"It has come at last?" I responded, for I guessed what he meant.

"What has come?" he asked, with a thrill of fierce anger in his tones.

"The evil I prophesied. I told you a Sunday-school was no place for Maggy. You can't mix oil and water, and it's no use to try."

"How did you know there had been anything wrong at the school?"

"I didn't know. I only guessed. I knew it would come, and that it was likely to come any day. Well, what was it?"

He told me all he knew.

"Are you going to let Maggy and the boys go back there to be picked at and insulted after this fashion?" I asked.

"They'll never go again, if I have my say," he replied. "But it won't do to interfere with Maggy, poor thing! She must have her will. I can't say no to her. And Jane is so anxious about Harvey and Willy, and wants them in the Sunday-school. I don't know what to do."

We were interrupted by customers. Not long afterward our bar-tender, who had been up stairs in answer to calls for liquor, said to me aside, that Lloyd might not hear,

"Tom's up stairs."

"Not Tom Lloyd?" I answered.

"Yes, and he's been in a muss with somebody, and got battered up dreadfully. He don't want his father to know he's here. Says, won't you come up and see him?"

As soon as I could get away from customers I went up to see the boy, who was going to ruin fast, I am sorry to say. I found him in a wretched condition. His face was cut and bruised, and the fingers of one hand badly hurt, swollen and very painful—broken, it proved to be. He had been drinking. I gathered from him that he had been across the river with a gang of rowdy boys and young men, and that he had got into a fight with one of them, that two or three joined against him, beating and kicking him about the body and in the face in a most savage manner. I wondered, from his account of the way they set upon him, that worse injuries had not been the consequence.

"Don't let father know about it," he said, in a piteous way. "I can't stand any more."

"He'll not do anything to you. Don't be afraid," I replied.

I then examined his hurts as well as I could.

"There's a broken bone here, I'm afraid, Tom," said I, after turning his hand about and examining the swollen finger, "and we'll have to send for a doctor."

He groaned from pain of mind as well as body.

"Will father have to know?" he asked.

"I don't see how it is to be helped, Tom," I replied. "I'll see him first, and have a talk with him."

He shut his eyes and closed his mouth tightly. Poor boy! My heart ached for him. Two years before he was such a nice lad, more like his sister Maggy than any of the other children. He was a favorite in the bindery, all spoke well of him, and all prophesied that he would grow up to be a good and useful man. Alas! what a change had come over him! In less than two years he had been transformed into a coarse, profane rowdy, the slave of evil passion.

I went down, and as soon as I could get Lloyd by himself, said,

"Tom's got into trouble."

A scowl darkened his face.

"What's the matter? Where is he?" he asked, harshly.

"You've got to be cool about it, Tom," said I. "It isn't a case for anger, but care and concern.

He's been badly beaten, and one finger is broken, I'm afraid."

The fierceness went out of his face.

"Oh dear!" he almost groaned. "There's no end to trouble."

"You'd better send some one for Dr. ———," I suggested.

"Is it so bad as that?" he inquired.

"If it's no more than a broken finger, there will have to be a doctor," I replied.

"Where is he? At home?"

"No; he's up stairs."

He seemed relieved at this, saying, "I'm glad he didn't go home. They're in trouble enough there, as it is."

I went up stairs in company with Lloyd. I did so in order to keep him from breaking out angrily. It was no time for a passionate assault upon the unhappy boy.

The face of Tom, swollen, cut, blood-marked and purple in spots from knuckle strokes and kicks, as he raised his head and looked in a wistful, frightened way at his father, was a sight to shock anybody's nerves. I did not wonder at the exclamation of pain and alarm that fell from Lloyd as his eyes first rested upon him.

A doctor was sent for, and the boy examined carefully. His finger, as I feared, was broken. There was a deep, ugly bruise on one of his cheeks, his nose was swollen to double its usual size and one of his eyes was black. On his body were several bad bruises. He had been kicked in the side just above the hip, and from the pain he felt there, the doctor feared there might be an internal injury.

After setting the finger the doctor very naturally asked how Tom came to be beaten in so shocking a manner.

"It wasn't in Sunday-school, I guess," he added, before there was time for an answer to his question.

I saw Lloyd wince a little.

"I never heard of Sunday-school boys fighting like dogs and beating their companions after this savage fashion," added the doctor.

Neither Tom nor his father felt inclined to go into particulars.

After the doctor went away we held a consultation as to what would be best to do with the boy. If he did not come home that night, his mother would be frightened about him, and if she were told of what had happened, she would be made wretched beyond description. Oh, but he was a dreadful object for a mother to look upon!

"Better keep him here for to-night, at least," I counseled. "It will never do for his mother and Maggy to see him as he is."

"But what can I say at home?" asked Lloyd. He looked like a man lost and bewildered.

"Trump up some story that will pass muster. Say anything except the naked truth. That will come soon enough."

"It's easy to talk," he answered, fretfully. "If you had two or three women to manage, you wouldn't see it all so clearly."

"Which, thank Heaven! I have not," was my fervent reply.

It was decided to let Tom stay where he was, and get up some story to explain his absence.

On the next day he went home to lay another sorrow on the heart of his mother.

I had not seen Harry Glenn but two or three times since the night his brother-in-law made an assault upon him. He felt the disgrace so deeply that he did not go back to work in the office, but got in somewhere else. He went down very rapidly after his wife left him.

One evening about this time he came shuffling into our bar-room, a most forlorn-looking object. His clothes were shabby and dirty, and he presented the appearance of a man who had been on a spree for a week or more. His eyes were bloodshotten and had a wild, restless way of glancing about that suggested mania. All his motions were nervous. He came up to the bar, and leaning on the silver-plated railing, bent his face over toward me, and said in a hoarse, shaky kind of voice,

"Brandy."

I did not often refuse men, drunk or sober. But I felt an impulse to say no to this wretched man, fallen so deep and in so short a time. I remembered that he was a sober man with a wife and child and a home when we opened "The Retreat," and I saw what he was now. It all passed through my mind in an instant, and I said kindly but firmly,

"You've had enough, Harry, for to-night. I wouldn't take any more if I were you."

"Brandy! Brandy, Hiram!" he answered, in a wild, eager way, reaching out his hand. "I want brandy or whisky, or any kind of spirits. Quick, Hiram!" and I saw him glare over his shoulder with a nervous, half-alarmed start, as if he thought some one had followed him in.

"I've been trying to shut down," he added, in a lower voice and in a confidential way, "but it don't work right. Just a glass, Hiram. Ugh!"

And he gave a quick spring backward, while fear and disgust writhed in his face.

"Give him brandy," cried old Jacobs, who was present, and who had been watching Glenn very closely since he came in. The old pressman came forward as he spoke, and taking the miserable-looking man by the arm, drew him again up to the bar.

I hesitated no longer. The brandy was set before him. With a kind of desperate eagerness, Glenn reached out his shaking hand toward the decanter, and was lifting it to fill a glass when he let it fall, with an exclamation of alarm. There was a look of abject horror on his face.

"Don't be a fool," said Jacobs. "'Tisn't outside of you. Here! Drink! Quick!" He had filled the glass hastily, and now held it toward the agitated man.

There were two or three of the rougher and more unfeeling kind of bar-room loungers present.

"Ho! ho!" laughed one of them, starting up and coming to the bar. "The old chap's after him, dead sure! Snakes and lizards, devils and crocodiles, and all that fancy crew! Bad company, my friend."

And he eyed Glenn with the excited interest of a bully enjoying a dog-fight.

In the mean time, Glenn had clutched the glass with both hands and was gulping down the brandy.

"Steady, man!" said the last speaker, his face twitching with merriment. "That's the way. Fight 'em with brandy."

But the fiends had too strong a grip on the poor fellow. His eyes as he drank were looking suspiciously into the glass, and before the last drops were drained, he saw in them some horrid thing of life. A cry, a start of fear and a dashing of the glass to the floor followed.

"Got him, sure!" chuckled the man to whom I have referred, and two or three joined in the laugh. "Give him another dose."

By this time Glenn had rushed desperately across the room, and was crouching behind a table trying to hide himself. Jacobs followed, and sought to allay his fears.

"'Tisn't anything outside of you, Harry! 'Tisn't in the room here. I don't see anything. I'm not afraid," he said, bending down over the frightened man and laying his hand upon his shoulder. "I know. I've had it. It's only an ugly kind of dream."

"Maybe it is," Glenn answered, partially assured. "But I never had it before, you see. It—"

He gave another start and cry, almost throwing Jacobs over, and bounded across the room, where he stood crouching and shivering against the wall.

"Go for a policeman," Lloyd said to the bar-keeper, in a cold, half-indifferent way.

"Don't do any such thing," spoke up Jacobs, angrily. "It isn't a case for the police."

"Go, I tell you!" Lloyd waved his hand to the bar-keeper.

"I say don't!" cried Jacobs, in a tone of command. "Gentlemen"—and he appealed to the company—"it's a shame! We know what's the matter. This poor fellow mustn't go to the lock-up. He might die. He's a fellow-creature, and not a dog to let perish in the gutter."

This had the desired effect. The company were unanimously against Lloyd, and the police were not sent for.

A second glass of brandy was given, but it did not do the work. Glenn's unstrung nerves would not respond and tighten their loosened fibres. Horrible things, great and small, filled the air around him, crept into his bosom, twined about his neck, grinned in his face, crawled over his hands, stretched great claws to seize him, swooped down upon him from wall and ceiling, sprung upon him from the floor. It was an awful scene. The poor man's cries of horror and calls for help and looks of deepest terror made the flesh creep. Even the rough, unfeeling men who had laughed at first, grew sober and silent.

We got him up stairs, so as to relieve the barroom of his presence, and there we worked with him for hours before exhausted nature retired from the struggle.

I noticed, as they were taking him out of the barroom, the pale, frightened face of a boy who had retreated near the door. He was one of our Sunday-evening guests, a lad from the bindery and the only son of a widow. He had been losing ground pretty fast of late. I could see the love of liquor growing on him steadily. He did not seem to care for it at first. Other lads in the bindery had told him of the nice evenings they spent at "The Retreat," and so he had been enticed to come. He was social, and liked games. There were dominoes, cards, checkers, backgammon and bagatelle and boys he knew—quite enough to lure him, and more than enough, when the taste for drink was formed, to hold him upon our enchanted ground. But this taste for liquor grew, and of late I had often seen him too much under its influence.

I gathered from what journeymen said to him occasionally that he was not doing as well in the bindery as he should.

Now and then he would slip away from his work in the daytime, and come in to have a little rest and play at backgammon or bagatelle with some other boys, idlers like himself.

"You here!" I had often heard a journeyman say to him in reproof. "You'd better be at your work. You'll have Ashley down on you."

"Not afraid of Ashley," he would answer, jauntily, or, "Look out for Ashley yourself."

He had learned to swear as well as drink, and could talk dirty talk as freely as any one. His face had changed noticeably. It was coarser and more sensual, and the boyish innocence had gone out of his eyes.

As Glenn was taken struggling and crying from the room, I saw this boy's pale face vanish through the door. He never came back again. It was the first time he had seen or heard of the drunkard's strange, appalling delirium—a delirium of which every one who drinks steadily and freely is in danger—and it so filled him with dread and horror that he turned his steps out of the way he had entered, and never went back into it, so far as I know, again.

Poor Glenn had been running down fearfully of late. He had drank until appetite for food was nearly gone, and kept himself up almost entirely by stimulants. There always comes an end to a state of things like this. Stimulants cannot take the place of food. They excite, but do not give nutrition—they diminish waste, but cannot build up. In the end, if too much relied on, they fail. The time comes when reaction ceases—when the bow will not pull against the string. Then follows the struggle for life.

In such a struggle this young man found himself. It was a death-struggle indeed. A doctor was with him all night, and it was only by the greatest care that he was saved. If he had been given over to the police and taken to a cell in the station-house, he would have died there. I said so to Lloyd on the next day, and he answered gruffly,

"It would have been the best thing for him. When a man gets as far gone as he is, he ought to die."

I was hard enough and indifferent enough, but not so brutal as this.

"If he were your son," I replied, with the covert contempt I felt for him at that moment trembling in my voice, "you might have something else to say."

"I'd rather see a son of mine dead than ever come to that," he said, dropping his high manner, and with a change of tone I did not fail to notice. I had meant to touch him in a tender spot, and was successful.

It was not until the afternoon of the day following Glenn's attack of delirium tremens that he was in a condition to be taken away by his friends. His presence in the house annoyed us very much. We didn't propose to keep a hospital, much less for diseases of this kind. It was our business to make men sick, not to nurse and cure them. Other people might do that if they had a fancy for it, but it wasn't in our line.

I noticed that a number of our regular drinkers tried to taper off after this. The ten-glass-a-day men cut down to six or eight, and the six-glass men to four or five. But it didn't last. After a few days they went at it as of old, and rather increased than diminished the supply. This is the usual result when a steady drinker sets himself to cutting down. The system has adjusted itself to a certain amount of stimulant every day, and if it gets that, is generally satisfied, though in the long run this amount is imperceptibly increased. But the moment you begin to cut down, a want is felt. The whole system is disturbed. The man feels restless and out of sorts all over. Food does not supply his want: it is the lost stimulant he craves; and so in a little while he goes back to the old number of daily drinks, but now these do not satisfy him as of old. Restriction has made desire restless and clamorous. He has to make up for what has been lost, and in the making up appetite gains a new strength and persists in a new demand.

So, as I said, the tapering off did not last. But there were two or three besides the boy whose frightened face I noticed on the Sunday night Glenn had his tussle with the demons who did not visit us again. They were occasional customers, dropping in for beer or ale now and then—young men in good places and getting along all right, but who had nothing special to do in the evening. They had heard, no doubt, of delirium tremens, but, I take it, had never seen a case before. A single exhibition of that disease, and in the desperate type they happened to witness, was quite enough for them. One of them was heard to say,

"If the road to that country lies through a tavern, I'm going some other way. Don't like the inhabitants."

This was told in the bar-room one day, and caused a laugh all round, but some, I think, felt sober while they laughed.

CHAPTER XVII.

THINGS were dull one evening. A good many came in and lounged about, but not being of the thirsty kind, were satisfied with cigars and a chat with acquaintances. They had come more for company than for drink. I sat behind the bar pretending to read a newspaper, but really waiting for the call I expected each moment, and beginning to feel rather cross.

A young man, clerk in a wholesale store on Market street, dropped in about nine o'clock, and looked through the room as if searching for somebody.

"Oh, you're here! I thought I should find you," he said to a couple of young men who were sitting at a table talking.

They made room, and as he sat down one of them said,

"Aren't you out of your latitude, Bland?"

"A little," he replied, a pleasant smile breaking over his handsome face, that was as free a face as ever was from sign of dissipation. "You see, I was kept late at the store this evening, and thrown a little out. It was too early to go home and too late to get myself up for a call on the ladies. So, as I was feeling dull and lonesome, like, I thought I'd look in here, and maybe I'd find somebody I knew and kill a little time."

"Glad to see you," was the cordial reply, and then the three young men put their heads together and had a good talk, sometimes speaking low and confidentially, and sometimes laughing merrily. They had enough of interest to converse about to keep them excited, and did not feel the want of any other stimulant.

I waited and waited, expecting every moment to hear one of them say,

"Come, let's have a drink."

But they kept on talking and laughing until I could stand it no longer. I knew a way to fetch them, but it would cost four drinks, and I held off. At last, as there seemed no prospect of their getting through, I said,

"Rather dry work, gentlemen. Come, drink with me ;" and I set down four glasses. I saw a shade creep over young Bland's face as he arose from the table with his companions, who responded without hesitation. He had not come to drink. But there was no get off for him, and so he took a glass of ale.

The young men resumed their places and talked on for a while longer. At last Bland said, rising as he spoke,

"I shall have to bid you good-evening, boys."

"Not till we have another drink," returned one of his friends. "Come, drink with me."

I was waiting for that. They couldn't drink at my expense without following suit at their own. So they ranged themselves at the bar and drank again. Two glasses were pretty heavy for Bland, who was not used to much liquor. They sat down and talked on for a while longer. Bland made a second move to go, but the other friend said,

"No, not till you drink with me."

I knew how it would work. It was an old dodge, and rarely failed. A bait of three or four glasses often gave us the profit on a dozen or twenty.

So up they came again and drank. It was stretching things for young Bland. I could see the color rising in his face, and his eyes getting shiny. When he spoke, his voice, which was clear and full on every word when he first came in, sounded thick.

They were noisier when they sat down for the third time, and one of them sang a song. After a while, Bland started up, saying,

"I must be off. Come, let's have another drink before I go." He had to treat, of course. His steps were unsteady as he walked up to the bar. Three glasses more—four apiece in all. It was too much for one whose head was hardly good enough for a single full tumbler of strong ale.

I saw him lurch against the door as he went out alone soon after.

"Got more aboard than he can carry, I'm afraid," said one of his friends.

"Isn't used to it," remarked the other. "Will

have a glorious headache to-morrow morning, I fancy."

He had worse than a headache, poor fellow! Morning found him in a station-house, minus watch and pocket-book, and with a pair of black eyes. How he came there, or who had beaten and robbed him, he knew not. All was a blank from the time he went out of our saloon until he found himself in the station-house and awoke to a sense of wretchedness and humiliation it would be hard to describe.

Bland was sensitive and proud, and felt the disgrace into which he had fallen most keenly. He could not go to the store in which he was employed with a pair of black eyes. So he feigned sickness. But that wouldn't save him. The truth had to come out. It was told of him to his employers that he had been on a drunken spree and got his eyes blackened, and as the leading man in the firm was a little over-righteous, and consequently very hard and unforgiving toward wrong-doers, he was discharged without pity.

I heard it talked over in the bar-room, some blaming and some excusing the act. One said,

"A case like this should have the kindest consideration. The young man was taken unawares. He wasn't used to liquor. Any one is liable to be caught in this way."

And another answered,

"They have to mark these things with a black

cross as a warning. Dissipation among clerks is getting to be a serious evil. Business is hurt and hindered by it in more ways than outside people imagine. I know a house that won't have a man in it who drinks a drop."

"Things get hitched with them, I fancy, now and then," was replied to this.

"Not a bit of it. All goes on like clock-work. Sober heads are generally clear heads. The buyer makes no blunders in buying and the seller none in selling. I don't blame a house that insists on having strictly temperate clerks. I'd do the same myself if I were in business."

"I'm afraid your example would be against you," said the other, laughing.

"When I go into business I'll swear off," was answered. "Men can't drink and prosper in business—your common run of men, I mean. There are exceptions, of course, but they only prove the rule. Drinking is against prosperity. It muddles the brain, and so confuses the judgment. One-half the mistakes that are made in business could be traced, I doubt not, to a glass of wine or beer or spirits taken just at the wrong time.

"There's Peter Stang: you all remember when he was at the top. A shrewder business-man was not to be found on the street ten years ago. He knew just when to buy and how to buy—had the market at his finger-ends—rarely if ever made a mistake. I know plenty of men who used to watch him like a hawk and take his judgment against their own in almost everything.

"He's only a clerk to-day. Why? He lost his clear head. How? Got too fond of wine. Used only to take it for dinner, when the best part of his business-day was over. In the morning his brain was as clear as light. But wine got ahead of him. The single glass of sherry was not enough. It took two glasses to meet the growing demand, then three, and at last—I don't know how many. He came to be a little unsteady in the morning—nerves not toned up. A glass of wine tightened them, so he took his morning glass, and then his forenoon glass. And thus he lost his clear head, and began to make blunders, and he kept on making them until he went under.

"Don't you believe it? Well, you needn't. It's a free country, and men can believe as little or as much as they please, but if you are in business, I'd advise you to steer clear of liquor during business-hours."

"Just as true as preaching," spoke out a man who had been listening to the conversation. I knew him very well. He had once been in a good trade, but failed a few years back, and was now loafing around, living on his wife's income, which was small. He was a pretty hard drinker.

"Just as true as preaching," he said, striking his hand upon his knee. "I could tell you a story to the point if I chose."

"Let's have the story," urged two or three, gathering about him.

He dropped his eyes, and sat a few moments with a serious air.

"Come, let's have some liquor first," said one of the company; "what'll you take? and you, and you, and you?" glancing from face to face. Half a dozen came promptly to the bar, each giving his order, and quite willing to drink at another's expense.

"Now for the story;" and all drew around the broken-down merchant.

"It isn't a story I like to tell," he began, with a little roughness in his throat. "I'd rather forget than remember it. Brings too many things back."

"It won't do, Tom," said I, "to let him sail off on this tack. He'll give 'em a regular-built temperance lecture before he's through. We must choke him down in some way."

"How'll we do it?" asked Lloyd.

"Can't we get 'em at cards?" I suggested.

"They'll suspect us if we try that. No, it must be something else, and we must do it quick. Gentlemen," he called. All the company looked toward the bar. "Gentlemen," said Tom Lloyd, putting on his best smile and taking down a bottle, "we got in, to-day, a few bottles of Jersey apple-jack ten years old. Came out of the cellar of a farmer who died last week, and is the nicest thing of the kind that's going. I want you to taste it and give me your opinion."

There wasn't a word of truth in all this. He held in his hand a bottle of the commonest kind of apple whisky, well charged with fusil oil.

There was an instant uprising of the company and movement toward the bar. All drank, and all said it was prime.

"And now, Andy"—Lloyd spoke to a short, rather stout young man who stood at the bar—"it's your turn to treat." Andy looked a little disconcerted, for he wasn't usually flush with money. But Lloyd quickly set him at ease by adding,

"The company to a song."

Singing was one of Andy's accomplishments. He had a very fine tenor voice, clear and sweet, and often sang for our amusement.

"Yes, a song, Andy! A song!" and one and another repeated the request.

Andy cleared his throat, and sang one song after another, as it was called for, until the broken-down merchant was forgotten.

We had often to resort to tactics of this kind to stave off disagreeable things. There was no counting on the people who came in. A man half tipsy is a very uncertain kind of a customer. You are never sure of him. Some grow quarrelsome as soon as they get down a few glasses, some grow merry and talkative, some familiar and obtrusive, and some begin to tell you about their troubles. A sot is sure, in imagination, to have everybody against him. This man is his enemy and that man is trying to do him some wrong, and when liquor sets his tongue free, he will fill your ears with complaints. It isn't his fault that he is going to ruin. Oh no. It's the fault of everybody else. He has no chance in the world. Everything he puts his hand to fails—everybody stands ready to give him a kick.

And it must be confessed that the lower a man gets, the less he is cared for and the easier it is to give him a kick. I know of none who get so little consideration as the poor wretches that rum has degraded lower than the beasts. They are rejected by all and despised by all. No matter how abused and wronged, few, if any, come to their aid. Coarse, unfeeling brutes in human form sport with their helplessness and infirmity, children taunt and torture them in the streets, and when the station-house or prison closes its hard doors upon them, God only knows what they are sometimes doomed to suffer.

The men whose business it is to get gain by debasing them are usually the most unpitying of all, the cruelest of all. I have seen things done that it makes me sick to think of.

We had a bar-keeper for a few months whose very delight it was to chafe and worry and play practical jokes on men who got drunk. We let him do a great many things that we hadn't the heart to do ourselves, because we didn't want worn-down sots about. They were offensive to our better customers. Many a man has gone home from our saloon with his face blacked, or his nose painted red, or his coat turned wrong side out, or the rim of his hat cut half away, or with a piece of ice down the back of his neck. Any mean or cruel joke that a devilish ingenuity can invent may be played off on the poor wretch who ends his day's debauch by falling asleep in a tavern, and there is no one to take his part.

I knew a case where a young man belonging to a respectable family, and having a wife and two little children, had his face shamefully disfigured. It did not happen with us, though our bar-keeper would have done it without hesitation. This young man had been going down, down, down, for a year or two, until he was at the bottom of the ladder. His wife had left him and gone to her friends. He was out of a place, for no one in business would have him.

One night about eleven o'clock he was found asleep in one of the boxes of a well-known restaurant, where he had emptied his pockets of the few small coins he had borrowed from some old acquaintance who could not deny him.

"Dead beat!" exclaimed a man who had his attention called to him.

"Dead beat it is!" responded another, with a laugh. Both knew him, and knew from what a height into this fearful depth he had fallen.

"I'm going to label him," said a bar-keeper, and he took from a drawer a stick of caustic. Three or four men looked on without a word of remonstrance, and saw him write the letters D. B. on the young man's forehead. He was then turned into the street with the red brand burnt on his flesh.

It was meant as a bit of cruel sport, but wrought the young man's reformation. When he looked into a glass on the next morning to see what gave the strange hot tightness to his forehead, and saw D. B. there in great red capitals, he was so shocked and pained and humiliated that he made a vow never to pass through the door of a tavern again so long as he lived.

As far as I know to the contrary, he has kept his promise. It was a great many weeks before the red letters faded away, and before he ventured on the street again. But when he did go out, he went earnestly to work in the store of a relative who was moved to give him a chance. He is to-day in a good business, steady and prosperous, with his family around him.

In another case the son of a well-known lawyer in the city who had his wine for dinner and served it to his guests fell naturally into drinking habits. At twenty-one he was a very fast young man. At twenty-four he was clear out of his depth, a sorrow and a shame to his friends.

He came into our place one bitter cold night in winter, tipsy as a lord, and drank with a couple of cronies who were with him. Afterward they tried to get him away, but he was growing very stupid and refused to go. So they left him. He got a newspaper after he was alone and tried to read, but soon fell asleep. It was after eleven o'clock when he came, and it was getting on toward twelve.

"You must get that fellow out, Bill," said Lloyd to our bar-keeper.

"All right," answered Bill, who went over to where the young man sat asleep in his chair. His head had fallen back and his mouth was wide open. His young, almost boyish, face, marred so sadly by dissipation, had a sad and suffering expression. None but the hardened or cruel could look upon it without pity.

"Time to go!" said Bill, giving him a rough shake.

But he might almost as well have tried to arouse the dead. He was sleeping the drunkard's heavy sleep.

Then with his huge hand he gripped the back of his neck and lifted him by main strength.

"Stand up, sir! There, now!" and Bill tried to steady him on his feet. But the nerveless limbs gave way, and the sleeper fell heavily on the floor, striking the back of his head against the leg of a table.

No one interfered or offered any remonstrance.

"I'll fetch him," said Bill, with the lively interest of one engaged in some favorite sport. We always had hot water on the stove ready for making punches. He filled a pint measure half full of this, and put in enough cold water to keep it from scalding. Then he opened the shirt bosom of the poor wretch and poured in the warm water, pushing the vessel first to this side and then to that, so that the water would go all around his body.

Even this did not wake him. Bill stood him up, and I saw the water, which had run down both legs, coming out over his boots upon the floor. His stockings were saturated. But I said nothing, and made no movement to prevent the outrage. Lloyd swore impatiently, not at the bar-keeper, but at his unconscious victim.

"Got to come!" Bill now exclaimed. He was getting angry. A castor used at lunch time stood on the bar. From this he took a box of red pepper, and before a word could be said threw a portion of the contents up the young man's nose.

"Ha! ha! Knew that would bring him!" laughed the brute as the sleeper started up wildly and struggled to his feet, stung by sudden pain into wakefulness and partial sobriety.

"Travel, sir!" was the greeting that fell on his rum-stopped ears, and ere he was conscious of where he was a strong hand on the back of his neck had thrust him toward the door and out into the freezing night.

Think of his condition! A pint of warm water had just been poured into his bosom, and it had saturated his clothes to the skin and down to his feet. It was a bitter cold night—one of the coldest of the season. He could not have been out in the street a minute before its icy touch was upon him, nor ten minutes before his wet garments were stiff about him—frozen, it might be, to his very flesh.

"Had to go when I took him in hand," chuckled Bill as he returned behind the bar. But no one answered him or echoed his laugh. Now that the thing was done we all felt, I think, that it had been overdone.

How the poor fellow got home, or what his condition was when he arrived there, I never heard. He did not visit us again. But a pistol-ball in Bill's elbow one dark night not long afterward, fired by an unknown hand, followed by erysipelas and amputation, was suggestive of revenge.

CHAPTER XVIII.

MAGGY LLOYD went back to her work among the poor; she also took her place in the Sunday-school, and through her influence and that of her mother kept her two younger brothers there for a few months longer.

But there was not a child in the class to which Harvey and Willy were attached who did not know that their father kept a bar, and that it was open every Sunday, and scarcely a Sunday went by that one and another did not throw it into their teeth.

It is not surprising that they rebelled against going to school, nor that their father, when they told him how they were taunted and picked upon all the while, set his foot down at last and said they should not attend any longer.

His will in this case ruled, of course. Harvey and Willy refused to go to Sunday-school, and the mother could not force them when the father said " No."

Poor Maggy! It was another stone taken out of the foundation of her life. She loved these little boys with a love made doubly sensitive by the unhappy condition by which they were surrounded, and by the unusual perils that lay in their future.

She had hoped much from the good influences and associations of the Sunday-school in giving their young minds a love for things pure and pious, but this hope was swept clean away.

Another stunning blow came soon after. She had missed a dear little girl from her class for two Sundays, and on asking if any one knew whether she were sick or not, a scholar said,

"No, ma'am, she isn't sick."

"Do you know why she stays away?" asked Maggy.

"Yes, ma'am, she told me," answered the scholar.

"What is the reason?" inquired Maggy.

"Don't like to tell," returned the child.

Maggy's heart stood still for a moment. It divined the reason. She did not press the child for an answer before the class, but after school took her hand as they were going away, and drawing her aside, said,

"You'll tell me now why Mary Lingen doesn't come to school?"

"It's because—because," was answered, "her mother says no rum-seller's daughter shall teach her child in Sunday-school."

When Lloyd next saw Maggy, she was lying still as death with her white face to the wall.

I knew something had gone wrong again at home by the dark clouding of his face, by his restlessness and irritability, and by the unusual freedom with which he drank. What it really was I did not know until some time afterward, and then such a tirade against churches, ministers and religious people generally as he indulged in one rarely hears. He wished there wasn't a church in the world, and as for ministers, they were all a set of hypocrites who swindled the people out of money under false pretences, and if he had his way of them, he'd hang one half and banish the rest from the country.

Maggy struggled up again, weaker, sadder, paler, than before, and went out to do her work among the poor, many of whom had sadly missed her helping hand, her comforting words and the religious strength she sought to give them. She kept on for a few months longer, and then the end came. It was a sad and sorrowful end, and every time I think of it a dull ache goes through my heart.

She had struggled up again, as I have said, and gone out to her work among the poor, giving her life for the good of others. One stormy day in winter a woman called late in the afternoon and asked to see her. She was poorly dressed, her face was thin and worn and marked with sorrow and suffering. The snow was white on her thin dress and lay melting in her hair as Maggy met her in the parlor, where she had been shown by a servant.

"Miss Lloyd?" the woman queried as Maggy advanced toward her.

"That is my name," Maggy replied.

"I've heard," said the woman, "that you are kind and tender-hearted, and so I have come. I don't want to trouble you, but I am heart-broken and in despair. It is all nice and elegant here "—the woman cast her eyes about the room—" but I have nothing left — no carpet on my floor, no comfortable chairs to sit in, no warm beds for my children, scarcely food to eat, and yet there was a time when I had all these;" and again she threw her eyes almost desperately about the room.

"I once had a sober, good husband," she resumed, "and our children had a kind father."

Poor Maggy began to tremble. She sat down from sheer weakness. The woman sat down also.

"Maybe it isn't right to come to you," the woman said, looking into the pale, shocked face of the girl, and comprehending something of her feelings. "'Tisn't any fault of yours—I know that—but I thought if you'd speak to him about it, he wouldn't take my husband's money for liquor. Oh, if you'd just speak to him! My husband's name is Gordon. Tell your father that he spends everything for drink, and that we are starving."

Mrs. Lloyd, who had followed Maggy down stairs, was standing in the entry near the parlor door and heard all this. Knowing her child's weak condition, and fearing some ill effect, she came into the room. As soon as Maggy saw her mother she got up and staggered toward her, laying her head upon her bosom and sobbing.

"Poor thing!" said the woman. "Maybe I've done wrong. But they said she was good, and might have influence with her father. Oh dear! Oh dear! It's dreadful! Everything is hurt;" and she went on in a bewildered way, wringing her hands.

Mrs. Lloyd drew Maggy out of the room, and got her up stairs to her chamber, almost carrying her for a part of the way. It was the old story. The white face turned to the wall again, and now for the last time.

When Mrs. Lloyd went back to the parlor, the woman had gone.

As night closed in, the storm which had begun late in the afternoon increased in violence. The wind was high and swept the snow along in blinding gusts, so that it was difficult to face it when it got an open sweep or was driven around corners or through narrow places in eddying whirls.

Maggy did not stir, nor seem to heed the roar and rush and sobbing of the tempest. Her mother went in and out of her room every now and then, feeling strangely anxious. The shadow of some great calamity seemed resting on her soul. She felt the dread of a coming evil.

At tea-time she sat down with her two younger children. Tom had not been home since morning, and she did not know where he was. After she had helped the children, she poured out a cup of tea and took it to Maggy's room. Entering softly, she bent over the bed for a little while, but Maggy did not stir nor in any way recognize her mother's presence. Then Mrs. Lloyd spoke to her, but she neither answered nor gave any sign. She bent close down over her, listening for the sound of breathing; it came faint and slow, and she lifted herself with a sigh of relief. If she were sleeping, better so.

Half an hour afterward she went to her room again. Maggy was sitting up in bed as she entered, and looked at her strangely. There was something unusual in the expression of her face, something wild and wandering.

"Oh, it's you, mother," she said, a slight tremor in her voice as if she had been alarmed.

"Yes, dear, it's me. Do you want anything?"

"No, thank you;" and then, with a heavy sigh, she dropped back upon her pillow and shut her eyes.

How pale and wasted and sad she looked! The mother's eyes grew blind with tears. Mrs. Lloyd put the two younger children to bed, and then sat down alone, trying to do some mending. The storm swept its clouds of fine hard snow fiercely against the windows of the room where she sat, and sobbed and wailed in the air, causing her to shudder every now and then with a kind of vague terror. Her oldest boy, where was he to-night? He was not out of her troubled thoughts for a moment.

It was nearly ten o'clock when the pressure on her feelings became so great, and the sense of loneliness so deep, that she could bear it no longer. Putting aside her work-basket, she went up stairs, intending to sit in Maggy's room until Tom or his father came home. As she opened the door and went in softly she missed her daughter from the bed. She glanced quickly about the chamber, but she was not there.

"Maggy!" she called, passing into the next chamber. But there was no answer, and the room was empty.

She ran hurriedly from one room to another, calling her daughter's name. But no sound of voice nor footstep nor rustle of garments came to her ears.

Half wild with affright, she went up and down and over the house from attic to cellar, but without discovering a sign of Maggy. The servants had not seen her, though one of them said she was sure she had heard the front door shut softly at least an hour before.

The truth dawned slowly on the mother's mind. The right suggestion came. Maggy, in a half-crazed state, had gone out on that dreadful night to find her way to the saloon and beg her father not to sell any more liquor to the man whose despairing wife had called that evening and implored her help. How long had she been away? It was nearly two hours since she last visited Maggy's room. If she had been gone for that length of time, there was small hope of her ever being found alive. Word would long since have come from her if she had visited the saloon. Weak, bewildered, chilled and blinded by the storm, the chances were all against her. So the mother thought in her agony and fear.

A servant was sent in haste to the saloon, but she

had not been twenty minutes on her way when Mrs. Lloyd heard the rattle of her husband's key in the door.

"Is Maggy here?" he asked, in an eager, panting voice, as he met her in the hall. His question was answered by the deathly pallor of his wife's face. Her lips moved, but no sound came through them.

"When did she go out?"

Mrs. Lloyd only shook her head. Terror made her dumb.

"How long has she been gone?" demanded Lloyd, with a solemn sternness of manner that roused his wife.

"I cannot tell," she replied. "I only missed her a few moments ago."

Like one beside himself, Lloyd turned from his wife and rushed from the house, leaving her more frightened and in a state of wilder uncertainty than when he came in. Out in the storm she went after her husband, bare-headed and without shawl or cloak, as one crazed, calling frantically after him. But he vanished from her sight in the darkness. After going for the distance of a block she came back with such an awful pressure on her heart that it seemed as if she should die.

CHAPTER XIX.

IT was on this same dreadful night that I took home through the blinding storm Mr. Ashley's drunken son, standing him against his father's door, and letting him fall in upon the vestibule like a log, and at the feet of his mother.

I went away with her cry of pain and terror in my ears. All the way back, as I waded through the snow and bent to the storm, which threw its blinding missiles in my face, that cry seemed coming after me.

I had heard the boy's head strike the floor with a heavy jar—too heavy, I feared, not to occasion serious injury. A feeling of anxiety began to creep into my heart. What if his skull had been cracked or his brain hurt? A policeman had seen him in my hands, and knew that I was taking him home. If he should be badly hurt and die in consequence, I might get into a serious scrape. I did not think of his mother's sorrow and suffering, but of the trouble that might come to me.

The snow had fallen so heavily on the tracks that no cars on the lines leading in the direction I wished to go were running, so I had to return as I went, walking the whole distance. It took full half an hour.

It was nearly twelve o'clock as I drew near the neighborhood of Harvey street. I had not met a single person by the way. As I turned from one of the main streets into the narrower one leading to that in which our "Retreat" was hidden, I thought I saw something unusual on the pavement close beside the step leading up to a doorway. It was on the opposite side of the street from that along which I had come after having taken John Ashley home. A lamp dancing in the wind that crept in by the smallest openings threw a flickering, weird sort of light on the spot. I stood still as if from an impulse not my own. For a moment or two my heart ceased to beat. Strangely into the outlines of a human form seemed to grow the snow-covered object which had arrested my attention, and the longer I looked at it, the clearer these outlines grew. A feeling of awe, as when one stands in the presence of the dead, stole over me. Then I pushed a foot carefully into the heap of snow, and touched what I knew on the instant to be a human body. A chill ran along my nerves and down into my heart.

I stooped hurriedly, thrusting in my hand where I thought the head and breast must lie. Catching hold of a garment, I drew it upward. The snow fell away, and I looked into the dead face of Maggy Lloyd. The lamp shone down upon it, making every feature distinct. There was no distortion, no mark of pain, but a restfulness and peace I have no words to describe.

It was only half a block from "The Retreat." How long she had been lying there no one knew, but it must have been for nearly two hours, the drifting snow having completely covered her over.

I took the frail body in my arms—how light it felt!—and ran to the saloon. Lloyd was standing in the middle of the floor as I entered, having just come in from a fruitless search.

A blank horror whitened his face, his eyes stood out, his hands were thrown forward in a convulsive motion. I laid his dead child tenderly down. He did not come toward her, but seemed held back by a spell he could not break. I saw him shiver.

"It's all over with her, Tom," I said, in a choking voice. "God help us!"

I saw him shiver again. He tried to speak. His face was working terribly. He clutched out with his hands as before. At last a cry broke from his lips—a strong sobbing cry—and he covered his face and sat down, trembling violently. It was for me to act. Lloyd was utterly unmanned. The thing to do was to get the dead girl home as quickly as possible, so I sent for a carriage. It was no easy matter to get a vehicle of any kind at that hour and on such a night, and it was nearly half-past twelve before a carriage came to the door. By this time Lloyd had gained some little self-control. His grief was excessive, for he had loved this child with a tenderness his vicious life and habits had no power to extinguish.

I think, from some sentences wrung from him by pain, that he fully comprehended the cause of all this ruin. It seemed a fitting conclusion to the tragedy of his daughter's life that her dead body should first be taken to the saloon against which her heart had broken, and that her father should reap there from the seed he had sown this harvest of unspeakable woe.

When the carriage came to the door, I lifted the dead body again and bore it out, Lloyd following like one half stupefied. I got in, still holding the body, Lloyd taking his place on the opposite seat. And so we were driven to his home. Such a ride! All the way Maggy's cold form lay in my arms, her wet hair on my face and hands, while her father sat opposite, silent and motionless as a bit of marble. I cannot, as memory goes back, recall that ride as a real life-experience, but rather as some awful dream.

Mrs. Lloyd was standing at the window when we drove up. The moment she saw the carriage stop she came flying out, and was at the door before it had been thrown open. Lloyd got out first.

"Have you found Maggy?" she asked, in a voice I did not recognize, it was so changed.

"Yes," replied her husband. And his voice was as unnatural as hers.

"Oh, thank God!" broke upon the mother's lips.

How it chilled me! for I was bearing to her no relief nor comfort, but a sorrow that might break her heart. She stood back from the door of the carriage after her husband got out, and waited for Maggy. I gathered the lifeless form closely in my arms and came out backward, Lloyd assisting me. Mrs. Lloyd stood close up to the carriage. I heard a startled "Oh!" as she saw that we were lifting Maggy out bodily. A moment after she looked on the face of her child, and then two insensible forms were borne into the house, one in Lloyd's arms and one in mine, mother and daughter, and it would have been difficult to tell from their faces which was living and which was dead.

"The Retreat" was closed for the next three days and crape hung at the door. A tragedy like this could not be kept away from the public. The family physician said that he could not give a certificate for burial, and that there would have to be a coroner's inquest. It was in vain that Lloyd and I urged every possible argument to induce him to give a certificate as to the cause of her death. The sorrow was deep enough, without adding thereto a needless public exposure. But he could not be moved. There was for him but one course, he said. The law was plain. When a body was found dead in the street, a coroner's jury must be called, and the cause of death ascertained if possible.

So, on the next morning, the coroner came to the house with twelve jurors, when Lloyd and his wife, their children and servants, myself and our bar-keeper had to appear and answer as to what we knew touching the cause of Maggy's death. The poor mother fainted during the ordeal. The verdict was, "DEATH FROM EXPOSURE."

It all went into the newspapers, with a variety of detail and comment. In one case it was more than intimated that the father had driven his child mad by cruel treatment, and in another, things worse were hinted at. It was hard that one so pure should have the taint of a foul suspicion cast on her name. But it is accepted almost by common consent that where anything evil is said of those who deal in liquor it must be true. Maggy, saint, angel, as we knew her to be, was the daughter of a man who kept a drinking-saloon, and so anything wrong or vile that might be spoken of her would be accepted, without question, as true.

Happy change for her! Death was her kindest friend. No evil thought or word could pain or harm her spirit. But for many hearts the world was darker and sadder for her absence.

After the funeral Lloyd came back to the saloon. He fortified himself for meeting his customers by drinking freely. I had been fearful that a trouble so hard to bear would throw him off of his balance, and I was sorry to see the evidence so soon. He was very quiet, never speaking to any one unless addressed, and seeming to be in a kind of dream all the while, but drinking almost double his usual quantity.

After a few weeks his reserve began to wear off,

but he still kept on drinking freely. Sometimes, by evening, the effects of what he took became so marked as to be noticed by almost every one. His affliction did not soften him, but rather left him harder and more irritable. If anything went wrong, he grew angry, and at times almost abusive.

How matters were going on at home after Maggy's death I did not know. I asked Lloyd a few times about his wife, but the question worried him, I could see, and as he did not give satisfactory replies, I ceased to make any reference to his family whatever.

One night—it was three months after Maggy Lloyd's death—on going to the hotel where I boarded, I found a young man of rather rough appearance waiting to see me. His face was coarse and sensual and bad in almost every line. He had been drinking.

"There's a young chap at the station-house that says please won't you come down and see him."

He said this in a half-rude, half-hang-dog kind of a way, not looking me in the eyes.

"Who is he?" I asked.

"His name's Tom Lloyd," he replied.

"Tom Lloyd! What's he doing in a station-house?" I said, in surprise. I had not seen him since the day of his sister's funeral.

"Got nabbed in a cock-pit. Most on 'em got off, but he was slow, and so they gobbled him. It's ten dollars fine, and if he don't pay it, he'll be sent down below. So he says please won't you come and see him."

"Where is he?" I inquired.

"In the —— street station-house."

This was nearly two miles away, in the upper part of the city, and it was now nearly twelve o'clock at night.

"Why didn't he send for his father?" I asked. "It's no affair of mine."

"Guess he's afraid. Mightn't be healthy," answered the fellow, with a chuckle.

"Where was the cock-pit?" I inquired.

"Back of Teddy Ryan's."

"Where is Teddy Ryan's?"

"Oh, you tip-tops don't know Teddy! Well, Teddy's one on 'em! You go out of Craig street, down through Little Mary street, to the right. Phil Moore's saloon is at the corner; you'll know by that just where to turn off. He's got a bully big gas-light, with red stars on blue glass. Half way down Little Mary street you'll see a door with a round window in it. That's Teddy Ryan's. His name's on the door. It doesn't look like much of a place, but I tell you lots of fellows go there o' nights, specially when they're going to have fightin' in the pit."

"Boys as well as men?" I suggested.

"You may bet on that," he answered, laughing. "Half on 'em's boys. The pit's away back. You go out through a door behind the bar, and down cellar, then along a narrow passage and up into the yard. You don't see anything nor anybody. The pit isn't there. But if you know the ropes, you'll just tip your toe against a little gate in the fence, and open it comes. Then you go along between two fences until you come to another gate. Push it, and you'll find the pit. It's been there for a year, and the police never came down on it afore to-night."

"How many were nabbed?" I asked.

"'Bout twenty, and a good many more got off."

"Are they all in the station-house?"

"No, siree! Most on 'em put up their double V's or got somebody else to do it for them."

"The fine's ten dollars for being caught in a cock-pit?"

"Yes, sir, that's the damage. But I guess you'd better look after this chap, if you're going to."

I had by this time made up my mind as to what I would do about Tom. I could not get over my old kind feelings for the boy, and pitied him. His father was not to be trusted in a case like this. His dealing would be so hard and harsh as to push the poor lad farther away from him and out into more perilous depths.

"Very well," I said. "I'll look after him. Thank you for taking the trouble to come here on his account."

"Better go to-night and have it all settled," he urged. "He may be sent below before you get round in the morning. Then it will all come out in the papers, and that wouldn't be healthy for Tom, you know. He's a nice chap, and I don't want to see him get into too bad a mess."

I promised to go that night. After Tom's messenger went away, I got a carriage and drove up to the —— street station-house, and had Tom released, after paying his fine of ten dollars.

It so happened that I knew the lieutenant of police who was on duty at the station-house. When I asked for Thomas Lloyd, he said, a little curiously,

" Not our friend Lloyd's son?"

"Yes," I replied.

He shrugged his shoulders in a meaning way, remarking, " He ought to keep his boy at home."

" Easier said than done, I'm afraid," I returned.

" Better shoot him at once than let him go to school in a cock-pit," said the lieutenant, emphatically.

I took the boy home with me, and gave him a bed for the night. He was a good deal cut down and frightened by the arrest, and promised that he'd never get into another such a scrape.

But it wasn't two months before a second haul was made on Teddy Ryan's cock-pit, and Tom was caught again. I didn't stand between him and his father this time, not thinking it best to do so. He sent after me, as before, but I refused to go.

On the morning afterward, in looking over the report of police cases, I saw an account of the haul at

Teddy Ryan's, which was spoken of as one of the worst dens in the city. Among the names of those who had been arrested was that of Thomas Lloyd. It was mentioned that he with several others had been committed to prison until their fine was paid. As I stood with the paper in my hands, undecided whether to speak to Lloyd about it or let him discover it for himself, a man sitting at a table reading called out,

"Hallo, Tom Lloyd! Is this your boy they've sent down below?"

Lloyd started as if he'd been shot.

The man then read aloud an account of the arrests made at Teddy Ryan's, and the names of those who had been sent to prison. As he finished reading he looked up and saw Lloyd's face.

"Why, bless me, Tom!" he exclaimed. "Didn't for a moment suppose it was your son. Was only jesting."

Lloyd did not answer, but I saw the surprise and trouble in his face give way slowly to an angry and cruel expression. He stood in silent debate with himself, his countenance growing harder and harder.

"If it is my boy," he said, at length, with an oath that made me start, "he's got to lie in the bed he's made. He'll be safer down there than in a cockpit."

While he was speaking a man came in and handed me a note. It was from the poor boy. I read it, and then gave it to his father. He read it, struggled with himself for a little while, and then said to the messenger, with a coolness I did not expect,

"All right, sir. Tell him it's all right."

The man said,

"But, sir, you're not going to let the boy stay down there?"

"All right, sir. Didn't I say all right, sir?" answered Lloyd, his voice rising in its pitch and quivering a little with the excitement he was evidently trying to keep down.

"But what shall I say to the boy?" the man asked, with a kindness of feeling in marked contrast with the hardness and anger of the father.

"Haven't I told you what to say?" almost shouted Lloyd, now half insane from passion. "It's all right. Tell him it's all right. Yes, sir, it's all right."

"Hallo! What's up now?" broke from the lips of Jacobs the pressman, who came in at this moment and heard Lloyd's passionate ejaculations. The old man had been going down very fast during the last few months. Drink had finally mastered him. He could no longer hold appetite in any sort of check. Its cravings had become so strong and incessant that resistance was over.

Poor old man! In his time he had been the best pressman in the city, commanding the largest wages. Now he was out of a place, the foreman of the office in Harvey street having been compelled to discharge him on account of his unfitness for work. No job was safe in his hands, nor could he be depended upon as to time. And so, with pity in his heart for the broken-down old man, the foreman had to send him away. This had occurred over a month before the time about which I am now writing, and since his discharge Jacobs had been loafing around, spending his time in taverns, and giving us the largest part of his society—something we would have gladly dispensed with.

He had no means of living, being unable to get a situation in any office in the city. Money for drink he obtained by borrowing small sums from one and another of the scores of printers he knew, and who could not say "No" to him, sometimes taking scarcely any food all day beyond the lunch he could get for nothing if he paid for a drink. He stayed about our place a great deal because he knew all the printers and most of the bookbinders in the Harvey-street establishment, and was sure to be asked to drink half a dozen times a day. He was getting to be a great nuisance, not only on account of his shabby and dirty appearance, in which respect things grew worse all the while, but especially because of his talkativeness. There was no repressing him. His oar went in on all occasions, and he was sure to pull against the rest or splash about in a way to worry and annoy us. Lloyd was very rough on him at times, but Jacobs always paid him back in words that hurt because of their truth. He was still a sort of pet or favorite with most of the men who came in to drink because of his free and saucy speech, and some of them took a half-malicious pleasure in setting him off on the evils of intemperance.

"Hallo! What's up now?" broke from his lips, as just said, on coming into the bar-room while Lloyd was going on in the excited way I have described.

"They've got his young hopeful down below," some one said to him, in a low voice that Lloyd could not hear.

"Ho, ho!" he ejaculated. "The crops a-growing. The chickens are coming home to roost. Bad business! Bad business!" and he came up noisily to where Lloyd and I were standing. Tom looked at him with an expression of fierce impatience in his eyes.

"What's the matter? What's the boy been doing?" questioned the old man, with an unseemly intrusiveness that was very irritating.

Lloyd cursed him with a hand half raised to strike him down.

"Swearing won't help it any," said Jacobs, with a coolness that strongly contrasted with Lloyd's excited manner. "I only asked what the boy had been doing. Is there any harm in that?"

"It's none of your business, and you'd better take yourself off," answered Lloyd, roughly.

Jacobs turned away at this rebuff, and walked to the other side of the room, muttering aloud as he went:

"It's all coming out as I told 'em. There's no good in rum-selling, and somebody's always getting hurt. Poor Tom! Sorry for him. Wonder what it's all about?"

"Nabbed in a cock-pit and sent down below," was said to him in an undertone.

"Oh ho! That's it! Poor boy! Knew he'd come to grief sooner or later. Hadn't any chance! In a cock-pit! Oh dear! Sorry! sorry!"

Jacobs did not lower his voice, and all this was heard by every one in the bar-room. Lloyd's face grew almost livid with anger and shame.

"Nabbed in a cock-pit! Well, well! Doesn't that beat all? Tom Lloyd's son nabbed in a cock-pit!" droned on the old man, talking partly to himself. "I told him long ago he'd better look after his boy. I saw where he was going. But nobody minds what I say. Well, well! The chickens are coming home to roost. They always do."

Lloyd was in no condition to bear such probing as this. It maddened him. I cannot record here the shocking oaths that broke from him as he sprang suddenly across the room and struck Jacobs a heavy blow. The weak old man fell from his chair stunned and half insensible.

"You'll pay for that!" said a journeyman printer, who sprang forward and caught Lloyd as he was lifting his foot in his blind fury to kick the fallen man. Another, less able to control himself, struck him squarely in the face, cutting his cheek to the bone. I sprang forward to the side of Lloyd, but saw in an instant that all were against him, and that we would have no chance in a fight. There was a pause long enough to let the blood cool down from its fever heat, but a bitter, incensed, angry feeling remained.

Jacobs was lifted from the floor and placed on a chair. He was evidently hurt, but it was impossible to tell how badly.

Language was hardly strong enough to express the indignation felt by many of those who were present. Lloyd's act was denounced as cruel and cowardly, and I think there was not a man who looked in his cut and bleeding face who did not say in his heart, "Good for him!" or, "Served him right!" He got out of the way as soon as he could, as well to have his hurt attended to as to escape from the little crowd of men, who were not over choice of their language.

Jacobs soon came to himself, and to the many questions asked as to how he felt said he was all right, except a queer singing in his head, that hurt when he moved it. He was not inclined to talk, but sat in a dull kind of way, as if drowsy.

"He'd better be taken home," said one. "I'm afraid he's hurt more than we think."

"Where do you live, Jacobs?" asked another.

"Live?" inquired Jacobs, rousing himself.

"Yes; where do you live?"

"Don't live anywhere now," he replied, with a

strange, sad humor in his voice. "Pitched me out last night."

"Where did you sleep?"

"Oh, I crept into the press-room round here, and they let me cuddle down in a corner. The boards weren't very soft."

One and another now began to go out, and it was not long before I was almost alone with the old man, who still sat very quiet and inclined to sleep. I felt uneasy about him. Lloyd was up stairs washing the blood from his face and cooling off. He had acted like a fool and a madman. But day by day for a long time he had been losing control of himself, and was constantly doing and saying things that kept me nervously anxious all the while.

CHAPTER XX.

JACOBS had fallen asleep, and Lloyd was still up stairs. I stood leaning on the bar-railing, with a feeling of worry at my heart, when a man whom I knew to be a constable came in and inquired for Lloyd.

"What do you want with him?" I asked.

"He must come round to the alderman's."

"For what?"

"Arrested for assault and battery, and maybe worse. Two men came and swore to the case, and the alderman's given me the summons."

"Where did it all happen?" I asked, feigning ignorance.

"'Tisn't any use shamming," the constable answered, with a slight laugh. "It all happened here, as you know. Tom Lloyd lost his head—he's apt to do that of late—and pitched into a customer rather severely—a poor old toper who had no chance with him. They swore that the man was badly hurt, and that the injuries might prove fatal. They're waiting round at the office, and say they're going to see the thing through. Where's Lloyd?"

"About the place somewhere. I suppose the alderman will take me? How much is the bail?"

"Oh, not more than a thousand dollars."

"Very well. Wait a moment, and I'll go after Lloyd."

I found him all cut down, sitting with his elbows on his knees and his head between his hands. As he looked up on my coming into the room where he sat, I saw an ugly scar two inches long on his right cheek, out of which blood still oozed.

"A pretty mess you've made of it!" I could not help saying, for I was angry with him for bringing all this trouble about.

His reply was an impatient oath, to which I returned,

"You've got yourself into an elegant fix! There's a constable after you."

"What?" and he started up.

"You'll have to go round to an alderman's and give bail for your appearance in court," said I.

"For what?"

"For assault and battery on old Jacobs. The constable's waiting for you."

An expression of blank amazement came into his face:

"It's impossible; I can't go. See what a figure I cut!" and he looked into a glass at the great red and purple scar on his cheek.

"Can't be helped," I returned. "So come along, and get the thing done as quickly as possible. I'll go round with you and stand bail. The constable is waiting."

There was no escape. He had to go to the alderman's and give the required bail. As we came back, and drew near "The Retreat," I noticed a quiet-looking man with a grave, pleasant face standing near the door. He was about going in as we came up, but held back for a moment as he saw us turn to enter, letting us pass in, and then following. He stood for a little while near the door, his bright gray eyes ranging about as if in search of some one.

Jacobs was still sitting in the chair where we had placed him, but now awake, silent and serious. The man on seeing him stepped quickly across the room, and laying a hand firmly on the old pressman's shoulder, said in a kind but earnest voice, "It's not too late yet, Jacobs."

And as he spoke he took a card from his pocket and held it in his fingers.

"'Tisn't any use, Charley;" and the old man shook his head. There was a mournful undertone in his voice that I had never before heard. "I'm past cure," he added, his head dropping forward in a helpless kind of way. "I'm in the street now, Charley. Pitched me out last night, bag and baggage; though as to the baggage," he added, a slight touch of the old humor in his voice, "that didn't count for much."

"Yes; I heard about it a little while ago," answered the man, "and I said, 'Now's his last chance. He's got to the end of the lane and must turn back or die.' I guess you'll turn back, my friend.

There's good stuff in you yet. The best pressman in the city is wanted. They want him in Harvey street, and down in Sixth street, and over in Sansom street. There are half a dozen places waiting for him. And then we want him. He's been long enough a standing monument of the evil of intemperance, and now we want him as a monument of what the 'TEMPERANCE BLESSING' can do. I want you to help me, friend Jacobs. And God wants you. He has sent me to offer you another chance. Here! sign this pledge, and all will be well."

"'Tisn't any use, Charley," he answered, but in a voice that betrayed a rising hope. "I'm too low down. Couldn't stand up square to anything. God help me!"

And the old man broke down.

"That's just it," was returned in a voice of tender encouragement. "God will help you, and no other can. I heard about you a little while ago, and God put it into my heart to come right round here. I was going somewhere else, and tried to think I must go, but something said to me, 'No, no! Old Andy Jacobs is on his last legs, and if he isn't saved now, it's all over with him!' So, you see, I'm here as one sent to you from God. Don't be afraid to trust him. Sign this pledge, and that's stopping, you know—stopping stock still and planting your feet down. I'll keep by you, and if you feel weak, you shall lean on me. Then you'll turn about and go the other way, and I'll stand by and help you along until you can walk by yourself. I know all about it. I know what's to be done."

"If you think it any use, Charley—" Jacobs looked up into the face of the man wistfully.

"Of use! I've seen many of them come up out of deeper pits than the one into which you have fallen, Andy Jacobs, and their feet are now on solid rock! Here!" and he laid the card down upon a table and handed Jacobs a pencil; "write your name just there."

"What does it say?" asked the old man.

"I'll read it;" and the pledge was read aloud in our bar-room. Here is a copy of a similar pledge now before me:

TEMPERANCE BLESSING PLEDGE.

I, ...
do solemnly promise to abstain from the use or sale of all Spirituous or Malt Liquors, Wine or Cider, and that I will not provide them as an article of entertainment; neither will I offer them to my associates, or provide them for persons in my employ. I also pledge myself that I will, under all suitable circumstances, discountenance their use as a beverage,

GOD BEING MY HELPER.

Dated this.................day of 187

Jacobs took the pencil and with a shaking hand wrote his name on the card. A breathless silence fell on the room. Lloyd and I and all that were present were too deeply impressed by the scene to utter a light or disapproving word. I do not know that I ever felt more solemn in my life. I was glad for the degraded old man that there was hope of his being held back even for a little while, but I had no faith in any permanent reformation.

"The best day's work you have done for a long time," said the man, cheerfully. "And now let me give you a certificate, and if you are ever tempted to take a glass, or a friend—no, an enemy—asks you to drink, look at it and say 'No!'"

He then filled up the blank of another card and handed it to Jacobs. I give a copy of that also:

"PERSEVERANCE, FORTITUDE AND FIDELITY."

This is to Certify,

That MR. ANDREW JACOBS

Signed the **PLEDGE** *of the Temperance Blessing*

On June 10, 18 .

Attest: CHARLES HERITAGE.

Then he took the old man, and said, "Come."

"I haven't any place to go to, Charley," replied Jacobs, rising slowly and heavily, and putting one hand to his head as if it pained him.

I noticed this movement of his hand, and glanced at Lloyd, who must have noticed it also, for a look of uneasiness passed across his face. There was no knowing what might come of the blow Jacobs had received.

"I'll find you a place," was answered in an assuring voice. "It's all right now. So come along."

And they went out together.

"And that's brother Heritage! God bless him!" fell from the lips of a man who stood leaning on the bar-railing.

"The man of the 'Temperance Blessing?'" remarked another.

"Yes; the man who in less than four years has got over three thousand persons to sign his 'Temperance Blessing' pledge."

"He won't make much out of old Jacobs," growled Lloyd. "No such good luck for us."

"He's managed a great deal worse cases than that," said the other.

"Don't believe it," growled back Lloyd.

"I happen to know," was answered. "Some of you remember Phil Oldham? Well, he got so low at last that he was sent to the almshouse. He would have died of cold and starvation in the street if the guardians of the poor hadn't taken care of him. A year ago last spring he came out of his winter quarters over the Schuylkill and tried to keep sober, but it wasn't a week before he was down in the gutter again. He couldn't stand alone, and there was no one to help and encourage him in the right way, so he fell, in spite of his good resolutions."

A number of men had come in to drink during the past fifteen or twenty minutes, and they were all more or less interested in what had occurred and in the conversation which was growing out of it. Most of them knew Jacobs very well. They now gathered in a close group about the man who was speaking. Among them were two or three hard drinkers—men who had become slaves to appetite, who were almost helpless in the morning until a dram steadied their nerves. Wilson the bookbinder was one of these. He was going to ruin fast.

The man went on:

"I had a long talk with Phil Oldham yesterday—or, I should say, rather, Philip Oldham, for that's the way it reads on the sign over his door. I never saw brother Heritage, as some of them call him, until just now, and I said 'God bless him!' for Philip Oldham's sake. I got the whole story, and it almost made me cry sometimes. There's nothing just like it in any book I ever read."

"What story?" asked one.

"Phil Oldham's story," he replied.

"Has he reformed?"

"I should think so. Has a nice little store full of goods," was answered.

"Tell us about him, won't you? Reformed! That is news! Why, I remember Phil as the hardest case going."

"It isn't a short story," said the man, "but it didn't seem long to me in the telling."

"Let's have it!" "Fire away!" came from one and another.

"Gentlemen," called Lloyd, who didn't like the

course things were taking, and who wanted to get in some interruption, and so prevent, if possible, further talk in that direction.

The company turned to him.

"Take a drink all round, gentlemen, and then have the story."

A few came toward the bar, but the man who had been speaking said, in a clear, decided voice,

"You can't have the drinks and the story too. It's only a flank movement to get me out of the way. I've seen it done a hundred times. So if you're going to drink all round, I'm off."

"Stop, stop!" cried two or three. "Let's have the story."

"All right; we'll have that first. The drinks will keep," was added, and the company closed about the man again.

"Not if I know myself," said Lloyd, angrily, as he set back the decanters he had placed on the bar. "Now or never!"

CHAPTER XXI.

THE tide was setting against us, and I yielded passively, as I had learned to do on such occasions. Lloyd fretted and fumed and swore fruitlessly. Let me recall as accurately as possible the true story told in our bar-room that morning. I grew interested in it in spite of myself, and did not wonder that many were touched or deeply moved by the narrative. The man resumed:

I'm going to tell you Phil Oldham's story just as he told it to me. You may think it's Phil himself talking. This is what he said:

"I was dead beat at last—clear down. My poor wife, who stuck to me while there was any hope, had left me and gone to her friends. My children were scattered about here and there. I was a helpless vagabond, with only one distinct consciousness, and that an ever-present, irrepressible desire for liquor. To get that I was ready to stoop to anything—to beg, to sponge on others, even to steal had the opportunity come in my way, but not to work, for I had lost that control of head and hand which work requires.

"My days, as I look back to them now, were passed as in a suffering, uneasy, troubled dream, with only one thing palpable and clear—an intense, unsatisfied craving for strong drink. I had no home. I could not pay for lodgings, and there was no one who cared enough for me to see that I had a place in which to lay my miserable body. If I fell asleep in a saloon, I was rudely shaken up and turned out of doors, often with some cruel trick played off upon me. No one cared for me—no one seemed even to pity me. All men turned away from me with disgust. And yet, somehow, I managed to get, by soliciting one and another, by false pretences or downright lying, a few pennies every day with which to buy liquor. Food I got by begging when I felt hungry, but hunger didn't trouble me so much, a little satisfied that—it was drink, drink, drink, that I craved with an appetite nothing could appease. I slept at night as I could, creeping in here and there, often finding myself in the station-house when morning broke.

"Last winter a year I was picked up in the street half dead with cold and sent to the almshouse, where I stayed until spring. When I came out, I tried feebly to get on my feet again, but I had no employment, no home, no one to care for me. I was walking along the street wondering what was to become of me, and in my poor way trying to hold on to good resolution, when I met an old acquaintance.

"'Hallo, Phil! Is this you?' he said, with rough familiarity, grasping my hand. 'I thought you were dead long ago;' and he eyed me all over. 'Rather seedy-looking,' he added.

"'Yes,' I replied. 'It's rough with me. When a poor devil gets going down hill, there isn't much chance for him.'

"'Come, let's have a drink,' he said; 'I know you're dry.'

"There was a tavern just opposite. He moved in that direction as he spoke, and I went with him as passively as a boat towed by a steamer when the engine moves. I drank, and it was all over with me again. That night I slept in the entry of a printing-office on Seventh street, hidden under the stairway. In the morning I was stiff, aching with rheumatism, thirsty and wretched. I crawled out, and going into the press-room, begged for something with which to get my breakfast. Two of the men gave me ten cents each. I got only liquor, reserving part of my money for lunch-time, when I could get some soup or hash as well as beer. I loafed about all day aimless and miserable. I felt myself going down helplessly and hopelessly, and the people who knew me seemed more inclined to push me down lower than to help me up higher. I got from one and another during the day over sixty cents, and I spent all but ten cents in drink; that I reserved for a morning dram, when I knew my craving would be the worst. I slept in the entry and under the stairway where I had found shelter on the night before.

"On the third day after I came from the almshouse I was not so successful in raising money. Everybody seemed gruff, out of humor and quick to deny me. I spent my ten cents early in the morning to get steadied up; after that I could get nothing. I went here and there, asking this one and that for the loan or gift of a trifle, but up to one o'clock had not been able to quench the craving thirst that grew stronger and stronger every moment. At last, in a desperate way, I went into a tavern down town, and going up to the bar, called for a glass of whisky. The man eyed me suspiciously as he set down a decanter. I took it and filled a glass half full, then adding a slight dash of water, poured down the fiery fluid. Ugh! It was a dose, tasting more like a mixture of benzine and soap-suds than anything I can describe. It burnt all the way down.

"What was I to do next? I had not a cent with which to bless myself. But I must get off somehow. I thrust my hand first into one pocket and then into another, with as much make-believe expectation of finding money there as I could put on, the tavern-keeper eyeing me all the while in an evil way that caused me to feel afraid of him.

"'It's here somewhere,' I said, going from one pocket to another in a nervous way.

"'You'd better find it pretty quick,' the man said, roughly, and with a threat in his voice, at the same time coming round from the bar. I instinctively backed away toward the door; we were alone, and I saw no pity in his face. I still kept going through my pockets, protesting all the while that there must be money in them somewhere. He cursed me as a cheat and a swindler. I turned in fear and ran for the door, getting it open before he could reach me. As I was passing through he kicked me with a force that threw me half across the pavement and over on my face.

"I was not much hurt, but a good deal frightened. A crowd came about me as I gathered myself up, but no one took my part or expressed any sympathy. Vicious boys and girls, white and black, began pulling me one way and another, calling me names and throwing dirt and garbage upon me, while the tavern-keeper stood in the door laughing and encouraging them. Hearing the noise, a policeman came up, but, instead of dispersing the crowd and protecting me, ordered me to 'make tracks,' or he'd put me in the lock-up. I got off as best I could, some of the crowd following and hooting.

"My poor knees trembled as I hurried up Sixth street. I felt weak and ready to fall. On reaching the square, I went in and sat down. Oh, I cannot tell you how heartsick I was. I knew into what depths of suffering and degradation I had gone down before the almshouse opened its doors for me, and thither my steps were again tending, and there was none to hold me back—none to save me.

"As I sat in this wretched frame of mind, wishing I were dead, a man whom I had known in better days came loitering through the square. He saw and knew me. Stopping, he said,

"'Why, Phil Oldham!' and he reached out his

hand. I took it, glad to be recognized and spoken to kindly. 'How are you, old friend?' he asked.

"'Not much to brag of,' I replied. 'Used to be some account, but when the tide turns against a man, his friends turn too. It's a hard world to live in.'

"'Guess you're right there,' he answered, falling in with my mood. 'What are you doing now?' he inquired.

"'Nothing,' I replied. 'Got run down—been sick—half dead with rheumatism. Couldn't come up to time, and so got out of work. It's easy going down hill when you once get started, and most men stand ready to give you a push.'

"'That's so,' was returned. 'I know all about it. You're all cleaned out, I suppose?'

"'Not a penny to bless myself with.'

"'And dry as a fish, no doubt?' he said, smiling.

"'Haven't had a good square drink to-day,' I replied. 'Look!' and I held out my hand that he might see it tremble.

"'Come, then;' and he moved on, I following. We had no occasion to search for a tavern: drinking-saloons were all about us. We could not turn in any direction without seeing one or more.

"After drinking with me twice, my old acquaintance gave me a dollar and said good-bye.

"I felt rich and in high spirits for a little while. Two strong glasses of ale set me on my feet, toned me up, satisfied the craving which since morning had almost driven me beside myself.

"I was never able to tell what became of that dollar. I found myself, near daylight on the next morning, lying on an ash-heap in an alley into which I must have staggered and fallen on the night before. I had a faint recollection of having had a fuss with a bar-keeper about change. I have no doubt now that I never got back any change for that dollar after offering it in pay for a drink, or, if any change at all, only a small part of what I should have received.

"And here let me say that there is a great deal of sharp practice in this matter of change. I have gone into a saloon with five or ten dollars in my pocket, and after staying half an hour or an hour come out with only a dollar or two left. Of course I drank enough to get my head confused, and then I was game for any scamp of a bar-keeper who wished to swindle me. Let me tell you how this is sometimes done. Take a Saturday night, for instance, after men have been paid off. Business in certain taverns is brisker then than usual. Customers are flush and feel generous, drinking and treating and having a good time all round. The bar-keepers are busy, drawing beer and ale, mixing punches and toddies, taking money and giving change. A man, after drinking with a friend or two, hands over, it may be, a two- or a five-dollar bill. The bar-keeper, who knows his customer, flings the bill into a drawer, hurriedly picks up the change and pushes it over the bar, then goes quickly as far off as he can get to attend to somebody else. On counting over the change it is found to be half a dollar short. The man waits until he can come at the bar-keeper again, who is too busy to look at or attend to him. When the matter is brought to his attention, he bluffs the customer off, or, if he be a cool-headed fellow, courteously tells him it is impossible, he must have dropped the change on the floor.

"Or a man half drunk hands over a bill. The bar-keeper says, 'In a moment,' and goes to another customer without giving the change. A friend comes up, and the man turns away to talk with him and forgets about his change. If, after a while, he thinks of it and returns, the bar-keeper tells him rudely or blandly, as seems best, that he gave it to him long ago. Sometimes there's a flare up, but in most cases the matter ends there.

"Well, as I was saying, I was never able to tell what became of that dollar, but some bar-keeper knew, without doubt. For about a month longer I went on in this way, until I was lower down than ever, and began to have symptoms of that utter nervous prostration that ends in mania. I could not get liquor enough to keep me up. Beer and ale had not sufficient strength, and I drank whisky at the cheapest places, so as to get the most for the little money I could raise.

"One evening about seven o'clock, after a day of terrible suffering from unappeased thirst, an old acquaintance whom I met in the street gave me ten cents. He refused at first, saying that he would not give me money for drink. But I told him I had eaten nothing since morning and was dying for food. Doubt mingled with pity in his eyes as he gave me the money.

"I must husband this. I must make it go as far as possible. So I went to one of the cheap whisky-mills and called for a three-cent glass. It was horrible stuff, fiery and strong. I poured it down, unmixed with water, and went out quickly, for I was sure it would not stay, nor did it. My diseased, over-taxed, sensitive stomach threw the nauseous potion out. I went back and drank another glass, and stood for a moment to note my feeling. The poor stomach rebelled again. I went out and did as before. My third trial was successful. The liquor held its own against the baffled organ.

"I knew that it was pretty much over with me now. There was not strength enough in that single glass to keep me up. My mind was pretty clear. I saw the awful gulf that opened at my feet, and knew that unless God helped me I must go down. Unless God helped me! Yes, my poor despairing heart had a deep sense at that time of the only hope, of the only arm, that could save. Never before had I felt it as I then did.

"I wandered aimlessly up Sixth street until I came to Chestnut, where I stood for a little while, and then turned down. As I came opposite the State-house I saw in one of the windows a transparent sign bearing the words,

> TEMPERANCE BLESSING.
> FREE TO ALL.

"'The Temperance Blessing!' I said to myself as I stood still, looking at the letters glowing in a soft warm light; 'what is that?' Men and women were entering the State-house door, and through the window above the transparency I could see the heads of many people. 'The Temperance Blessing,' I repeated to myself over and over, and then there came upon me an impulse to go in. So I followed. The court-room at the right was full of people, the number so large that many had to stand. I was a loathsome object, and men moved away from me, but I crowded in and got a seat back near the wall.

"On the railed platform or bench on the western side of the room were about a dozen little girls. At the desk in front stood a man past the middle age, with iron-gray hair and a mild, kind face. He held some slips of paper in his hand, and was saying that the evening's exercises would be opened by singing 'the Temperance Blessing hymn.' He then distributed the slips of paper containing this hymn through the audience. When everything was ready, a lady started the tune, and all sang with as much freedom and earnestness as if they had been in church. I give you the first verse of the hymn:

'Temperance! source of every blessing,
Safeguard of the old and young,

>   Let those now thy joy possessing
>   Praise thy virtues trumpet-tongued.
>   From a dire career of madness
>   We were plucked like brands from fire;
>   Joy now dwells where once was sadness:
>   We have conquered fierce desire.'

"It was years since I had been to church. How the singing, in a tune once familiar almost as my mother's voice, took me away back! How it melted me down! How it overcame me! Old tender, sacred and religious impressions returned. I was strangely moved while the singing went on. At its close the chairman of the meeting, whom I have mentioned, said, to my surprise, 'Let us pray.' I had not looked for that. Some stood up; most of those present merely bowed their heads where they sat, but I got down upon my knees: I couldn't help it; and when the chairman prayed for a blessing on the assembly, and for especial help from God for any poor drunkard that might be there, I groaned in spirit, 'God help me!' Somehow, after that prayer, I felt as if I were going to be helped, as if God had led me there, and surely it was so!

"After the prayer was over the chairman said, 'Now we will have a temperance song from one of our little friends.' At this one of the girls I have mentioned stood up and sang something that sounded very sweet. Her innocent face took my heart back to the children that once made music in my home. I felt strange and tender.

"Then the chairman talked for a while about the

'Blessing,' as the meeting held there every Tuesday evening was called, and told of many who had signed the pledge of the 'Blessing,' and were now sober and happy. He read the number of the last signature on the pledge-book: it was two thousand five hundred and twenty-seven! I felt oppressed and in a maze, but there was just enough of excitement in the scene to keep me up. He said that the pledge-book was now open, and would lie open all the evening, that if any wished to sign, to make in that hall where national independence was first declared a declaration of personal independence, the opportunity was here given. 'Come now, or at any time during the evening,' he urged. 'The moment you feel an impulse to do so, come forward. The sight will gladden our hearts. Come over on our side and help us, and we will help you.'

"After this one of the girls recited in a clear, well-trained voice, and with admirable effect, a poem bearing on temperance. At its close two or three men went forward and signed the pledge. I was strongly impelled to go, but did not rise from my seat. 'What good would it do?' I said to myself. 'There's no one to help me; no one to take me by the hand; no one to hold me up. I have no home; where can I go? What can I do?' A feeling of dumb despair came over me, and I felt helpless and hopeless. For some time after that I hardly heard what was going on. But after a while I saw that a man was on the floor speaking. I listened, and he told how he had once been away down almost as low as I was, how he had seen the 'Temperance Blessing' sign one night, just as I had seen it, and how he had come in just as I had come, and how he had signed the pledge, and how 'brother Heritage,' pointing to the chairman as he spoke, had taken him by the hand, and stood by him until he was able to stand alone. How eagerly I listened to every word!

"When he had done speaking, the chairman called one of the little girls by name, and said, ' Now give us that song you learned last week.'

"The child stood up. She was not over ten years of age. I felt my heart give a strong beat as I looked into her dear young face, she was so like one of my own children. I wiped my dim eyes and strained them toward her. Oh what a tide of old feelings came rushing back upon me! But I knew it was not my Lucy. She had gone to a better world long ago.

"Out on the hushed air of the room stole the sweet voice, tender, sad and pleading, in the words, 'Father, come home!'

"It seemed like the voice of my own child calling to me. Home! Come home! God help me! I had no home!

"The song went on, the singer pleading with the imaginary father to come home, and I sat listening as if to the voice of my own child.

"'If there is any poor wanderer here to-night,' said the chairman as the song ceased, 'let him come home now—home to the 'Blessing.' He will find it an ark of safety and a haven of rest.'

"I made an effort to rise, but something seemed to hold me down. Almost with a cry I started to my feet and moved blindly forward, saying in my thought, 'I will go home! I will be free, God helping me!' One and another gave way as I moved. The chairman's quick eyes saw me, and he came forward to meet and led me to the table where the pledge-book lay.

"My hand shook as I lifted the pen; my sight was so blurred that I could hardly see the page before me. But I set the pen down resolutely, and wrote as best I could my name. A card certifying that I had signed the pledge of the 'Temperance Blessing' was then put into my hand.

"I can't recall much of what was said and done after that. There was speaking and singing and talking by the chairman, while every now and then some one came up and signed the pledge, but it all passed as if I were dreaming. The singing of the Doxology, 'Praise God from whom all blessings flow,' by the whole assemblage at the close of the meeting, roused me to a clearer and a better state of mind.

"The little card certificate was in my hand. I was holding on to it tightly, very much with the feeling, I think, of a man overboard with the end of a slender rope in his hand that he feels may snap at any moment, while the angry waves roar about him. In this little card I felt lay, somehow, my last and only hope.

"I sat still as the people went slowly out. When I left that room, where was I to go? What was to become of me? I had signed a pledge not to drink again. Could I, without food, without a physician, without a place in which to lay my head, hope for anything? I felt the chill of utter despair come creeping over me, and then I cried, turning as best I could my poor heart to the Saviour who died for me—the Saviour I had, when a little boy at my mother's knee, so loved to read about—'Lord, save me, or I perish!' There never went up a cry to God from a lower depth of despairing helplessness than the one my heart sent up that night. Even as I prayed I felt a hand laid on my shoulder, and there was something in the touch that gave me hope.

"'Brother Oldham.' It was the chairman's voice. How tender and interested it was! 'Brother Oldham!' How did he know my name? I did not rise, but sat trembling, for my poor unstimulated nerves were fast giving way.

"'Where do you live?' he asked.

"'I have no home,' I almost sobbed. I was breaking down.

"'Then I must find you one,' he answered, cheerily. 'Come!'

"I got up and followed. How differently things looked in the street as we came out! How or in what they were changed I could not tell, but somehow I had to them, or they to me, a new relation. They spoke to me in a language I had not heard for a long, long time.

"We walked for several squares, the chairman of the 'Blessing' talking all the while hopefully, and saying that I'd find plenty of friends to stand by and help me if I kept true to my pledge, and I answering over and over again,

"'God helping me, I will!' Weak, broken, almost gone, I was now desperately in earnest. I said to myself, 'I will stand or die!'

"My God-sent friend went with me to a house down in Seventh street, where I was taken in and kept for a few days. At first I was refused admission. But my friend would take no denial. He pleaded for me as if I had been a son or a brother. I heard him say, 'God has sent him to your door, a lost sheep of his fold just ready to perish; you dare not refuse to take him in. It may be the salvation of a soul precious in his sight.'

"And so he prevailed. I had a warm bath, a clean shirt and a clean bed to lie down upon, a strong cup of coffee and something to eat. My filthy garments were all taken away, and my friend said, as he left me for the night, after having brought in a physician to give me something to take the place of liquor in my worn-out nervous system, and so keep me if possible from mania, 'In the morning I will bring you some better clothing.'

"What a night that was! I was afraid to lose

myself in sleep, lest I should be seized by delirium. I got up and down, sometimes walking about the floor, sometimes kneeling and begging God to help and save me, sometimes so overcome with fear and despair as to cry like a child. None but the unhappy ones who have had similar experiences can imagine anything of what I suffered.

"Toward day I fell asleep, and when I woke, dear brother Heritage was sitting at my bedside. He took my hand and said, 'It is well.'

"'God bless you!' I sobbed, and tears made me so blind that I could not see his face. He had brought me an old suit of clothes. They were lying across a chair. He pointed to them, saying,

"'We're going to have you all right, brother—going to give you a good chance, going to help you up and make a man of you again.'

"I tried to rise, but sunk back weak and trembling. All my strength was gone. I was like a man just over some crisis in a long sickness. But oh, words cannot tell the deep thankfulness that was in my heart. I was on the shore, far inside the breakers, yet with their awful roar still sounding in my ears.

"The woman to whose house I had been taken had now become interested in my case, and she cared for me as if I had been her own son. May God reward her! as I know he will.

"Entire rest, with nourishing food, gave a new life to the forces of nature, which were wellnigh exhausted. In a few days I was strong enough to go out, and now the peril came.

"'Dear brother,' I said to the friend who had rescued me as I stood on the brink of destruction, 'what am I to do?'

"'Go to work, of course,' he answered. 'It won't do to be idle. You'd be down again before three days went over your head.'

"'Where am I to get work?' I asked. 'Nobody that knows me will have me about.'

"'What can you do?' he asked, 'and who do you know?'

"I told him what my business had been and who had known me in my better days. As I went over name after name he listened, and when I mentioned that of Mr. H——, he said,

"'All right. I know H—— very well. He'll give you a chance.'

"And so he did. I got into his store to do some odds and ends, for which he paid me five dollars a week to begin with, and said if I did well he would increase my pay or help me to get another place.

"But I wanted more than this for safety. Employment would only help me through the day, but what was I to do in the evening? I should not dare to go on the street. In every square, and at almost every corner, hung red alluring lights. I could not turn my eyes in any direction without an invitation to drink, and appetite, only repressed, not destroyed, would arouse and plead for the draught so long denied.

"My friend and brother knew all this, for he had himself walked the same dreary and perilous way, and walked it safely. He knew just what I needed and how the strength to keep on my feet must come. So he said to me on the morning of the day I went to work,

"'I will call for you this evening at your boarding-house. I want you at the "Blessing."'

"So I waited for him after supper.

"As we walked toward Independence Hall he said, 'Now, brother Oldham, as God has saved you, you must gratefully consecrate yourself to the work of saving others. That was what I did. I was just as near destruction as you, and in my weakness and despair I looked to my Father in heaven, and he helped me, and as I felt a little strength of purpose coming in answer to my prayer, I promised that if I were saved I would give my very life to save others, if that must be. And so as soon as I had strength to get out I began to work among the intemperate, and my heart got so full of this work in a little while that I had stimulus enough, and so the old craving died. Now, what I want you to do to-night is to tell in the "Blessing" the story of your deliverance. It will come home to somebody, and help somebody. And I want you, if you see a poor worn-down drunkard drag himself up and sign the pledge just as you did, to look after him as I looked after you.

It is God's cause, and his strength will go into you if you put your hand to his work. It will make you strong and brave. You will soon be able to pass the most inviting saloon in the city, and not feel the smallest desire to enter its fatal doors.'

"I went to the 'Blessing' and told as best I could my story, not without tears. The whole company was greatly moved. I saw many eyes as wet as my own. As I sat down a white-headed man rose from his seat, and coming forward, stood by the railing and faced the audience.

"'Mr. Chairman,' he said, in a clear, earnest voice, and like one used to public speaking, 'I noticed your sign a little while ago, and came in to see what you were doing. I am an old worker in this cause, but not in your city. I have seen a great many men sign the pledge and a great many break it. I have seen one movement after another gain favor with the people, and then lose its hold upon them. I have myself lost heart many times and felt like giving up. They that were against us seemed more and stronger than all who were on our side. Now, I learn that in three years over two thousand five hundred persons have signed your pledge. Are they keeping it? I have been out of heart with the pledge. I have even gone so far, sometimes, in my discouragement, as to think it utterly useless. But I stand on higher ground now. I believe in the pledge, because it is a man's act, and what a man does always gives him strength beyond what he can possibly have by mere willing and thinking. The good purpose is made strong by the good act. And so every man who has signed your pledge to-night is stronger for sobriety than he was before, and more able to resist than he was before.

"'But what I want especially to say is this: The mere act of signing a pledge does not give all the strength a man with a craving appetite requires. It takes from him a sensual enjoyment that has been indulged for years, and gives him little or nothing in its place. Good resolutions, as we all know, are weak when a repressed appetite begins to assert itself and clamors for the old indulgence.

"'Shall I tell you how to supplement the pledge?—how to give it a power against which the very gates of hell cannot prevail? Let every man who pledges himself not to drink consecrate himself at the same time to the work of saving others. If you have been low down—low as the brother who has just spoken—you will know better than any others the need and peril of those in a like condition. You will know that they must be wisely cared for, helped and encouraged, and you will be more patient and watchful and tender with them than others might be. Oh, brothers, you must work if you would be in safety.

"'Shall I tell you how, in this living and working for others, there are strength and safety? It is all very plain. A child can understand it. Two thousand years ago our dear Lord and Saviour came down to seek and to save that which was lost—came down to the lowest and the vilest—came down visibly to the eyes of men and invisibly to their souls. He withdrew from them only as to the visible and external, but remained ever after invisibly near—God with us; a present help in time of trouble; a Saviour and a deliverer, a guide and refuge and comforter for all who look to and desire him. You all believe this. Well, the work of saving men is God's work, and whoever becomes a co-worker with him gets nearer to God, and the nearer we are to him, the farther off we are from hell and all its enticements. Go over, all of you, to the side of God in the work of saving men, and you shall surely dwell in safety. Make your pledge of freedom something more than a mere effort to save yourselves; let it be a sign that you are set apart to the work of saving others.

"'It is because this is not done that the pledge so often fails. It is because men try only to save themselves, not caring, it may be, who else goes to ruin. Nearly three thousand names on the pledge-book of the "Temperance Blessing!" What an army for work and battle in our good cause! There is not one in this great army who might not, if he set himself earnestly to work, rescue some poor soul from the pit or hold back some heedless one whose feet are wellnigh slipping. Brothers, be up and doing. If you would be in safety, give yourselves to the work of saving others, and you shall stand secure, firm as the everlasting hills.'

"As this man spoke a sense of power and safety pervaded my soul. I understood him thoroughly. I saw that in going out of myself, and giving will, thought and effort to the work of saving other men from misery and degradation, I would be lifted so far away from old desires, habits and associations that they could have little or no influence over me. And then, too, I would be on God's side, working with Him for the salvation of men, and being on His side, nearer to him and so farther away from hell, I would be encompassed by the sphere of His protection, I would be safe, not through the power of the pledge I had taken, but safe because His arm was about me.

"From that hour I have been doing all that I could to lead men out of the paths of intemperance, but especially to help, sustain and encourage those who have been down into the mire, and now, with clean garments, are trying to walk in safety. I never went back a step. The old appetite often returned, but I was too much interested in my work to give it any heed, and so it was never able to take me unawares. I soon had my wife and children again around me, and to-day I do not think there is in all this great city a happier home than ours."

CHAPTER XXII.

ONE and another dropped in while this story was being told and drew to the little crowd about the speaker, instead of coming to the bar. Lloyd was almost furious. But I got him away by telling him that his face looked dreadfully, and that he had better go up stairs or home, and keep out of sight for a while.

Very few of those who heard the story called for anything to drink after it was ended. They broke up into groups as they happened to be acquainted, all talking about Phil Oldham and the "Temperance Blessing."

There was a marked falling off in business that day. Not many men came in from the bindery. Most of these were among the hardest drinkers in the establishment. But even they were not cordial toward us, as of old. There had evidently been an excitement about the assault on Jacobs, and I gathered that a strong feeling had been aroused against us. I did not imagine this would last long. I felt pretty certain that our good cheer was stronger to attract than any little excitement over a miserable old toper was to hold men away from our tavern. I put the case here as it shaped itself in my own thoughts.

I wasn't very far wrong. In a day or two we had in nearly as much custom from the printing-office and bindery as before.

About a week afterward a printer, while drinking at the bar, said,

"Old Jacobs is back again."

"Back where?" I inquired.

"In the office."

"No!"

"Fact! And what's more, he's as sober as a judge. Signed the pledge."

I laughed incredulously.

"You may laugh," he returned. "It's all so. The old man looks as if he'd come out of a spell of sickness. But I tell you he is in earnest—has roped in old Wilson already."

"How roped him in?" I asked.

"Got him to sign the pledge."

"Faugh! They'll both be as full as their skins will hold before a week goes over their heads," I replied, with some contempt and a good deal of irritation.

"Will you take a bet on that?" demanded the printer.

Before I had time to reply, another printer who stood at the bar said, looking at me,

"There's mischief brewing round in Harvey street —mischief for you, I mean."

"Indeed! Who's at the bottom of it?"

"Old Jacobs."

I thought of the blow he'd received from Lloyd, and made answer,

"I guess he'll not do much harm. Can't show any special damage. But anyhow, it's Tom Lloyd's affair, not mine."

"Oh, 'tisn't about the assault-and-battery case," was returned. "It's your affair just as much as Lloyd's."

"Out with it, then! Let's have the worst;" and I put on a mock serious air.

"He's going into a conspiracy against you—means to cripple your business."

"Indeed! Well, tell him from me to go ahead."

"Oh, it isn't any joke. Jacobs means business. He's going to get every man in the establishment to sign the pledge."

"You don't say so!" I responded in affected alarm. "Then I guess we'd as well shut up at once."

"It wouldn't be healthy for your business if he should succeed," our customer said.

"No, not exactly," I replied, dashed at the suggestion in spite of myself. I remembered at the moment what I had heard a little while before about the self-consecration of a few reformed drunkards to the work of saving men from the terrible depths of suffering into which they had fallen, and out of which they had come as brands plucked from a fire. I thought of the three thousand men who had, through the efforts of a single earnest, untiring worker in the cause of temperance, been led to sign the pledge in less than four years, and how this very man had lifted old Jacobs out of the mire and stood him on firm ground. Jacobs was strong willed, earnest and resolute. If he put his hand to work like this, it would have to move. There was no help for it. For good or for evil, a single strong-willed, restless, persevering, one-idea man often exerts a vast influence. I understood this. The old pressman I had despised and almost loathed a week ago now commanded my respect. He stood before my thought as one having power and influence, and I will confess it that then and there I feared him.

And I had cause. On the next day I missed two printers who had been in the habit of spending not less than three or four dollars a week in our saloon.

"Is Tom Hagan at work?" I asked of one who came in from the printing-office late in the afternoon.

"Yes," was replied.

"Oh! Ah! I thought maybe he was sick."

"You haven't seen him here to-day?" I saw a comical look in the man's face, as if he were enjoying something at my expense.

"No," I replied.

"Got him, too;" and the man laughed. "Old Wilson yesterday, and Tom Hagan and Bill Wines to-day. Jacobs is a whole team. No getting away from him. Pitched into me this morning, and blamed if I hadn't the hardest time to get away from him. Expect to be caught before the week's out. Fact!"

And he laughed in a serious kind of way. It was the last time he came to our bar. I heard of him on the next day as over on the other side. Jacobs had "roped him in" also.

The tide had fairly set against us in the Harvey-street establishment. Day by day we missed one familiar face after another, and in little over a week, instead of our forty or fifty customers from the bindery and printing-office, we hadn't much over a dozen. Things began to look squally. We received regular reports of what was going on, and affected to laugh over it as a good joke, but the laugh was a little too far on the wrong side of the mouth. The falling off in our receipts was beginning to be a serious matter. Something must be done. What? We were entirely at fault. Our best customers had gone over to the enemy, and still the defection went on, until we might as well have been in China for all the good Harvey street did us. A nightly band of music helped a little, but "The Retreat" was too far out of the way to gain much by a diversion of this kind. Our day custom had fallen off until it was hardly worth keeping open for.

Meantime, an association called the "Harvey-street League" had been formed, with Jacobs at its head. Its members not only pledged themselves to total abstinence, but to the work of saving others from the evils of intemperance. They had already got nearly every one of the hardest drinkers in the establishment to break off, and were standing close about them, holding them up and giving them the strength of a brotherhood.

I looked, day after day, for the return of old friends, but they came not. Our lunches stood almost untasted on the bar, except for those who dropped in from neighboring stores and manufactories.

"What's the matter?" was often asked by those who missed the lively crowd that usually filled the saloon from ten to twelve o'clock every day.

"Better shut up this place," said one of the few who came in occasionally from the printing-office. "The last man in the bindery joined the league to-day, and only six printers are holding back. Jacobs will have them before a week, sure."

"It's nothing but a mere spirt," I replied. "Can't last long. These things always die out in a little while."

"I don't know," he replied, "how it's going to be. Good, I've heard it said—and I guess it's true—is stronger than evil and must prevail in the end. And there's no getting away from the fact, friend Hiram, that liquor-drinking is a great evil, cursing our land in all its length and breadth. You understand this as well as I do, and perhaps better. You've had a chance to know. Maybe there's going to be a new order of things. There certainly is a great rising of the people all over the land. They are getting terribly in earnest, and when the people move against anything, it must go down."

I pooh-poohed, but felt uncomfortable. It might be as he said. As to the evil that was being done, he was right in saying that I knew as much about it as he did, and perhaps more.

The movement, under the lead of old Jacobs, did not prove to be a mere spirt, but took the form of a strong and effective organization, and in a little while changed its character, and became aggressive as well as protective. It was in vain that we got up new, costlier and more tempting lunches. We had "game lunches," and "snapper soup lunches," and "kidney lunches," but the Harvey-street men were on guard and watchful over each other. We could not draw them in, and it didn't pay to keep up this style of attraction. The lunches cost more than we got for the drinks.

All this had a bad effect on Lloyd. He drank still more freely and grew more and more irritable. It was as much as I could do, often, to keep him out of quarrels with men as irritable and full of liquor as himself. Our lighter business, now that we had lost the Harvey-street men, gave him an excuse for being away a great deal. I did not like the men with whom he was beginning to associate. They were a fast, reckless, unscrupulous set, without any regular business, ward politicians many of them, and some of them gamblers by profession.

I had my suspicion that Lloyd was losing money.

There was something in his silent, brooding, troubled manner when he came to the saloon in the morning that boded no good. After Maggy's death he had lost, apparently, all interest in his family, and never spoke of them. His wife, as far as I could learn, was a sad and almost broken-hearted woman. Tom was going fast to ruin, and she had no power to hold him back. The reader already knows how far along this road the boy had gone. Love of liquor, as well as love of vicious company, had both done sad work upon him. The taste formed in his father's saloon had been fed ever since, and was now an appetite against which he opposed no restraint. I had heard often of his being seen with half-tipsy boys and men, as much the worse for drink as any of them. It was because his father knew this that he refused to interfere when he was sent to prison until the fine for being caught in a cock-pit was paid. His "All right!" which seemed utterly unfeeling, was not born wholly of anger or indifference. The lesson and restraint of a few days or weeks in prison might, he felt, have a good effect, and he was too blind with excitement to act or speak in any other than the way he did.

Three weeks had gone by, and still Lloyd gave no sign of relenting toward his poor boy. I spoke to him about it two or three times, but he said he might lie there: 'twas a safer place than low groggeries and cock-pits. I would have paid the fine and got Tom out, but I didn't care to take the responsibility of going between him and his father. And I wasn't sure that a few weeks' imprisonment would do him any harm. It might do good.

One morning I was pleased to see the face of an old friend from the bindery. A great many dollars of his hard earnings had gone into our till—quite enough during the past two or three years to have paid the rent of his house. You think this a pretty strong statement? Well, count it up for yourself. Five drinks a day was his lowest average. At ten cents a drink—what he always paid at our bar—the amount would be fifty cents a day, or a hundred and eighty dollars a year.

I was pleased, as I said, to see his familiar face. He was one of the men old Jacobs had " roped in."

" Good-morning, Fred. Glad to see you," fell in a hearty greeting from my tongue. " Thought you were dead and buried."

" Not yet, thank God!" he answered, with a gravity of tone and manner that dashed me considerably. " Where's Lloyd?"

" About somewhere," I replied. " Do you wish to see him particularly?"

" Yes." His eyes looked into mine coldly and steadily. I did not feel at ease.

Lloyd came into the bar-room at this moment.

" Good-morning," said our visitor.

" Oh! Good-morning, Fred. Glad to see your face again. Thought you'd left the city."

I noticed that Lloyd's voice, which was hearty at

first, toned down rapidly, and was not very cheery at the close.

"I have a note for you;" and the man handed him a letter, watching him keenly as he read it. My eyes were also on him. I saw him glance at the signature and then knit his brows in a hard, angry way. But when he read the letter a change that I could not understand swept across his face. It was not out-and-out pleasure, though relief of mind was plainly expressed. Twice he read the letter, and then, as he folded it, said, in a repressed voice,

"Very well," and turned away. Our old customer eyed him curiously for a moment and then went out. He didn't call for a drink.

Lloyd made no remark on the incident, but seated himself at a table with his back toward me and leaned his head on his hand. He sat for a long time like one half asleep, he was so still.

"Hiram," he called, after nearly ten minutes had gone by. I went to him, and he handed me, without speaking, the letter he had just received. I opened it and read:

"DEAR FATHER: Harry Glenn came down to the prison this morning and said if I'd take the pledge and join 'The Harvey-street League' the men would pay my fine and Mr. Ashley would give me a chance in the bindery, and I've done it. I've seen Mr. Ashley, and he's spoken kindly to me, and says if I'll go to work and do right he'll be my friend. I'm to begin to-morrow, and am to have three dollars a week now, and more when I can earn it. I'm sorry I've done so badly, and mean to be a better boy. I'm going right home to see mother.

"Your affectionate son, Tom."

I don't think I was ever taken more aback by anything in my life. I read the letter again, and then, without saying a word, handed it to Lloyd and went back to the bar. A customer came in at the moment, and I was glad of the diversion.

Lloyd went out, and I did not see him until the next day. He came in about ten o'clock in company with a professional gambler, and seemed more excited than usual. They went up stairs together, and I did not see them again. Late in the afternoon Lloyd made his appearance, but so much the worse for drink that I had to get him out of the way of customers. I began to feel very much troubled about him—troubled on my own account as well as his. Our interests were too closely bound together for one to make sudden shipwreck without damage to the other. Three years of liquor-selling, profitable as the business proved, had not made either of us rich. We could not afford to retire. Our "pile" was yet a thing of the future. Lloyd was in the hands of a set of men who would rob him of every dollar he possessed with as little compunction as we had felt in our work of getting gain. And if he were utterly fleeced, and involved in gambling debts besides, where would I be?

Troubles seem never to come alone. Something occurred almost every day to keep my mind in a worry. A year before, I felt safe in one thing. The main chance, as we called it—that is, the money chance—was all right. We were heaping up our "pile." "The Retreat" was a success, and no mistake. I would get rich, whatever else might happen.

But I was beginning to feel less confident, to have uncomfortable doubts, to be conscious of a weight resting all the while upon my feelings. A shadow of coming evil had fallen on my path. With an unaccountable unanimity, temperance men had aroused themselves, and were showing front in all directions. No movement yet attempted looked so disastrous as that in favor of "local option," or the right of the people of each ward or county to decide at the polls whether they would have bars and drinking-saloons or not. The matter was often discussed in our barroom, and I did not fail to observe that the weight of argument as well as sentiment of a majority of our customers, even the hardest drinkers among them, was on the side of the new movement. There was one man who always put the argument in this form, and I never heard it successfully combated. He said:

"Let us take fifty men. They settle together, and go to work to build up a town. Their interests being mutual, they meet for consultation, and adopt certain laws for protection and government. They say the freedom of the individual must be maintained, and yet the good of the whole secured; therefore every man shall be permitted to follow the occupation he chooses, provided it does no harm to his neighbor. The carpenter, the baker, the merchant, the manufacturer, the tailor, the blacksmith, the gardener, and all who produce or help the people in any way, shall be free in their callings. But no business that hurts, depraves or in any way injures the people shall be carried on among us. We will not have dram-shops and liquor-saloons, nor gambling-hells, nor obscene shows, nor vile publications, in our town. No man shall have permission to get gain by hurting or corrupting his neighbor, and if any violate our laws against these evil things, he shall be punished."

Who will say that this community of fifty men has not a natural as well as a civil right to do all this? And if a community of fifty men has this natural and civil right, is it any less the right of a community of a thousand or of five hundred thousand? As just said, I never heard the argument answered, and could never answer it to myself.

"You can't get the Legislature to pass any such law," was boldly affirmed by a liquor man one evening when the subject of a "local option" law was under discussion. "I've been to Harrisburg a good many times, and know the ropes about as well as the next man. Politicians can't get on without whisky. The liquor interest rules the State. We have too much money. I could tell you a thing or two if I chose. It was tried last winter, and the temperance men thought they had the game. But it was no go. It cost us a good many thousands of dollars, but we were ready to put down twice as much more if need be. Why, gentlemen," he continued, "pass a local option law, as it is called, and four-fifths of us might as well shut up shop. Give the people a right to say whether we shall live or no, and it's all up with us. I don't believe there are five wards in this city—maybe not one—that, if fairly polled, wouldn't vote down the saloons."

"I'll bet on that," returned a half-tipsy customer. "Hurrah for local option! I'm on that side. Told Betsey only yesterday that I was going for that ticket."

"And what did Betsey say?" asked one who was amused at the man's drunken enthusiasm.

"Why, she just put her hand on my shoulder and said, 'Pray God the time come soon, Andy!' And I said 'Amen.' I hadn't been drinking anything for two or three days. But, you see, one can't go a square without being tempted. 'Tisn't possible for us poor devils to pass a hundred or more saloons every day, and not feel a craving for liquor. If I were off in the country, or anywhere out of sight of your man-traps, I could keep sober as a judge, but, confound it! it's no use to try, with your gilt signs and red lights and windows full of bottles staring me in the face at every turn. Yes, sir! Give us a local option law, and we'll vote you all out of existence. Hurrah for local option, say I."

"It's bound to come," said another, in a confident

voice. "The great body of the people seem to be getting awake on this subject, and if they once move against anything, it must go down. Rings break into helpless fragments and combinations lose their power. Nothing is too strong for the people. Whatever exists in our social or political organizations, for good or for evil, is by sufferance of the people. They set up and throw down at will."

"They'll never stop the sale of liquor," was answered to this. "They can't do it."

The response was so weak that everybody laughed.

"What is to hinder them, if they resolve to do it?" some one inquired.

"They won't stop it. They can't stop it," was returned in a dogged, half-angry way. "It's a free country. It's against the constitution. I'd like to see them stop me."

I didn't feel much comforted by the line of argument taken by this man.

CHAPTER XXIII.

EVERY day the aggressive movement of the temperance people was becoming more and more pronounced. Morning after morning I read in the papers an account of some ward local option meeting. Petitions were being circulated asking the Legislature to give the people a local option law, and public opinion seemed steadily setting in that direction. In our own ward this movement was very active, and had its centre of influence in Harvey street.

And now a new demonstration was begun. There was a law forbidding the sale of liquor on Sunday—our best day—but it had been for years a dead letter, because the people themselves were indifferent and suffered us to violate this law with impunity. Most of the constables were in league with us, and so no official notice was taken of the matter. Now and then, under pressure from some judge who saw and deplored the evils that sprung from this Sunday traffic, the grand jury would in solemn inquest, present the matter. But it ended there, and we laughed. It was nobody's business to see that the law was executed. Mayors were appealed to in vain. They had no authority to shut our doors or close our windows. Somebody must see somebody drink on Sunday, and must be able to swear that what he saw drawn or poured into a tumbler and drank therefrom was actually malt, spirituous or vinous liquor, and he must swear to the paying of money for the same, or else there could be no conviction. And even if all this were sworn to, if a liquor-seller could be got on the jury conviction was impossible. So it had been.

But there came signs of a change. It was the people's business. If they let it alone, judges, mayors and grand juries were powerless. But the people were beginning to move—the sleeping lion was arousing himself. Some of the temperance men, in asking for more legislation, had been told that they already had laws governing the sale of liquor that lay as a dead letter on the statute-books, that it was useless to give them more laws while they did not see to the execution of what they had, and they were referred to the law punishing with fine and imprisonment the sale of liquor on Sundays, and to minors, and to known drunkards. While there were from seven to eight thousand licensed and unlicensed taverns open in the city every Sunday in violation of law, what encouragement was there to give new laws? See that the laws you have are executed, they were told, and then, if further legislation is needed, let us hear from you.

There was no getting away from this. It bluffed off the temperance men, as it was meant to do, but set some of their leaders to thinking in the right direction. "Let us take what laws we have," they said, "and make them felt as far as they go. It is our fault that they lie dead. The Sunday traffic can be stopped if we will it."

And so they went into council to consider the ways and means of shutting up the dram-shops on Sunday. We heard of it, and laughed, but there were some of us who felt, even as we laughed, that our enemies were deeply in earnest, and that they were combining and organizing their forces in a way that looked dangerous. One of the worst auguries that showed itself was the change that had come over the daily press. Papers that once spoke lightly of all prohibitory movements, that picked flaws in the sayings and doings of temperance men, that talked of sumptuary laws as unconstitutional, that favored our side so plainly that all could see it, now ranged themselves on the other side, and entertained their readers with prison and pauper statistics of the worst kind, and charged on us the responsibility of filling the prisons and poorhouses of the country. I had almost come to feel nervous while looking over my morning paper, for hardly a day passed that some story of rum's fearful doings was not told, and the comment thereon was sure to be a thrust at us as the worst class of men in the whole community.

So long as the daily press was careful about what it said against a business in which a large number of wealthy, respectable and influential citizens were engaged, liquor men felt no serious alarm. Public opinion was formed or determined by the press. If the press did not favor a movement, it had little chance of success. If it opposed the movement, it would remain feeble or die.

But the press was steadily ranging itself against us. It talked of the fearful weight of taxation imposed on the citizens through pauperism and crime, nearly all of which it charged upon the liquor-dealers. It dwelt on the social and political demoralization consequent on the traffic. It gave reports of temperance lectures, and kept its readers advised of what was being done to destroy the "monster vice," the "deadly cancer that was eating down to the vitals of the nation." Any man who wanted to say hard and bitter things against us had now the opportunity. In a word, temperance had become popular, and the papers were not afraid to speak out.

It didn't look well. I began to feel as if we were going to fall on evil times. Another aspect of the case was threatening. Our judges were beginning to show their teeth, and the growl of the Bench was unmistakable. At every good opportunity word went forth that liquor men must be on guard, that they would be dealt with summarily and severely if they should get tripped. Constables were called up, sternly reminded of neglected duty in the matter of unlicensed dram-shops, and warned of consequences if longer derelict. Grand juries were charged as to their duty of presenting violations of law by saloon and tavern-keepers, and the law read and expounded to them. In any convictions of petty offences against the license law, sentences were noticeably severe. Juries, too, were beginning to take the popular side, and lawyers of character and standing in the community were coming to be ashamed of law-defying liquor men as clients.

I did not like the new aspect of things. It boded no good.

One Saturday evening a printer whom I knew very well, an old customer of "The Retreat," came in. He was looking remarkably well, and was better dressed than I had ever seen him. His skin had a fair, healthy look, his eyes were clear and his step firm and manly. I could not but remark to myself how much he was improved since I saw him last. Then he was slovenly in attire and sick-looking, had rheumatism, dyspepsia, and I don't know what all— one of your miserable sort of men, fast going down hill. He was one of our old eight-glasses-a-day men, and his custom worth having, of course—spent at one time nearly half he earned in our saloon for drink.

He came up to the bar, handed Lloyd a paper, and then bowing gravely, went out. He had returned our rather cordial greeting very coldly.

"What in —— is this?" growled Lloyd as he unfolded the paper. He ran his eyes over it hurriedly, and then with an angry imprecation threw it on the floor and spit upon it.

After waiting until he had cooled a little, I asked what was in the paper.

"Oh, we've got to shut up shop to-morrow," Lloyd answered with a mocking contempt.

"Who says so?" I asked.

"Our good friends in Harvey street."

"Indeed!" I was angry at the impertinent interference, and yet amused at what seemed its comic solemnity. Lloyd stooped, and lifting the soiled paper from the floor, opened it with the tips of his fingers, and read an extract from the law forbidding the sale of liquor on Sunday. The extreme penalty was fifty dollars fine and sixty days' imprisonment for each offence. I knew all this—had the law at my finger ends. Below the extract was a notification by the "Harvey-street League" to all tavern-keepers in —— ward that on any further violation of this law information would be given and prosecutions instituted. The notice was signed by Andrew Jacobs, as president of the league.

"We'll shut up, of course," I remarked, trying to look amused and affecting to treat the matter as a joke.

"Yes," rejoined Lloyd, with a snarl of defiance in his voice, "at twelve o'clock on Sunday night." Then he stamped about and swore frightfully.

A similar notice was served on every tavern-keeper in the ward. Some were frightened, and closed their doors on Sunday, but we paid no heed to it whatever. Business was too poor, now that we had lost the Harvey-street custom, to justify dropping out our best day. If we must shut up on Sunday in the present state of affairs, we might as well shut up altogether.

Lloyd came late on the next morning, crusty and moody, as usual, and went away before twelve o'clock. I was alone at the bar for two or three hours. We had in our usual Sunday customers, and there was considerable talk about the effort that was being made to close the taverns. One man had counted twenty places in the ward with shut doors and windows. I noticed during the day several men come in whose faces I had never seen before. Some of them drank and some did not. One of them called for a glass of lemonade, and sat down with it at a table, where he read, or appeared to be reading, for at least half an hour. I watched him pretty closely, and caught him several times looking over the top of his paper at men who were drinking at the bar.

I began to feel uneasy, in spite of all I could do to bolster up my feelings. What if I should really be arrested? The thought began to worry me. It would be bad enough to go into court as an offender against the law, but what if I were convicted of the offence? The fine was nothing. But sixty days in the county prison! The thought of it made my heart sink. We had been fairly warned, and by men who were in earnest, and in the face of that warning had gone on in open defiance of the law. Such thoughts began crowding on me as the day declined, and all the evening I had a feeling of worry and a sense of danger. I dreamed that night that I was arrested, tried, found guilty and sentenced to ten years' imprisonment, and awoke as an officer put his hands on me. My forehead was wet with perspiration. I never felt such a sense of relief in all my life as when I found myself awake.

There is an old adage that dreams go by contraries, and I tried to comfort myself with the thought that this dream was an assurance of safety. But the comfort was very small. Lloyd came along about ten o'clock on Monday morning. His first act was to drink a large glass of brandy. I noticed that his hands were unsteady, the glass shaking as he raised it to his mouth.

"That's bad, Tom," I remarked.

"What's bad?" he asked, turning on me with a look that said, "Take care!"

"The way you're going on," I returned. "If you don't taper off a little, you'll see sights before long."

He looked very much annoyed, and swore between his teeth. After that he was moody and silent, as usual. He helped at the bar for an hour, and then asked me to let him have five hundred dollars. I had some money in bank, and he knew it. I had already loaned him over two thousand dollars to complete his payments on a lot of ground purchased somewhere up town. He had promised to give me a mortgage on the property, but had not yet done so.

"What do you want with five hundred dollars?" I asked.

"Got a payment to make on some property I bought last week," he answered, not looking me in the face. "It's a great bargain, and will double in value in a year or two."

"Where is it?" I inquired.

"Away up town," he replied.

"You haven't given me the mortgage you promised on that other property," I said.

He fired up and got into a little rage, swore considerably, and wanted to know if I thought he was going to swindle me. I told him it was no use getting into a passion. Business was business. He had already borrowed two thousand dollars, and so far neglected to put the security agreed upon into my hands. If he wanted any more, he must first execute the mortgage. I kept my eye fixed steadily upon him, and showed by my manner that I was in earnest. He fretted and swore for a while, but cooled down.

"I must have the money this morning, Hiram," he said, at last, in a coaxing way. "Your mortgage is all ready, and has been for a month. I didn't know that you were thinking about it. I'll get it for you this afternoon. Give me a check this morning. I don't wish to lose the chance I have for securing a great bargain.

I gave him a check, but reluctantly; I had lost faith in him. He might be going to buy a property, but

I had my doubts. I did not see him again that day, nor the mortgage he had promised.

Time passed on until the middle of the afternoon, and the nervousness I had felt since morning was beginning to wear away. After all, the notice we had received was only a threat meant to scare us off. Or if more was intended, sufficient evidence had not been procured to warrant the commencement of a suit. I was laughing over the matter with a customer who had referred to the movement against the Sunday traffic, when through the opening door appeared the face of the constable who had served the warrant on Lloyd after his assault on Jacobs. The laugh died in my throat. He came up to the bar, and leaning over, said to me in a low voice,

"You're wanted round at the alderman's."

"What for?" I asked, not able to keep my voice steady and clear.

"Got a case against you."

"For what?"

"Selling on Sunday."

"When must I appear?"

"Now. The witnesses are all present."

There was no help for it. I had to go. At the alderman's I found four or five men waiting for me. Three of them were old and good customers who had drank at our bar every Sunday for months and months. They had been in on the day before, and I had sold them liquor. Had they turned against me? I felt my knees give way. If that were so, I was indeed in peril. The case was opened, and these three men, who had been seen going into and coming out of "The Retreat," were put on oath, and against their will, I could perceive, compelled to give evidence against me—compelled to testify that I had sold them whisky and ale and beer on Sunday, and that they had paid for the same and drank it standing at the bar. Two of them were well-known business men with families of grown-up children, and the other was a young man, the son of a well-known clergyman, but a little fast. I saw that they were very much annoyed at their position and the discreditable notoriety they would obtain if the matter went to court and they were compelled to appear as witnesses.

The alderman had no alternative. The evidence was too clear. I had to give bail for my appearance in case the grand jury found a true bill against me, and on the Monday following the bill was found.

The Harvey-street men were in earnest. They had employed a good lawyer, and instructed him not to let the matter sleep. So he arranged with the district attorney for as prompt a hearing of the case as possible. In less than two weeks I was in the prisoner's dock, with all eyes in a crowded court-room upon me.

In the mean time, our liquor-selling friends had rallied around us and employed counsel, promising a thousand dollars fee if the case went in our favor. Lloyd was so scared that he took to drinking harder, and kept so full all the while that he was of little or no account. He was under bail to appear in court on a charge of assault and battery, as the reader knows. The grand jury had found a bill against him also, and his trial was to come on in two weeks after the day fixed for mine. An effort had been made to compromise with old Jacobs, but he said the matter had gone out of his hands. As much as five hundred dollars were offered to settle, but it couldn't be done. Our enemies were determined to drive us to the wall. There was no hope but in fighting to the death.

On the Sunday following my arrest "The Retreat" struck its flag, closed its doors and windows, and its rooms were as empty and silent as those of any store or manufactory in the neighborhood. I did not go near it all day. I could not bear the sight.

The case, after a brief examination of the three reluctant witnesses, who testified clearly to facts, but with shame marks in their faces, seen and noticed by every one, was argued by counsel on both sides. The prosecution was solid and strong, the defence intemperate of speech, captious, wild in its range of discussion and desperate in its appeals to the jury. But through all I saw only defeat. The law and the testimony were against us.

There was no mistaking the animus of the Bench when the jury was charged. "The law in this case is very clear," said the judge. And then he read the section prohibiting the sale of liquor on Sunday.

"Laws are made for the public good," he went on, "and good citizens cheerfully obey them. All who violate them are bad citizens, criminals through this violation, and must be punished. This Sunday law has for years been treated with open contempt, and by a class of men who, not satisfied with plying their wretched business of making paupers and criminals during six days and six nights of the week, licensed thereto by the commonwealth, keep on in defiance of law through the seventh, making the Sabbath a curse instead of a blessing to thousands of their fellow-citizens. What can our four hundred churches do against seven or eight thousand grog-shops and drinking-saloons? Gentlemen of the jury, the law in this case is as explicit as words can make it— clear in the intent and plain in the expression. It is a good law, a needed law. Its violation is working the saddest evil in this community. I need not amplify here. You know it all as well as I do. Gentlemen of the jury, if the evidence in this case has proved to your satisfaction its violation by the defendant, you are bound by your oath to convict."

CHAPTER XXIV.

THE jury retired, and I sat for half an hour in a state of miserable suspense it is impossible to describe. For three years I had openly defied the law. For three years I had felt as safe in this defiance as if I were obeying it to the very letter. I had felt strong in the power of the great interest I represented, and laughed at what seemed the futile efforts of a few fanatics to break that power. But now the law had its hand upon me, and the grip was iron-like. I felt it to the bone. I had watched the judge's face while he charged the jury, and saw in it no mercy. If I was convicted, nothing could save me. Prison! To be locked up with vile criminals! I shivered as the picture grew vivid in my thoughts.

There fell a silence upon the court. I lifted my head and saw the jury coming in. My heart gave a bound, and then beat like a hammer in my breast. Perspiration started from every pore.

After the jurymen had arranged themselves, the judge said:

"What say you, gentlemen of the jury? Is the defendant guilty or not guilty?"

The foreman rose. I held my breath. "Guilty!" he said. I did not see nor hear anything for several moments. The court-room appeared to be turning round. Then I felt a hand on my arm. There was no mistaking the touch. It was the hand of the officer of the court, and I was a prisoner.

"Come," he said, in a cold, imperative voice.

Two or three friends had been around me during the trial, but they moved off now with changed, blank faces. I arose, thinking I was to be taken out and conveyed at once to prison, but, instead, I was escorted to the dock in the centre of the court-room, and set down there with a dozen other criminals of all grades, sexes and colors. This was a humiliation I had not expected. I looked helplessly toward my counsel, but saw no assurance in his face.

"The prisoner will stand up," said the judge. I arose, striving to look calm.

"Prisoner at the bar"—so the judge addressed me—"you have been tried for the breach of a wise and good law, and a jury of your countrymen, after hearing the evidence, has found you guilty. It now remains for me to declare your sentence, and in doing so I shall be governed solely by considerations of public weal. Your offence is a very serious one. I need not dwell upon its character here: that has been fully exposed during the trial. You represent a large class who have been long engaged like yourself in setting at defiance the law for a breach of which you are now to be punished. The public conscience, so long and so strangely indifferent to the evil work you were doing in open violation of law, has become aroused to a sense of duty. The people are beginning to move, and the court hails the movement in this direction as the beginning of better things. Your conviction will give it strength. And now, prisoner at the bar, I pronounce upon you the full sentence of the law: Sixty days' imprisonment in the county jail and a fine of fifty dollars. I trust that, after a residence there of two months, you will come forth in a better mind."

As the judge ceased speaking, I sank down upon my seat in the dock with a sense of disgrace so deep that I would have thought a prison cell a paradise compared with that crowded court-room, where I was the observed of all observers.

"Caught at last!" said a chuckling voice at my side, a hand punching me in the ribs at the same time. The mouth that opened to say this breathed into my face a rank odor of whisky, onions and tobacco.

"Never been down there before, ha!" went on the voice. "Guess you'll find it a little dull at first, but 'tisn't no account after you get used to it. I've been there twenty times."

I made no response to this familiar speech of the dirty vagabond at my side.

After a little while I ventured to look about the court-room from my new position. During the trial there had been not less than fifty saloon-keepers present, all of whom watched the proceedings with keenest interest. Many of them had come around me, speaking words of encouragement and saying that they would stand by me to the last, that any amount of money would be put up to defeat the course of law. I could not find one of these men in the court-room now. They had all deserted the place, and I was in the dock with thieves, vagrants and criminals of all degrees, a sentenced prisoner.

The business of the court went on, and I had time to observe more carefully my companions of the dock. One was a stout negro who had been sentenced to a year's imprisonment for cutting a woman with a knife in a drunken brawl. He had the face of a wild beast, and when I looked at him his eyes held themselves in mine with an expression that made me afraid. It seemed as if he were ready to spring upon me. Another was a boy of eighteen with all the signs of a dissolute man about him. He too had been in a drunken spree, and had used a knife on somebody. Another was a sneak thief, and another a poor wretch degraded by drink who had been pitched into the street by a tavern-keeper. His offence was the throwing of a stone through this tavern-keeper's window in revenge for the personal outrage. And another was a poor woman who sat with her face covered and a convulsive sob shaking her whole frame every few moments. She was an orderly and decent person, as I learned afterward, but poor and cursed with a drunken husband. A sister of this husband, not much better than himself, had come to her house one day and abused her shamefully. She had borne it as long as she could, but at last, exasperated beyond endurance, had pushed her out of the house. Being considerably in liquor, the sister-in-law, as she was forced upon the pavement, staggered and fell, striking her head against a tree and cutting it so that it bled some and left a scar. For this the poor woman had been taken from her children and sent to prison by an alderman in default of bail. The grand jury had found a bill against her for assault and battery, and she was here for trial.

As the woman sat with her face concealed, and the intermittent sobs shaking her frame, I saw a man with a kind, earnest face go up to one of the judges and talk a little while, looking every now and then toward the dock. I noticed that the judge shook his head once or twice, but on this the man became more earnest, pressing the matter under consideration, whatever it was, strongly upon him. From the judge he went to the district attorney, and considerable talk passed between them. I saw that the district attorney was not favorable to his plea, whatever it was. But the man was persistent, arguing and gesticulating most earnestly. At last he seemed to prevail, and the district attorney went to the judge and spoke with him for a little while. Then the man laid what seemed documents before them, and after they had looked them over, the judge spoke a few words to the man I have referred to, and I saw a gleam of pleasure light up his face. The judge wrote a line on a piece of paper, and the man came down and made his way to the dock, handing the paper to the officer in charge of us. He read it and nodded assent.

All this while the poor woman sat like a statue of despair, with her face hidden from view. The man came into the dock, and bending over her, said, kindly, "It's all right. I've got it settled, and you can go home."

"God bless you, Mr. Mullen," she said, lifting her face. It was pale and thin, but through its wasted tissues and sad expression there broke such joy and gratitude as I had never seen.

The prison agent—for it was he—took her out quickly.

For two hours I sat in the dock while the trials went on. One after another was convicted and sentenced, until I found myself in the midst of a wretched crew—thieves, roughs and vagabonds of the meanest class, and nearly all of them smelling of whisky.

At the end of this time we were marched out upon Sixth street, where the prison van and a crowd of curious men and boys awaited us. There were laughs and jeers from the hardened and thoughtless as we were thrust into the van.

"Hallo!" I heard a voice say as I crossed the pavement; "there goes Hiram Jones."

How my cheeks did burn and tingle!

Into this horrible carriage twenty human beings

were thrust and the doors closed upon them. My place happened to be alongside of the negro I have mentioned. Opposite me was a white man whom I had noticed in the dock as acting strangely. He was a dirty, ragged, forlorn, gutter drunkard. I cannot better describe him. The negro, too, had worried me a good deal by his jerks and starts and restless throwing of his eyes about as if in dread of something. I had a suspicion of mania. Scarcely had the van started when the negro gave a cry and a leap upward, striking his head against the roof of our prison on wheels, and at the same time the man opposite sprang from his seat and tried to rush to the lower end of the van, his eyes starting with terror. Cries and curses filled the air. Some pounded on the door, but the officer in charge gave no heed to us.

The negro sat still for nearly a minute after striking his head, and then, as the white man struggled back from the lower end of the van, grappled him with the savage fury of a maniac, and both went down upon the floor of the vehicle, where they yelled and struggled in the wildest desperation. It was in vain that we pounded on the door for help from the officer outside. Three or four of the stoutest men in the van—hard, savage-looking fellows—now threw themselves on the two struggling madmen and held them down, so that the rest of us were comparatively safe. I shall never forget their awful cries and shouts and curses while I live. In this way they were held down, yet not without violent struggles to get free that sometimes sent the men who had grappled with them back upon the alarmed and cowering inmates of the van, bruising and hurting them, until we reached the prison.

I never supposed that I would feel a sense of pleasure on entering a prison door, but the horrors of that ride made even a prison welcome. The two men crazy from drink were first dragged out and made secure. I heard the strange order given, "Take them to purgatory," and wondered what it could mean. Then we crept forth one after another in the stony vestibule of the prison, and each was placed in a cell. Mine was at the west end of a long corridor high up in the third tier. Before I was put in I saw them write on a slate that hung outside and close by the door, "HIRAM JONES. Selling liquor on Sunday; sixty days." And so every visitor who passed that cell could read my name and the crime that brought me there. Poor Hiram Jones! He had never counted on this.

I was passed through a low iron door in the wall, stooping to save my head, and in the next moment I heard the door shut behind me and the key turned in the lock. For a while I stood close by the door looking around the cell. It was about twelve feet long by eight wide, lighted by a narrow opening in the wall. A bed stood in one corner, and there were a small table and a chair. The floor was of wood. The air of the cell was pure, and I soon found that the ventilation was good. But what a different place to live in from my comfortable room at the hotel! I tired of that after a few hours. It was too confined for me. How was I to live here for sixty days? I felt a chill creep over me as this thought crowded in among the many unhappy ones that were filling me with bitterness and dismay.

And so it had come to this! Three years of liquor-selling, and here I was, a disgraced man! I threw myself on the bed, shut my teeth hard, closed my eyes and tried to force back into something like calmness my agitated feelings. I do not think I had lain thus for over a minute when I sprang up with a shudder. Such a cry of terror and suffering as smote upon my ears, coming apparently from one of the cells across the corridor, I had never heard. I shivered, and could feel the hair rising on my head. In a moment after, the cry was repeated. It was full of the wildest terror. Then it came again, more like the yell of a wild beast than anything else. I sat motionless and breathless, listening intently. I could hear voices as of two or three men under strong excitement and the noise of violent struggling.

All then grew still—so still that I could hear my watch ticking in my pocket. My forehead was damp with sweat; my hands were cold and clammy; I felt as weak as a child. I sat on the bed for two or three minutes, hearkening, but the silence was unbroken. Then, exhausted, as one after a long and severe effort, I fell back again upon the bed. But scarcely had my head touched the pillow when a wail of anguish smote my ears that it is impossible to describe. Only the extremest torture could have wrung such a cry from mortal lips. It was a mingling of terror and pain wrought up to their intensest expression. Then, as I listened with keenest attention, I could hear curses and words of deprecation and pleading, followed by renewed cries of agony.

I could bear it no longer, and so thrust my fingers into my ears to keep out the fearful sounds. But whenever I removed them, the dreadful cries would be heard. So it went on, with brief pauses, for nearly two hours, the strain on my nerves becoming so great that I felt sick and faint. Between five and six o'clock I heard a rumbling, as of a light wagon coming along the corridor. It stopped every little while, and then came on again, drawing nearer and nearer. At last it was opposite my cell. I looked toward the door and saw a little square place near the top drawn open outward, and then a small tin basin containing some liquid, which I found to be chocolate, and a piece of bread, were pushed in through the opening.

I came forward and took them, saying as I did so,

"For Heaven's sake, what's the matter over there?"

"Purgatory got the rams," was the brief answer, and the little opening was shut with a sharp click.

I put the basin of chocolate and piece of bread on the table and sat down. "Purgatory got the rams!" I said, taking a deep shuddering breath as the truth dawned upon my mind. I understood now the meaning of those dreadful cries.

"Take them to purgatory," had been said of the two men with mania-a-potu as they were taken from the prison-van, and it was no doubt the horrible ravings and struggles of one or both of them that I had heard. "Purgatory!" Well might the chamber of despair in which were thrust the poor wretches assaulted by rum demons be called "purgatory!"

I was sick at heart. By this time the wails and shrieks from across the corridor had ceased, the unhappy maniacs having been drugged into quietude, perhaps stupor.

My supper of weak chocolate and dry bread remained untasted. It would have taken daintier food than that to tempt my appetite.

As the darkness came on and I sat lonely and depressed in my cell, a few faint rays of light creeping in through a small opening from the corridor, a troop of miserable thoughts came like fiends to worry and torment me. I too was in purgatory—a purgatory of my own—and in spirit I cried out from pain and torture. It was coming out too sadly true, and in my own case, that the traffic, as I had so often heard it said, was accursed, and its harvests deadly. I had not cared much for the consequences that might fall on others, but now the curses had come home. I was in the fire of retribution, and it made a vast difference.

I did not sleep much that night. Every time I

lost myself the screams of some wretch in "purgatory" would startle me into wakefulness. Morning found me nervous and feverish. I tried to eat my breakfast of tea and bread, but could get down only a few mouthfuls.

All that day I paced at intervals my narrow cell, chafed and restless as a wild animal, or tried vainly, lying face down upon my bed, to stop the procession of tormenting thoughts. For dinner I had soup and bread and a small piece of meat. I could not do much with it. About four o'clock in the afternoon I heard a voice outside of my cell, then the thrusting of a key into the lock and the opening of the outer door. A hand pushed inward the inside grated door, and a slender youth stepped in. Then the clang of doors and turning of the lock followed, and we were alone. I looked at my fellow-prisoner.

"Tom!"

"Hiram!"

We both exclaimed in mutual surprise. It was Lloyd's son, Tom.

"What has brought you here?" I asked.

There was a look of deep distress in the boy's face. He had been taken out of prison only a little while before under promise of signing the pledge, which he had done, and gone to work in the Harvey-street bindery.

"I'm very sorry to see you here, Tom," I said. "I had hoped for better things."

"So had I," he answered. "But there isn't any

chance for me, Hiram. I've got a bad name, and there's the end of it."

"What have you been doing?" I asked.

"Nothing to bring me here," he replied, looking at me steadily.

"Then why are you here?"

"Because I've got a bad name."

"Tell me about it," I said, pitying the poor boy from my heart. I had always liked Tom.

"I signed the pledge, you know," he began.

"Yes."

"And I've kept it so far. Mr. Ashley gave me a place in the bindery, and I've been at work every day. Well, you see, the Harvey street men are in earnest about shutting up the liquor-shops on Sunday. They don't want the trouble of bringing the tavern-keepers into court and fining them if they can help it, and so are sending round notices again, warning them to keep the law, and hoping they will take heed. To-day I was sent to serve a notice on Crangle, who keeps the saloon just out of Sixth street: you know where it is. I went in and gave it to Crangle, and he threw it in my face and gave me a cuff on the side of my head. I couldn't stand that. I'm quick and fiery, you know. If I'd stopped to think, I wouldn't have done it, but I was so mad that I wasn't myself. In a flash a tumbler went past his head and smashed in among the decanters. I ran, but they caught me before I could get out and took me round to the alderman's. They swore against me, and had a witness to say that he knew me, and that I was the worst boy in town and just out of prison. So the alderman made out a commitment. I asked if somebody wouldn't go round and get father to come and be bail for me. But Crangle laughed, and said father was under bail himself to appear at court and couldn't be taken; so I was brought down here."

"But why didn't you send round to the bindery? The men would have stood by you," I said.

"Maybe so, and maybe not," Tom replied, gloomily. "I'm only on trial there."

"Well, suppose you are?"

"They'd have thought I'd taken a glass and got into a spree. But I didn't touch anything. It was all just as I've told you."

And the poor boy put his face down between his hands.

"How are things going on at home, Tom?" I asked, after a while. He looked up. His eyes were sad and troubled. His mouth twitched slightly as he began speaking, and his voice was low and mournful.

"Not very well," he replied.

"How is your mother?"

"Poorly."

"Has she been sick?"

"No, not exactly. But she's out of sorts, like, 'most all the while, and she's had enough to make her so. I thought maybe I'd be some comfort to her, but it's all over now."

His voice choked a little.

"I'll not be home to-night, you see, and she'll be sure I've gone off in my old ways, and it will put her in bed. Oh dear! I wish I'd died when I was a baby."

And the poor boy burst out crying. How I did pity him! After he had grown calm, I said,

"Is your father much at home?"

Tom shook his head as he replied,

"We never see him except at breakfast-time, and not often then. He don't come in until long after we're in bed."

"How is he in the morning?"

"Not right. It's as much as he can do to get a cup of coffee to his mouth, his hand shakes so. But he don't often come down until we're all done breakfast."

"Has he said anything to you since you signed the pledge?"

"No; hasn't even spoken to me."

"I'm glad you signed it, Tom," I could not help saying. "And you must stick to it. No good ever comes of drinking, and often a great deal of harm."

He looked up at me with a sudden surprise in his face, then answered slowly,

"Yes, Hiram, a great deal of harm. It was a bad day for us when you and father set up 'The Retreat.' Nothing has gone right since. It was the death of poor Maggy, and has 'most killed mother."

He paused, and I added, with the bitterness I felt, "And has put you and me in prison." The boy sighed heavily.

At this moment, piercing the air sharply, came a howl of fear from across the corridor. Tom started and turned pale.

"What is that, Hiram?" he asked, with quivering lips.

"Some poor fellow with mania," I replied.

"Oh, isn't it dreadful!"

Another and more prolonged cry, full of pain and terror, smote upon our ears, and we could hear struggling in the cells opposite. Tom's face grew whiter.

For nearly an hour we had to listen to these awful cries. Then they died away, and we were thankful for the silence that followed. We had commenced talking again, when we heard some one unlocking our cell door. It was swung open, and the man I had seen in the court-room that morning stepped in.

"Sorry to see you here again," he said, in a kind voice, speaking to Tom. "Thought you were going to sign the pledge and be a better boy? What's the matter? What are you here for now?"

Tom told his story, which was listened to attentively. When he had finished, I said,

"You may believe every word he says, Mr. Mullen. I know him."

"You do?" and the agent turned on me quickly. "How came you to know him?"

"I am in business with his father," I replied, not stopping to think what the business was.

"Oh, are you?" and he fixed his eyes on me so steadily that I had to look away from him. "Then all I have to say about it is, that it's a very bad business."

I turned from him abashed.

"And you've been a good, sober boy since you left here?" said Mr. Mullen, the old kindness and interest coming back into his voice as he turned to Tom.

"Haven't touched a drop of liquor. You can ask them at the bindery. Mr. Ashley will tell you. Oh, Mr. Mullen, if there's any way to get me out before mother knows it— It will be dreadful for her. I'm all the hope she has now. Oh, Mr. Mullen, help me if you can;" and he burst out crying.

"There! there! Don't take on about it," said the agent, kindly. "I'll see what can be done."

He drew his watch out from his pocket and looked at the time, stood thinking for a few moments and then said, with a twinkle of humor in his eyes,

"If I go your bail, you won't go back on me?"

"Not if I die for it!" answered Tom, quickly.

"Don't be afraid," I spoke up. "I'll make it all right."

He gave me a look that said plainly enough, "I'd rather take the boy's word than your bond!"

I turned away hurt and abashed. I was only a liquor-seller, capable in his eyes of any baseness!

"Very well. I'll see the alderman, and you shall be with your mother by six o'clock," said the agent, and he went away.

In about an hour he came back.

"All right!" he said, cheerily, as he entered the cell again. He did not take any notice of me, and was going out with Tom when I put my hand on him, saying,

"Won't you come and see me, sir? I'd like to talk with you."

"What about?" he asked, coldly.

I dare not say why I wished to see him, for were I to do so, I felt that he might deny me wholly. I wanted his influence to get me out.

"A good many things," I answered, evasively.

"Very well. I'm the prisoner's friend, and if I can help you any shall be glad to do so."

And he went out with the boy, leaving me lonelier and more depressed than ever.

CHAPTER XXV.

I SLEPT but little that night. The horrors of "purgatory" kept me awake.

I looked for Mr. Mullen all the next day, but he did not come. I heard his voice in the corridor two or three times during the afternoon, but he passed my cell without calling. A whole week of imprisonment, and I had not seen him again. I was losing heart. There was no hope for me if I could not get him to take up my case. Lloyd, to my surprise and indignation, had not come near me. "I might die like a dog, for all he cared," I said to myself. Nor had any other of my many friends. I was left alone in my calamity.

I was, besides, greatly troubled about my affairs. Lloyd had borrowed nearly all my ready money, and I more than feared its loss in gambling. He was too much under the influence of liquor all the while to be any match for the sharpers who had him in hand. If I could not get out of this horrid place in less than two months, everything would go to ruin. He was in danger of being cleaned out at any moment—would be, I doubted not, before I could be at hand to save myself. Then there was the assault-and-battery case to be tried in a day or two. He might be sent down here for six or nine months, and who was to take care of things until I could get out? I chafed and worried and tormented myself with evil forebodings helplessly and fruitlessly.

One afternoon, a little over a week after my sentence, I heard the key turn in my cell door. It opened, and the prison agent came in. I did not read the kindness and sympathy in his face that I had seen there when he interceded for the poor woman in court and when he spoke to Tom Lloyd.

"You don't find this quite as pleasant as a room in the Girard," he said, betraying a little sarcasm in his tones.

"Not quite," I replied, forcing as much indifference into my voice as was possible.

"Nor are your fellow-lodgers as agreeable," he added, giving his head a nod toward the corridor. I understood him, and felt irritated—would have answered roughly, but dared not do so, for I wanted him to befriend me.

"You wished to see me?"

"Yes, sir," I replied.

"I've been too much occupied in looking after the poor creatures rum has brought here to see you before. And now, what can I do for you?"

I saw no hope in his face. It wore a cold severity that seemed a stranger to it.

"I don't know that you can or will do anything," I replied, with the bitterness I felt. "Men like you don't have much charity for us."

"And why should we?" he asked, a softer tone coming into his voice. "You are not on our side. While we are trying to help and save, you are hurting and destroying."

"You judge us too harshly," I said.

"By their fruits ye shall know them," he replied. "What brought to prison the poor boy I found in your cell a week ago?"

I let my eyes fall from his. It was his father's work and mine—indirectly, but as surely our work as if we had of purpose corrupted him. I saw it all in a flash of perception.

"There are now in this place, convicted or awaiting trial, over eight hundred persons," he went on. "Of these, nearly four-fifths were sent to prison for crimes or misdemeanors committed while under the influence of liquor."

"It is easy to charge upon liquor every crime in the calendar," I replied.

"The exceptions are few," he returned. "We who have much to do with paupers and criminals have the best opportunity for knowing. Let me repeat to you, as nearly as I can remember them, a few sentences from a memorable charge made by Judge Paxson to the grand jury. He said, 'No one can sit for a week in this court, and observe closely the vast amount of criminal business transacted here, without coming to the conclusion that at least three-fourths of all the crimes committed in this city are the results, directly or indirectly, of intemperance.

This is an appalling fact. From this poisoned fountain flow out the streams which fill our prisons with convicts and our almshouses with poor. Nor is this remark true only of the lowest rank of crime. It applies with equal force to the highest grade. In a large proportion of the homicide cases the primary cause is whisky, or some wretched compound in imitation thereof. This is "the pinion which impels the steel." Maddened by its use, men who in its absence would be peaceable citizens and kind husbands and fathers become brutes in the domestic circle and outlaws in society. I have been sitting for the last three weeks in the oyer and terminer. During that time eight cases of homicide have been tried. With a single exception, the evidence disclosed the melancholy fact that intoxicating drink was either a direct cause of the crime or a potent agent in producing it. This fearful plague-spot has been spreading with great rapidity for many years. In 1847, as I am informed by Mr. Mullen, the efficient prison agent, the number of persons committed to the Philadelphia county prison for drunkenness, upon the charges of vagrancy, disorderly conduct and breaches of the peace, was two thousand seven hundred and fifty-two; in 1857 they had increased to seven thousand three hundred and ninety-two; and in 1867 to twelve thousand six hundred and ninety-seven. And the increase for the first ten months of this year is three thousand. This is far in excess of the increase of population, and proves conclusively that, notwithstanding the efforts heretofore made to check it, the evil of intemperance is steadily upon the increase.'

"There is no going behind this," the agent went on, while I sat as one dumb before him.

A shuddering cry came over from "purgatory." He watched my face for a moment, and then said,

"No trade but yours gives a harvest like that. In a single year over a hundred and sixty poor wretches have gone into the mania-a-potu ward of this prison and suffered the torments of the damned. Thirty-three died there a death of inconceivable horror.

"Have you ever," he went on, after observing me closely for a little while, "made yourself familiar with the statistics of your business?"

I shook my head.

"I wonder at that," he returned. "Men usually post themselves in such matters. Do you know how much is spent in the United States in a single year for intoxicating liquor? I mean in the taverns, restaurants, saloons and liquor-shops?"

"I have heard, I think, but do not now remember," I replied.

"Over a billion and a half of dollars, or more than one-third the amount received by retailers of all other kinds of merchandise. Is it any wonder, sir, that our prisons and almshouses are full? How many poor creatures, do you think, have been committed for drunkenness to this prison alone in twenty years? You would never guess. A hundred and ninety thousand!"

"Impossible!" I exclaimed.

"Too true, sir—too sadly true," the agent replied. "There is no need for exaggeration. The facts are appalling enough as they stand. I give you simply the prison record. And is it any matter of wonder? You have not been for years in this business without some knowledge of its practical workings. You can call to mind many, alas, how many! now worthless sots, paupers or criminals who were once sober, industrious men. Think of the fearful work that eight thousand bars and dram-shops, open seven days in the week, can do in a single city! Eight thousand dram-shops, and only four hundred churches and three hundred and eighty schools! How fearful the odds against virtue and religion! How many do you suppose are now in the almshouse?"

"I cannot imagine," I replied.

"Nearly four thousand. And do you think sobriety and industry brought them there? No, sir! I question if there is a single person in that institution who has not, directly or indirectly, been reduced to pauperism through the influence of liquor-drinking. Out of thirty-one thousand arrests made by the police of our city in a single year, fifteen thousand were sent to prison. Of these latter, one thousand were for assault and battery, five thousand for disorderly conduct, four thousand for drunkenness and thirteen hundred for vagrancy. Thus nearly twelve thousand out of the fifteen were committed to prison for misdemeanors clearly traceable to drink. Of the other fifteen thousand arrests made by the police, it is fair to suppose that three-fourths of them were of persons more or less under the influence of liquor. Sober, quiet people are not often troubled by policemen."

I sat with my eyes cast down upon the floor utterly speechless before this appalling array of facts and figures.

"And this, mind you," went on the prison agent, warming every moment under his theme—"this is for a single city. And the same work is going on in almost every city, town and neighborhood in the land, and everywhere the cry goes up—the bitter cry of poor women and children, for on them the crushing weight of this great millstone is heaviest, grinding out hope, happiness and often life itself. Let us take a wider survey, and try to grasp the aggregate of this monstrous evil. Carefully-prepared statistics tell us that there are five hundred and seventy thousand persons employed in producing and selling various kinds of intoxicating liquors, and that the sales of these reach the enormous sum of nearly a billion and a half of dollars annually. No wonder that in a single year (1868) criminal statistics give this frightful record of crimes: Four hundred and eighty suicides, six hundred and forty murders and eighty thousand cases of larceny and theft committed under the influence of liquor."

I made a feeble effort to throw in something about the impossibility of getting reliable statistics, and the tendency of those opposed to liquor men to exaggerate.

"Exaggerate!" he exclaimed. "Why, sir, it is impossible to exaggerate! Let any man in his sober senses sit down with the facts before him and ponder the subject. You can do it for yourself, and I trust you will do it, now that you have the opportunity. I will supply you with all the data you need, and you shall work out the question for yourself. In this city, with a population of over seven hundred thousand, we have had in operation for years past about eight thousand drinking-places. Extend this ratio to the whole United States, and you will have over two hundred thousand places where rum is sold. Call it a hundred and fifty thousand, and what a fearful aggregate you have! Estimate, if you can, the evil effects of a single well-frequented bar, and then try to imagine what sorrow and crime, what suffering and unutterable woe, must spring from a hundred and fifty thousand such moral pest-houses.

"You have never thought of these things? Ah, sir, it is time you were beginning to think, and that very soberly."

"You are not indisposed to give me the opportunity," I said, betraying both in voice and manner the annoyance I felt under the pressure of his crowding figures.

"I am glad of the opportunity," he replied, "to enlighten one who, if I read his face aright, is not all lost to considerations of humanity, is not wholly indifferent to human woe. How long have you been in this wretched business?"

"About three years," I replied.

"And you have had a fair run of custom during that time?"

"Yes."

"Can you remember a single instance, looking back over all your customers, in which you think a man was benefited by what you gave him for his money?"

I was silent.

"I am not now seeking to annoy you, not trying to fret and chafe you, because you are in prison and in a certain sense in my power," the agent said in gentle tones. "I only desire to get conviction into your heart. I only want you to see the fearful responsibility that rests upon the men who live by the traffic in which you are engaged. And now will you not, for the sake of getting down to the very root of this thing, tax your memory and answer honestly to yourself the question I have asked?"

I paused for a little while to let my thoughts, which were disturbed by his question, run a little clear.

"I can hardly say yes," I at length replied.

"Let me go farther, and ask if you cannot recall many cases in which men are worse off for what you gave them?"

I was silent again.

"I will not press the question," the agent said,

rising. "I leave it to you and your conscience. Answer it to your own soul, my friend, and answer it fairly. Go back bravely and resolutely over the past three years of your life, and be honest with yourself. Call up the unmarred faces of men who were allured to your bar two or three years ago, and call them up again as when you looked upon them last. Set them side by side in your imagination, and put the question soberly, 'How far am I responsible for the dreadful change now visible?' Think of the homes of these men, of their sorrowing, suffering wives, and of their neglected children, and ask again the question, 'How far am I responsible?'"

He moved to go. I arose from the bed on which I had been sitting, and said, earnestly,

"It is all very bad, sir, but men are not apt to stop and consider who is hurt by their business, more especially if it have the sanction of law. It is hardly fair to put all the responsibility on us. The commonwealth that sells us a license to deal in liquors must have its share."

I saw his eyes flash and a quiver of pain and indignation disturb his face.

"The commonwealth takes blood-money!" he exclaimed, almost passionately—"sells to unscrupulous men the right to make paupers and criminals, to consume the poor man's substance and beggar his wife and children, to break poor human hearts! It is an awful thing."

And he walked the brief length of my cell backward and forward in strong agitation.

"If the men who represent this commonwealth," he went on—"the men who are chosen to make its laws and secure the highest good of their fellow-citizens—could see a hundredth part of the evils of rum-selling that I have seen in the last twenty years in this city alone, they would sweep every license law from the statute-book and shut up every bar in the State. They would say to each citizen of the commonwealth, You shall be free to get gain by serving your neighbor, but not by hurting him. We will not license men to the business of corruption, we will not license men to make paupers, thieves and murderers, we will not license men to the business of eating out the poor man's substance and letting his wife and children starve or beg."

I did not venture to oppose anything to this. I could not. He walked toward the cell door, saying, in a changed and quieter voice,

"But I must go—have already stayed too long. There are three or four poor victims of your traffic sent down to-day that I must see after and get back to their families."

His hand was drawing open the inner door. I could not let him go without a word for myself.

"I cannot stay here for sixty days, Mr. Mullen," I said, reaching out my hands toward him eagerly.

He shook his head gravely: "There is no help for you, that I can see."

"Cannot influence be brought to shorten the sentence? It is hard on me. I am not the only offender. The court gave L—— but ten days."

"The court gave fair warning at the time L—— was sentenced," he replied, "that the next offender would get the full benefit of the law, and the court, let me tell you, is in earnest about this matter. I could not help you if I would."

And he went out, leaving me again in solitude, and with a bitter morsel under my tongue.

CHAPTER XXVI.

TWO days afterward I was sitting a prey to gloomy and self-tormenting thoughts, bitterly repenting that I had ever set my foot in the path that had led to places like this, when my cell door was opened and a man pushed in. He staggered a little as he came toward me.

"Good heavens, Tom!" I exclaimed, in sudden agitation. It was Lloyd.

We grasped hands and stood for a little while looking dumbly at each other. His face was congested, his eyes watery and blood-shotten and the purple scar on his cheek clear and strong. He had evidently been drinking more deeply than ever since I had seen him, and was now more than half stupefied with liquor. The muscles of his marred face began working like those of a sobbing woman as soon as he recognized me.

"And so it has gone against you?" I said, first breaking silence.

"Yes, Hiram. It's gone against me. They swore it all through, and I had no chance," he answered, piteously. All his brave manhood was gone.

"How long?" I asked.

"Ninety days," he replied.

I then began to ask questions about our affairs, but could get little satisfaction. His head was all in confusion. I gathered that he had not been at the saloon for two days.

"Why not?" I asked as I drew the admission from him. It had come out incidentally.

He did not answer, and I saw something in his face that awakened a suspicion of foul play.

"Why haven't you been at the saloon?" I said, pressing the question, and with some sternness in my voice.

"Oh, you needn't growl about it," he replied, in a dogged way. "It's done, and can't be helped."

"What's done?" I demanded.

"It's done, didn't I tell you?" he mumbled, turning away from me.

"Tom," I exclaimed, grasping his arm, "I don't want any nonsense. What has been done? Speak out!"

He shook my hand off angrily and showed his teeth like a dog, then cursed me.

There was no use in quarreling with him. He was too much under the influence of liquor to have any control of his temper, bad enough at any time. So I held down my feelings as best I could, and sought to get from him the meaning of his last strange sentences.

"Say, Tom"—I now spoke in a persuasive manner—"what has been done? You haven't told me yet. You only thought you did."

"It was the best thing for us," he replied. "'The Retreat' was played out, and all the Harvey-street custom gone."

"'The Retreat' played out! What do you mean, Tom Lloyd?" I grew excited and imperative again

"Oh, if you're going to curse and swear about it, I'm mum," was answered, in a thick, maudlin voice. "Did the best I knew how. No use crying over spilled milk. Couldn't help myself. Bad sort of business, any way."

"You don't mean," said I, speaking with forced calmness, "that you have sold 'The Retreat'?"

"Couldn't help myself. Had to do it. Got me all tied up."

His last sentence made everything clear. I had dreaded this. As soon as I was out of the way his sporting friends had come down upon him for gambling debts, and he had settled with them, while half intoxicated, by passing over our saloon, with its lease, fixtures and license.

I felt like striking him down, I was so filled with sudden rage against him, but held myself under control, keeping back even the bitter denunciations that were crowding for utterance.

I turned my back upon him with impotent curses in my heart. He laid himself down, and in a little while was fast asleep and breathing heavily. I tried to arouse him when our supper of bread and chocolate was handed in, but his stupor was so heavy that the effort proved fruitless. Night came down, but he slept on. I went to bed about nine o'clock and tried to sleep, but my brain was too busy and my feelings too sensitively alive. Rest was far from me.

It was near midnight before Lloyd's heavy slumber was broken. Then he became restless and talked in his sleep, but in a jerky, incoherent way, muttering and mumbling, and sometimes crying out in a clear, sharp voice. I began to feel uneasy. It flashed across my mind that the sudden withdrawal of liquor might result in delirium, and a chill crept over me at the thought.

Toward daylight I was awakened from a light slumber into which I had fallen by feeling his hand on me and hearing his voice.

"Hiram!" he called.

"What is it?" I asked, rousing up.

"Is there any water here? I'm burning up with thirst."

"You'll find a spicket over by the door," I replied.

He went shuffling across the cell, and felt about the wall, but could not find the spicket.

"Low down, on the left side," I called.

He fumbled a while longer, and then I heard the cup rattle against the spicket. But he could not open it.

"For heaven's sake, Hiram," he called, "come and find me the water."

I got up and drew him a cup of water, but he

spilled half of it in trying to raise the cup to his lips.

"Hold it for me," he said, his voice shaking.

I put the cup to his mouth, and he drank eagerly. He then went back to bed, muttering and cursing.

As daylight came creeping slowly through the narrow window into our cell, and I could make out his face, I saw that it was greatly changed from what it was on the day before. It was now haggard and pale. His eyes were restless and all his motions nervous. He took again freely of water. When our breakfast came in, he drank a basin of the tea that was served, but it did not allay his nervousness.

"Oh for a cup of strong coffee!" he exclaimed. "I'd give ten dollars for a cup of strong coffee."

As the morning advanced Lloyd's nervousness increased. I tried to get him to talk about our affairs, but he would not be drawn out. I urged him, and he grew angry and violent. I did not like the expression of his eyes.

When our dinner came, I urged him to take some of the soup, but he turned from it with loathing. He had no appetite for food.

"I'd give my right hand for a glass of brandy," he exclaimed, striding about the cell. "Brandy, brandy, Hiram! God help me if I don't get whisky or brandy!" and I saw him shiver.

I was beginning to feel very uneasy. And now there came a yell of agony from "purgatory" Another poor wretch was among the demons.

Lloyd started up—he had thrown himself on his bed a few moments before—and looked at me in wild alarm.

"What is that, Hiram?" he asked, in a hoarse whisper. I saw him tremble.

Could I answer him truly? I dared not do so, for he was himself near that world of horrors into which the wretch whose cries were in our ears had plunged, and a breath might topple him over. So I pretended not to know.

Again the fearful outcries smote our ears.

"They're murdering somebody, Hiram," he exclaimed.

"No," I replied. "They don't murder people here."

"Then they are torturing somebody. Hark!"

His face grew pale as a wilder scream of terror and the sound as of men in some deadly struggle startled the air.

"What is it, Hiram? If you know, for Heaven's sake tell me!"

I hesitated a little, and then said, throwing a light expression into my voice,

"It's from the delirium tremens ward, I guess."

He looked at me strangely, then drew his eyes away from mine and sat quietly for a little while. The yells and outcries still came at intervals to our ears.

"Oh, it's too awful! I'll never be able to stand it!" he exclaimed at last, starting up from the bed on which he had been sitting and looking wildly and helplessly around.

I tried to soothe him—told him to do as I had done at first, stop his ears. He shut his hands tightly over them, and stood for half a minute in the middle of the cell.

"It's no use, Hiram," he said, despairingly, as he withdrew his hands. "I hear it all the time just the same. I cannot stop it out."

And yet, while his hands were upon his ears, not a sound had come from "purgatory."

A long, long time the maniac cries were heard before the miserable sufferer became unconscious, Lloyd all the while manifesting the keenest sensitiveness. They had ceased altogether for about half an hour, and I thought Lloyd, who was lying down, had fallen asleep, when I heard him say in a quick, rather startled voice,

"See there, Hiram!"

I turned, and saw him gazing with wide-open eyes and mouth drawn apart into a corner of the cell.

"What are you looking at? I don't see anything," I returned, feeling a chill pass over me, for I knew too well what was coming.

"There's a devilish-looking thing in the corner, Hiram! There! Don't you see it coming out?" and he shrunk as close to the wall as he could get, his eyes staring into the corner of the cell.

"Pshaw!" I said. "Don't be a fool, Tom. Be a man, and shake this thing off."

But that was impossible.

"It's coming, Hiram, it's coming!" he cried out, his face convulsed with terror.

I went over and tried to soothe him, but he broke away from me with a yell of fear that rang out into the corridor. A few minutes afterward the little window in our cell was opened, and a voice said,

"What's the trouble in there?"

"Won't you come in?" I asked. "There's a sick man in here."

"A sick man, eh? Very well; I'll send the doctor."

In about ten minutes the doctor came. Meanwhile, Lloyd had been driving about the cell in a mad way to escape the horrid things that seemed to be after him, shaking in every nerve and muscle and crying out in terror.

Two strong, hard-looking men, with faces in which you saw no pity, came in with the doctor.

"Take him over there," was the prompt order, and the two men moved toward Lloyd, who leaped backward from them in a vain effort to escape. But they were upon him in a moment, and had his arms pinioned. Lloyd was a strong man, and now that he was in a delirium his struggle was like that of a giant. He struggled and kicked and roared frightfully, giving the two men quite as much as they could do. They were used to such work, however, and soon had him out of the cell and over into the ward opposite, from which came to my ears his cries and yells of fear and agony!

CHAPTER XXVII.

IT seemed the very climax of misfortune and misery. Nearly all the money I had saved in three years I had loaned to my partner, and he had lost it, and not only lost my money, but sacrificed my business. I would go out from this place, after fifty days, a disgraced and humiliated man, poor, almost, as when I turned from a useful trade to live by a calling that only the license fee makes less than crime.

I moved about my cell, stung almost to madness by these thoughts, much as a wild beast moves about his cage, stopping every now and then to listen as the cries of poor Lloyd came across from the ward opposite, smiting my ears with indescribable pain. What they were doing to him I did not know. But his groans and yells and abject supplications were dreadful to hear, and it seemed as if they never would cease.

It was more than two hours after Lloyd had been removed, and while his cries still came to me, wailing and wild with fear, that my cell door opened, and the prison agent came in. I had not seen him for several days.

"You had a fellow-prisoner?" he said.

"Yes," I replied, gloomily, for I was not able to shake off the depression I felt.

"The commitments are so large," he remarked, "that we have often to put three or four into a single cell. The pauper and criminal trade is very active. The State gets two hundred thousand dollars annually from the city for licenses to sell intoxicating liquors, and the city has to extort from her tax-payers a million of dollars every year to restrain and punish the criminals and support the paupers that are made by this licensed traffic. A shrewd and sensible business operation, isn't it? And now there is a call for enlarging this place. We have in the male department some three hundred cells and seven hundred prisoners, and the courts and aldermen are sending down scores daily. We want two hundred more cells, and it will cost our tax-payers an amount equal to the whole sum of this license trade for two years to build the required addition, and so there will be nothing during these two years to set off against the annual one million pauper and criminal tax. It sounds like fiction, doesn't it? A noble commonwealth to get gain by licensing thousands of men to scatter crime, pauperism and untold misery among its people! To compel a great city like this to have eight thousand nurseries of disease, crime and death scattered through its wards and precincts that not only corrupt and debase its citizens, but draw from their industry a million of dollars in extra tax every year! A million, did I say? It can easily be shown that our city pays over two millions a year for the maintenance of courts, prisons, almshouse, charitable institutions and extra police, all consequent on the debasement that flows from intemperance under our present license system."

It seemed as if he would never stop. His sentences hurt and stunned me.

"It is frightful to think of," he resumed. "Anybody may get a license from our noble State to make widows and orphans, to sow crime, poverty and death broadcast among the people. Character is not necessary. Any criminal who has served out a term in the penitentiary or county prison may apply to the clerk of Quarter Sessions court for a license and receive it, or for half a dozen licenses if he will pay the fee to each of the officials whose sanction is required. I know of one instance of a man who died recently in this city, leaving one hundred thousand dollars, every dollar of which he made within a few years by selling liquor in six different places, for each one of which he received a license. His dens were in the lowest part of our city, and he sold to the most depraved of mankind, and to the poorest of the poor, blacks and whites. He distilled the liquor himself, and supplied each of these known places with a compound of his own make which he called 'whisky' This man had served out a term at Cherry Hill.

"So, you see," the agent went on, while I would have pitched him out of the cell if I had dared, I was so chafed and worried by his pressure of this subject upon me, "our noble commonwealth don't require character nor standing in its agents of death. It only asks their money. If they can pay over fifty or a hundred dollars into the State treasury, all right. They are as free to work as the minister or the teacher.

"And that reminds me," he said, after a little pause, "of some other figures. You see I have studied up these matters. It costs the people of this country for intoxicating liquor nearly a billion and a half of dollars every year. Now, what do you think it costs for churches and schools? Thirty millions to sustain the gospel and forty millions to sustain our schools. A vast difference, that! Taking the population at forty millions, and we have a cost of one dollar per head for schools, seventy-five cents a head for the gospel and thirty-seven dollars a head for intoxicants. Think of that! Is it any wonder that crime and misery go stalking through the land?"

He paused again, looking at me keenly.

"You may have other company in your cell at any moment," he went on, changing the subject—"a rough sent down for biting somebody's nose off, or a poor drunken rowdy, or a sneak thief."

I turned on him with an imprecation I could .not keep down.

"You can't bear it," he said, in a softer tone of voice. "Still, the lesson and the pain may do you good. They will set you to thinking. The rough, the rowdy and the sneak thief are chiefly the products of the business in which you have been engaged, and it may be well for you to make their closer acquaintance—to see and hear and touch the humanity you have helped to degrade to so mean a level."

"I am in your power, Mr. Mullen," I said. "I cannot help myself. But is it fair? Is it generous?"

"Was it fair or generous for you—"

A shuddering cry came over from "purgatory," and checked his speech.

"The bitter, bitter fruits," he exclaimed, his voice falling. "No other business in the world curses a man like that. But come."

He moved to the cell door. I stood still.

"Come," he repeated, and I saw that I must go.

I went out with him, crossing the bridge that led over to the cells on the opposite side of the corridor. He walked along, I following, until we came to the last cell in the south-west corner. He opened the door and went in, I stepping in after him. The cell was unoccupied, but there was a door in the wall opening into the adjoining cell. Through this door I could see that five or six cells had thus been made to communicate with each other.

"Come," repeated the agent, and I moved on after him, passing through the cells until I came in sight of the last. Two men were in the door of this. Over it I read in strong black letters the word "Purgatory," and even as I read, the voice of my poor friend Lloyd came shrieking out in a long despairing cry that made the hair lift on my head and my blood seem to curdle.

The agent spoke to the two men—they were the same hard, unpitying men who had taken Lloyd out of my cell, prisoners selected for this dreadful work because they were known to have nerves of steel and hearts of iron—and they moved back from the door.

"I want you to look in there," said the agent. I stood in the door of this last cell. Let me describe in as fitting words as I can use what I saw. I shiver as I recall it. Lloyd was lying on the floor motionless with his face upward. I have no words in which to give a picture of that face as I see it now, and shall always see it in memory. It makes a chill creep over me whenever it becomes visible, as it often does. The eyes were distended with fear, the countenance pale and distorted, with all the muscles working as if from intensest physical pain. His head kept turning from side to side, as if he were watching the movements of frightful things that were about rushing down upon him in his bound and helpless condition.

I soon saw that he was fastened to the floor, and so completely that he could move only his head. His hands were encased in great leathern gauntlets and drawn with straps tightly across his breast, his legs were stretched out to their full length and fastened to an iron chain in the floor, while his shoul-

In Purgatory.   Page 343.

ders were secured in a similar way. He could not move a muscle of his body, except those above the shoulders. And there, sick with the direst of all diseases, helpless and alone with hard, unpitying attendants, he lay given up for torment to a hellish crew of demons.

I stood in the door of the cell and looked down upon his awful face. He saw and knew me, lifted his head a few inches, called my name, cried out in a voice of strong and pleading agony,

"Oh, Hiram! For God's sake, Hiram! Take me out of this place! Oh, Hiram! For God's sake, Hiram!"

A hand grasped my arm, and I was drawn firmly back from the cell door and hurried away. As I retreated I heard the cry "Oh, Hiram! For God's sake, Hiram!" wailing after me in tones of agony and despair. And in my cell I heard them, I cannot tell for how long after, as I sat shivering and appalled by what I had witnessed.

All became still at last—still, it seemed, as death. The agent did not come to my cell again. He had other work on hand. Nor did he come again for several days. I could get no word about Lloyd. Two other prisoners were put into my cell, which caused me to feel great uneasiness. Why had not Lloyd come back?

From one of these prisoners, a great, coarse, brutish-looking fellow who came in on the third day after Lloyd was taken out, I got a newspaper, and turned instantly to the column of deaths, running my eyes along it.

"LLOYD." I caught my breath at the word, and then read: "On the 10th inst., suddenly, Thomas Lloyd. Funeral from his late residence, No. — Poplar street, on the 13th inst., at ten o'clock."

I sat stunned and oppressed for a long time. It seemed as if God had taken up the cause against us, and was sending swift and awful retribution. I was afraid and humbled; I felt that a power greater than man's was at work, and that I was not able to stand against it.

From that time I schooled myself to submission. I had no hope of getting out until the expiration of my term. My fellow-prisoners—I had two others in the cell all the while I remained—were far from being agreeable companions. One was coarse and brutish, as I have said—a man of depraved instinct and vicious life; the other, a poor weak creature made criminal through bad associations. I got along with them as best I could, but against the intimate association I was compelled to have with such men, nature was in perpetual revolt.

Poor Lloyd! I could never get him out of my thoughts—never banish from sight his awful face as I saw it last—never get out of my ears his imploring cry, 'Oh, Hiram! For God's sake, Hiram!'

How had he died? Alone with unpitying keepers, in darkness, his soul went out from the pinioned body, and there was none who cared to tell the tale of mortal agony.

Over thirty such awful deaths in a single year, and in this one prison!

It is too dreadful to contemplate. I can dwell upon it no longer. What would I not give if the scene I have just pictured for the reader were for ever erased from my memory?

CHAPTER XXVIII.

I HAVE little more to tell. The strength of a good purpose which impelled me to write what I have written has kept me thus far to my task, and now that nearly all I need to say for warning and counsel has been said, I have lost the firm grip with which I held my pen. My fingers are nerveless. I would stop here.

But a few things remain to be told, and I will tell them in the quiet pages that follow.

I had to serve out the full term of my imprisonment. The court would not listen to any application on my behalf. I had persistently broken a good law and must suffer the penalty, and so I suffered it to the end. It was a long and bitter humiliation.

I came out at last, broken in spirit and with a depressing sense of weakness and shame. The self-poise and self-confidence I had felt while in the full tide of success—when I saw gains steadily coming in, when I pushed away all thoughts of responsibility and said in my heart, "Every man for himself, and the devil take the hindmost"—were all gone now. I shuddered with a feeling of repulsion when the thought of going back to liquor-selling crossed my mind. I could get a license for fifty dollars and do as one of my fellow-prisoners, a hardened criminal, said he meant to do as soon as he got out, which happened before my release—set up a drinking-shop and gather in money from the vicious, the besotted and the weak. I could, with the law all on my side, make ample provision for myself. But I did not debate this question a moment. I was out of the business, and I said in my heart, I will starve sooner than go into it again.

My first concern was to ascertain what I had left. The two thousand five hundred dollars I had loaned my partner, and to secure which he had promised to execute a mortgage, but never did, were all gone. The fixtures, lease and good-will of our drinking-saloon had been sold while I was shut up in the county jail, and the amount received therefor taken to settle Lloyd's gambling debts. I had, besides, only a few shares of gold-mining stock, which I had been foolish enough to buy from a man who sold it at a great sacrifice because he was hard up. They were going to make me rich in a few years. On inquiry, I found them next to worthless. The mine had been flooded and work abandoned.

And so I was out in the world with nothing to show for my three years' work at saloon-keeping but a gold watch and a diamond breastpin. I sold the latter for a hundred and fifty dollars, in order to get something to live on until I could look about me and determine what to do.

I did not call on Mrs. Lloyd: I had no heart to

do that—I felt that I could not look her in the face—but I made diligent inquiry in regard to her. She had, immediately after her husband's death, given up the house in Poplar street, for which seven hundred dollars rent was paid, and sold more than half her furniture. She was now living in part of a small house with Tom and her two little boys. Tom was at work in the Harvey-street bindery, and earning five dollars a week, which was all their income.

I was glad to hear good accounts of Tom. He worked faithfully, and took home to his mother every dollar of his earnings. Mr. Ashley, the foreman, was very kind to him, and often spoke an encouraging word.

Poor John Ashley! The blow he received on the back of his head, as he fell into the vestibule at his mother's feet on the night I took him home through the snow-storm, gave his nervous system a shock from which he never fully recovered. The concussion hurt his brain in some way. Fever and temporary delirium followed, and there was a time when his family had little hope of his recovery, but he came up slowly, and it was many weeks before he got out again. He now had some light employment in the bindery, but was not clear-headed or efficient.

About a week after I came out of prison, as I was walking along the street, I came face to face with Ned Allen. He was about passing me, but I stopped and held out my hand. He merely touched it, and then let it drop as though it hurt him. His face was ruddy with health and his eyes clear. I saw at a glance that it was well with him.

"All right, I hope?" said I.

"All right," he responded, and was about passing on. He seemed afraid of me.

"One moment, Ned."

He looked at me sharply, and I saw a shade of dislike and suspicion in his face.

"I'm glad to know it, Ned." I spoke with feeling and sincerity. "Keep away from saloons and taverns, and you are safe."

"Thank you for the advice," he answered, bluntly. "I only wish you had given it sooner."

"It would have been better," I returned, humbly. I felt abashed in the boy's presence, for his words threw instantly on the canvas of memory that sad and tearful scene I had witnessed, when his poor heart-broken father, with white face lifted upward, prayed that his unhappy boy, wellnigh lost in the mazes of sin, might be saved.

"Good-morning," he said, coldly, and hurried on, as if anxious to get away. Why, it slowly dawned on me. I was known as a liquor-seller, and he felt that to be seen talking with me in the street might hurt his good name, and he was right. A true man had given him a chance for his father's sake: he was doing well; but for him it was safest to shun even the appearance of evil. One is judged by the company in which he is seen.

I walked on, with mingled feelings of pleasure and

pain. I had long carried this boy in my thoughts. I had felt trouble on his account. It was too clear a case against us. We had lured his feet out of a safe way and set them in the road to destruction, and he had gone along that road with hurrying steps. I was never more thankful for anything in my life than for this clear evidence that he was in the right way again.

The "Harvey-street League" was still active and on the alert. Old Jacobs, the president, was a host in himself. "The Retreat" I found, as Lloyd had said, "pretty well played out." No custom came from the bindery and printing-office, and without this the new owner couldn't make his rent. It was too far out of the way for general traffic. Sunday saw its door closed and shutters up. After the example that had been made of me, the new proprietor felt scary. Sixty days in Moyamensing wasn't pleasant to think about.

I drifted around the city for many weeks, undetermined what to do with myself. The life I had led for three years unfitted me for the old work, and I could not make up my mind to go back to my trade. But what was I to do? To be idle is to be in danger. I was not morally strong. It was natural for me to gravitate toward the class of men with whom I had been in association for the past three years—fast men, saloon-keepers, bar-room loungers, idle politicians. I had learned in three years to drink considerably. I was master of my appetite, and yet, somehow, after the long repression consequent on my residence in prison, this appetite was singularly keen and restless under denial. I indulged in what I considered moderation—three or four glasses a day—but it was never entirely satisfied, wanted something more, and I often gave it more.

As time wore on and the money received for the sale of my diamond pin was nearly gone, I began to feel anxious. What was I to do? In this crisis of affairs a certain ward politician whom I met one evening in a saloon asked me what I was doing.

I answered, "Nothing."

"Anything in view?" he inquired, and I said, "No."

He called for a couple of glasses of ale, and we drank together at the table where we had been sitting.

"There's a scheme on hand," he said, confidentially, "and I think you are the man we are looking for."

"What sort of a scheme?" I inquired, with a good deal of interest. "And secondly, will it pay?"

"There's no doubt as to its paying," he replied— "that is, if it is managed right. But mind, if I let you in, you must be as close as the grave."

I was in a desperate mood, ready for almost anything but setting up a tavern. I was cured of that.

"You can trust me," I answered. "I never betrayed a friend in my life, and don't mean to begin now."

"Just so. I thought I knew you."

And then he unfolded a scheme, in which he and two or three other men of his class and profession were engaged, for an out-and-out swindle of the public through a bogus enterprise that was to have the sanction of a few prominent men deceived into giving an endorsement. The projectors were all too well known to secure confidence, and were in search of a new and unknown man with good address who would stand in the front and manage affairs in the public eyes, but as they directed.

I listened patiently to the whole scheme and its well-digested programme. If it could be carried out successfully, it would pay, and that handsomely. My share of the profit would be several thousand dollars. It was a tempting offer to a man hanging loose on society as I was, and waiting for anything that might turn up. But I did not fail to see that if I went into it I would be a cheat and a swindler. The evil counselors of my soul who came in upon me when I debated the question of giving up a useful trade to become a saloon-keeper, and told me that no man cared for me—that if I did not look to the main chance I would be flung aside as of no account—now came trooping about me again and urging me to close with the tempting offer. If you don't take the chance, they said, somebody else will. Your holding off won't stop the scheme. Go in, and get on to your feet. It's a duty you owe yourself. I tried to fight them off, but they stifled reason and conscience.

Just at this critical moment I saw, with surprise, the face of old Jacobs the pressman at the door of the saloon. He was standing a little inside and looking about the room. At first I thought he had come in for a drink, but I saw by his countenance, so calm and serious, that another errand had brought him here. I had not seen him since the night he was taken out of "The Retreat" by brother Heritage. He did not look like the same man. The change in his appearance was marvelous to behold.

As his eyes ranged about the room they rested on me. I had turned my head partly aside, hoping I would not be recognized. But he saw me, and coming over to where I was, said,

"You know old Wilson, who worked in the bindery?"

I answered that I did.

"Have you seen him here to-night?"

I said no.

"Have you been here long?" he then asked.

"Half an hour," I replied.

He stood for some moments, and then said,

"Hiram, I'd like to have a few words with you."

Glad of the opportunity to escape from the tempter, who had me already half bound, I started up, saying,

"I am at your service."

I saw a heavy frown darken the face of the man with whom I had been talking.

"You are not going?" he exclaimed in a tone of repressed anger and surprise.

"Yes," I replied. "Good-evening;" and I went out with Jacobs, feeling a strange sense of relief and safety, like one escaped from imminent peril. We walked for a hundred yards or so in silence, I waiting anxiously to hear what old Jacobs had to talk to me about.

"Hiram," he said, at length, in a very serious but kind and almost confidential way, "I want you to help me."

"To help you?" I returned, surprised at his speech.

"Yes; you can do it if you will."

"Then I will!" was my strongly-uttered response

"To help me do a good office for a weak fellow-creature who has fallen among—"

He checked himself, not uttering the word that was on his tongue.

"I have done, I fear, much harm in my time, Jacobs," I replied, "and if you will now show me how I can do any good, I shall be glad of the opportunity."

"Why, Hiram!" the old man exclaimed, stopping and turning round upon me. "Let me take your hand!" and he gave me a grip that almost made the bones snap. "The greater the sinner, the greater the saint, I've heard said. You've been an awful sinner, Hiram, for you sinned against light and knowledge. But if you have repented, just come over to our side, and we'll put you high up in the calendar."

I felt somehow stronger and safer for this speech of the old man.

"I don't expect to get very high up," I made answer. "Indeed, I'd rather keep out of sight. But what is it you want me to do?"

"I'm after poor old Wilson," he said. "He's broken his pledge and gone off on a spree. I've been looking for him in one saloon after another for an hour past, but can't find him. Joe's out after him too."

"Joe Wilson? His son?"

"Yes. Joe's a member of the Harvey-street League, and as fine and steady a fellow as you'd wish to see. Hasn't tasted liquor for over two months."

"Glad from my heart to hear it," I replied, in all sincerity.

"And I'm glad from my heart to hear you say so," returned the old man. "But we must find Wilson. He's in some of these taverns, but there are so many of them that one might almost as well look for a needle in a haystack. Just two hundred within four or five squares!"

I went into the old man's service, promising to visit every tavern in a specified area, and to bring out Wilson if I came across him. I was to take him, if found, to the hall or meeting-room of the Harvey-street League, the direction of which Jacobs gave me.

As I turned from the old pressman to commence my search, I was conscious of a new state of feeling and a sense of rest. Since I had come out of prison my soul had been like a ship tossed on troubled waters, and therefore this calm and restful state that fell so suddenly upon my spirit was something I could not but observe. With it came a feeling of concern for Wilson, who, but for his one great failing, was a man well esteemed by every one.

Two hundred drinking-saloons within an area of four or five blocks! Could that be possible? I thought Jacobs must be in error, but ere I had been long in search of Wilson I began to realize how fully up to the truth had been his assertion. Into one after another I went, hurriedly looking through each for the man I was seeking, and as I went I saw with new eyes and from a new standpoint. So many young men, clerks and mechanics, the promise of our mercantile and industrial life! And here they were side by side, and too often in free intercourse with the vicious and debased. I saw a fair-faced young man, the son of a well-known merchant, drinking with a notorious corner-lounger who had twice found it convenient to be absent from the city while certain police matters were being investigated. I saw another young man, clerk in a large Market-street house, laughing and talking familiarly with a miserable fellow who was bad and base enough for almost anything, and I saw them go out together, evidently with a common purpose. I saw a weak boy of eighteen, the only son of a wealthy and good citizen, treated by a gambler's stool pigeon—I knew him well—and then drawn away from the saloon. I had little question as to where they would be in less than half an hour.

I saw what I had seen over and over hundreds of times before, but how different the impression made upon me now! Then I was interested in the gain, and when I looked at the thirsty crew, young and old, rich and poor, steady and debased, that thronged our bar-room, it was with the feeling of a sportsman when he sees his game. My business was to bring them down and bag their money.

But I was seeing with other eyes now. I had not come for game, but for rescue, to save, not to destroy, and I was moved with concern by what I saw. As some idea of the extent of the traffic in liquor grew upon me, estimating, as I could not help doing, the whole city by the four or five blocks through which I was ranging, I felt almost appalled at its magnitude. Few of the saloons into which I went had less than three or four persons inside, often a dozen, and they were going and coming all the while. Take eight thousand of these, and give twenty visitors to each in a single night—many had hundreds—and the number is a hundred and sixty thousand. But one person will often go to two or three saloons in an evening, and this would reduce the actual number of individuals to sixty or eighty thousand. But what an aggregate! One tenth of the whole number of our people to be found every night in taverns, saloons, restaurants and whisky-shops!

In spite of myself I could not help running these figures through my mind. And as I did so I recalled the words of the prison agent, and felt amazed at the marvelous indifference of the people. All this was under sanction of law. The commonwealth had sold for money, and to any and all who applied, the right to set up places for the sale of liquor in our city, and with the full knowledge that such places work the saddest of evils, that they were nurseries of pauperism and crime, moral pest-houses, stumbling-blocks for the weak and unwary, and often hot-beds of infamies too deep to mention. And against all this the citizens had no remedy. Two hundred thousand dollars received by the State treasurer for the privilege of doing all this evil, and in its hopeless task of repairing the evil, the city spending over a million each year, drawn from the industry of its citizens!

How long, I said to myself, will the patience or indifference of the people endure all this?

But I had not meant to give so long a digression. It was one thing to hear all this from the prison agent when I was locked up in a cell, chafing at restraint and rebellious toward the law. It was another thing to think it over for myself under new circumstances, and to look at the evil from a new standpoint.

I went from tavern to tavern searching for Wilson. I had gone in and out of some thirty or forty, and was beginning to despair of finding him. At length

I stood at the entrance of a two-story mean-looking dram-shop with a broken lamp in front, hesitating whether to go in or not, when some one pushed open the door. I got a momentary glimpse of the inmates, and thought one of them looked like the man for whom I was in search, so I went in.

It was a poorly fitted-up place, with a few kegs, bottles and glasses, and half a dozen vile-looking men standing at the bar or moving about the room. I saw Wilson as soon as I entered. He was asleep in a chair, and one of the men present was standing over him with something in his hand that he put quickly out of sight as he saw me.

"Hallo, comrade!" exclaimed some one, in a familiar voice.

I looked to the bar, from which the words came, and saw behind it the well-remembered face of one of my county-prison associates — the hardened fellow who had declared his intention to buy a license as soon as he got out and go into the liquor trade. And here he was. "Comrade!" How like the stroke of a lash, cutting and smarting, fell the word on my ears! I did not think it safe to ignore him, for he was a wicked brute, and there were fellows just like him present — some of them old prison-birds, I doubted not. So I went up to the bar and gave him a not very cordial response. He reached out his hand, but I managed not to take it. He set down a decanter of whisky, but I declined, saying I had already taken enough. He scowled a little.

As soon as I could I turned from him and went to the sleeping old man, and putting my hand on him, called him by name.

"You know the old soaker?" said my prison friend, coming from behind the bar and looking at us with a half-ill-natured curiosity.

I did not reply, but called in a louder voice, shaking Wilson as I did so. It took me some time to get him fairly awake. At last he knew me, and exclaimed,

"Why, bless my soul, Hiram, is this you?" He got up and stood looking at me in a pleased way.

"And so you're out again! Well, well! Glad to see you, Hiram!" and he thrust forth his hand.

I took it, giving him a strong pull toward the door as I did so, and saying,

"Come with me, Wilson. I want you for something."

But he held back.

"Come," I repeated.

"Not till we have a drink," he replied. "It's a good while since you and I drank together, Hiram. What'll you take?"

"Nothing to-night, thank you, Wilson. Had enough. Come."

I saw my prison friend glance toward a couple of the inmates of his den, and they moved quietly between us and the door.

"Oh, I'll stand the treat," responded Wilson, and he turned toward the bar. "What'll you have?"

I was at a loss whether it were best to humor him or not. My prison friend went behind the bar and looked toward the decanters.

"We don't want anything more to-night, neither of us," I said.

"We don't? Well, now, that's a good joke!" Wilson answered, with a tipsy laugh. "Hiram Jones says we don't want anything more to-night. Never heard him say that before in my born days. Good for Hiram!"

I began to feel uneasy. The men in the bar-room came gathering around us, and I saw evil in their bad faces.

"Why don't you drink with him?" asked one of them in a tone that meant mischief.

"Because, as just said, we've both had enough," I returned, controlling my voice as best I could.

He laughed an ugly laugh. Wilson was moving toward the bar. I put my hand on him, and leaning to his ear, said, "Joe's looking for you."

He stood still instantly, not answering for some moments. I saw his head droop.

"Come!" I said again. He was passive now, going with me toward the door. But the men, seeing this, went round and intercepted us.

"Where are you going to take him?" demanded one of them.

"Home," I replied.

He cursed me. Out of his eyes flashed a cruel light.

"His son is looking for him," I said. "Let him go out, won't you?"

He cursed me again and put his back to the door. A sudden indignation fired me. I caught him by the collar, and with a wrench drew him forward and then flung him across the bar-room. It was a madly desperate act in such a place and in such company. I was beaten down in almost a second of time. I did not know much of what followed until I found myself in a station-house. In the morning, spite of all I could say in my own behalf, which went for little or nothing against the sworn testimony of some of the very men who had assaulted me, I was committed for drunkenness and rioting.

Old Wilson, as I learned, had been knocked about some, but not much hurt. He got off with a few bruises, considerably scared, and made his way home. On the next day he took the pledge again and went to work.

My cup was full—full of bitter wine.

"Here again!" exclaimed the prison agent, on coming to my cell an hour after its iron door had shut me in.

I told him all. He listened with deep interest.

"It curses everybody," was his response when I had finished. Then he added, "And so you do not intend going back into your old business?"

"Not if I starve!" was my reply.

He took the name of old Jacobs, president of the Harvey-street League, and went away, saying that he would see about my case. Two hours afterward I was at liberty again, but under bail to appear in court on the charge of drunkenness and rioting.

But I did not have to stand a trial for these misdemeanors. I had the prison agent on my side now, and when the case went to the grand jury, he laid such a statement of facts before them as prevented the finding of a true bill against me.

Meantime, I had come under better influences and into the hands of true men who were in earnest to help and save—even the men of the Harvey-street League. What I had done and suffered for old Wilson drew toward me a feeling of kindness, and when it was understood that I had renounced the business of liquor-selling, a new interest was awakened.

"What are you going to do?" asked Jacobs as I came forth from the prison. He had gone bail for me.

I shook my head gloomily.

"Go back to the bindery. You are a good workman."

"That's impossible," I replied, with decision.

"Why? Ashley will give you a place."

"I could never show my head there, Jacobs, after what has been," I said.

"Psha!" he returned. "It won't be any harder for you than it was for some of us."

"No, no, no!" I answered, emphatically. "Anything but that! I'd rather go and jump into the dock;" and that was my feeling at the time.

But I had no way to live honestly and with a clear conscience except by my trade. Two or three old fellow-workmen came about me, moved to do so by Jacobs and by the cause in which they were so deeply interested. They talked with me, and showed so much interest and hearty good-will that I was led at last to overcome my shame and reluctance and go back to the bindery. I took the pledge of the Harvey-street League, and am now an earnest worker in the cause toward which I stood for a long time in active antagonism.

And so you have the story of a three years' effort to get rich and "live like a gentleman" by means of liquor-selling. It didn't pay in my case. It doesn't pay in any case. The loss is always more than the gain.

"Many get rich, if you did not," I hear one say.

To which I answer in the words of a Book I read oftener when a child than since: "What shall it profit a man if he gain the whole world and lose his own soul?"

"Oh, that's cant!" is returned, with a sneer. "A liquor-seller turned preacher!"

Is it? Well, have it so! But I leave you the thought, and it may be wise to give it consideration.

THE END.

www.ingramcontent.com/pod-product-compliance
Lightning Source LLC
Chambersburg PA
CBHW020314240426
43673CB00039B/803